THE PSYCHOLOGY AND
TEACHING OF READING

Other books by Fred J. Schonell

BACKWARDNESS IN THE BASIC SUBJECTS
HAPPY VENTURE TEACHER'S MANUAL
ESSENTIALS IN TEACHING AND TESTING SPELLING
PRACTICE IN BASIC ARITHMETIC
RIGHT FROM THE START ARITHMETIC

With F. Eleanor Schonell

DIAGNOSIS AND REMEDIAL TEACHING IN ARITHMETIC
DIAGNOSTIC AND ATTAINMENT TESTING

THE PSYCHOLOGY AND
TEACHING OF READING

FRED J. SCHONELL
M.A., PH.D., D.LIT.

OLIVER AND BOYD
TWEEDDALE COURT, EDINBURGH 1
39A WELBECK STREET, LONDON W. 1

FIRST PUBLISHED 1945
SECOND EDITION 1948
THIRD EDITION 1951
FOURTH EDITION (REVISED AND ENLARGED) 1961
SECOND IMPRESSION OF FOURTH EDITION . 1962

PRINTED IN GREAT BRITAIN BY
OLIVER AND BOYD LTD., EDINBURGH

PREFACE

THE purpose of this book on reading is to provide some information on what constitutes a scientific approach to the teaching of reading. During the past fifteen years there has been a considerable amount of well-planned and carefully executed research into many problems associated with learning to read, and it is vital that teachers and parents should be acquainted with the proven and pertinent points arising from this research. Possessed of such information, teachers and parents can establish adequate standards regarding the means and materials by which children are taught to read. Too long have children been handicapped by unsuitable reading methods and by unscientific textbooks. In not a few instances textbooks have been badly printed, with little attention paid to the development of eye-span as determined by size of print and adequate spacing between words and lines. Choice of illustrations for these same books has revealed both low educational and low aesthetic standards on the part of publisher and author. But perhaps the worst feature of some textbooks by which young children are expected to learn to read is the too heavy vocabulary burden employed. Words are not chosen from children's vocabularies, and for the less able 50 per cent of pupils there are, in the early reading books, far too many new words per page. Informed parents and qualified teachers could do much to eliminate reading texts which show such blemishes as those cited above.

But more important than experimental findings on textbooks is the information now at our disposal concerning the early stages of reading instruction. Research shows that it is fatal to 'push' young children along in the initial stages of learning to read, particularly if there have not been activities to create a functional language background beforehand. Many children fail in reading because they are plunged into formal reading with an over-analytic method employing abstract symbols before they really understand what words and sentences mean in spoken, let alone printed, form. Young immature minds need opportunity and time to 'sort things out', to understand what they are doing, and to see the purpose in the operations with which they are confronted. My strongest plea in the teaching of reading is, don't hurry the children, don't expect too much in the early stages—do all you can to provide a language background. This slower, wider approach will repay doubly later on. The teaching of both reading and number would greatly benefit if we allowed children time to understand fully and assimilate, indirectly and informally, at their own pace and through carefully planned experiences, the fundamental concepts in these two subjects, namely, the meaning of language and the meaning of numbers.

All pupils develop at different rates in different subjects. Only today I have examined an intelligent boy aged $10\frac{3}{4}$ whose arithmetic age is almost 12, but whose reading age is barely 8. The same kind of variations in development, particularly in reading, are to be found in infant classes, and we must be ready to provide for them. For this reason the *teaching* of reading should be conceived as a kind of unitary educational activity ranging over the years 5+ to 10+. The fact that pupils pass at 7+ from one department, or one class, to another should not lead us to think that all pupils should be taught to read in the infant school. Some children will learn to read in the infant school, others will not. This is not because the infant teachers have not worked sufficiently hard ; in very many cases they do excellent work. My only wish is that some teachers would, particularly in early stages, do a little less 'work' and allow their charges to proceed somewhat more leisurely and informally, and hence intelligently.

The pupils of 7+ who cannot read at the infant school

stage can learn to read at 8+ or 9+, or as late as 10+ in the junior school, *provided they receive suitable instruction and appropriate materials*. There should be complete dove-tailing between infant school or section and junior school or section in respect to these pupils who have not yet learned to read. The main objective of all teachers, in either department, should be to get all pupils to learn to read, and continuity is an essential factor in achieving this objective. Reading is of immense importance to the child's whole mental development. Apart from the obvious limitations that disability in reading imposes on progress in spelling, English, arithmetic, in fact in all subjects, it produces in most cases personality maladjustment, so that normal mental health cannot be maintained if there is failure in reading. Every child, except the lowest mentally defective cases and rare cases of cerebral lesion, can be taught to read. Teachers and parents should distrust the pseudo-psychologist who glibly labels children as word deaf or word blind, because he does not know why they fail to learn to read and to spell. Word blindness and word deafness are extremely rare conditions.

Certain backward readers require special scientific diagnosis of their conditions to discover their difficulties and to plan methods to overcome their handicaps, but in nearly all cases of reading disability this is a practical possibility, as I have shown in some detail in *Backwardness in the Basic Subjects*.[1]

If teachers find that pupils are not making progress, they should do as much as they can within their power to find out why. Is the method right for this child ? Is the material suitable ? Don't let the child drift. Reading disability becomes increasingly difficult to treat the longer it persists. Similarly, parents should adopt the same enquiring yet not over-anxious attitude towards cases of backwardness in reading.

It is in this spirit that I offer to teachers and parents the material set out in the body of this book. In writing it I have been impelled by a desire to inform them, to help them,

[1] *Backwardness in the Basic Subjects*, by F. J. Schonell, 4th ed. (Oliver & Boyd)

to give them hope, yet at the same time to lead them to realise the immense importance of teaching every child to read, and hence the necessity of making a scientific approach to the whole problem.

1945   F. J. S.

PREFACE TO FOURTH EDITION

THE continued and extensive use of this book has led me to provide a fourth edition. In this edition, entirely reset and expanded, I have frequently cited results of recent research, but not always have I given detailed references. Too many footnotes would have been cumbersome, but readers may obtain additional information from *Summaries of Reading Research* by William S. Gray (University of Chicago Press) and *Review of Educational Research* (American Educational Research Association, Washington).

New chapters deal with the understanding and interpretation of what is read, and with the task of teacher and parent in developing in boys and girls an interest in reading, surely our most important educational objective.

It is reassuring to record the great advances that have been made in recent years in the teaching of reading through increased use of word whole/sentence methods, employing attractive and meaningful material. That millions of children, and hitherto illiterate adults, have gained skill and joy through the use of reading schemes based on the psychologically sound word whole/sentence method is one of the outstanding educational achievements of the century.

I would like to record my thanks to two of my staff, Mr J. McLeod, B.SC., B.ED., and Mr R. Cochrane, B.A., M.ED., of the University of Queensland Remedial Education Centre, for reading the proofs and making helpful suggestions. To my wife, my constant companion in thirty years of writing and research, I am for ever grateful. I would also like to thank Miss J. Thompson and Miss B. Mason for help with the manuscript and proofs.

BRISBANE 1960   F. J. S.

CONTENTS

CHAPTER I

PSYCHOLOGICAL FACTORS IN
WORD RECOGNITION

MALCOLM, aged 4½, is intrigued by a new game. It is the
game of 'reading'. In his room he has three names printed
in capital letters on separate pieces of cardboard, and he
proudly informs one that he can read these words.

They are :

MALCOLM

PAT

BARRIE

A few questions soon show that he can 'read' the names
correctly no matter in what order the words are presented
or in what form the questions are framed, as for example,
'What is this one?' or 'Show me Barrie's name'. How
is it that a boy aged 4½ can respond accurately to these printed
words, although he does not know the names of more than
two or three letters nor the sounds of any of the letters? What
are the factors which have produced this accurate discrimination of word patterns?

In the first place it is obvious from our knowledge of
Malcolm's acquaintance with letters and sounds that he is
responding primarily to the total visual pattern of the whole
word. This is in keeping with our experimental knowledge of
young children, namely that they perceive objects and forms,
at first, as wholes. It is the marked differences in the visual
patterns of the words as wholes which enable him to recognise
each word. The length of the word and the nature of the
letters which make up its visual pattern are the determinants
in this discrimination. For example, his own name, MALCOLM,
starts with M and finishes with M ; this gives it a certain

discriminatory characteristic apart from its length. BARRIE finishes with E, a letter that Malcolm remembers from his attempts ' to write' the name of his friend PETER, when he was told that E ' has three arms, one long one at the top, a short one in the middle and a long one at the bottom '.

Had Malcolm's name been JIM and those of his friends TOM and PAT it is quite possible that he might not have shown the same facility and the same degree of accuracy in his early ' reading' reactions. The fact that all the names would have been of similar visual pattern would have made his task of recognition, i.e. of word discrimination, much more difficult.

Now although distinctive visual pattern was the primary means by which Malcolm recognised each of the three words, yet we must remember that he had heard these names many times and that they had maximum interest and meaning for him. The words Barrie and Pat were symbolic of all kinds of friendly social relationships and pleasant play experiences. Furthermore, Malcolm had made several attempts to copy his own name—imitative efforts more nearly resembling drawing than writing, but nevertheless helping him to recognise the visual pattern of the word when he came across it in other places.

Thus we see that the factors which had contributed to Malcolm's accurate ' reading' or recognition of the three printed words were fourfold :

(a) the visual pattern of the words

(b) the saying and hearing of the words

(c) the meaning of the words

(d) the impressions gained through tracing or writing (or trying to write) the words.

Now of these four contributors towards word recognition, the most important is the *visual pattern* of the word.

There is now a wealth of research evidence to show that words are first perceived as visual wholes, that is to say it is the total pattern or schema or gestalt of the word that young pupil and mature reader alike first observe—mature readers, of course, may take in two or three word wholes in a perceptual span or unit.[1] In this total pattern both length and individual characteristics of the word aid in its recognition. But it should be remembered that word recognition is also intimately bound up with meaning and with any other clues available, such as illustrations.

With the young pupil word recognition in the initial stages often involves also a careful scrutiny of parts of the word, a searching for clues as to its familiarity. For this reason scientific compilation of material for basic reading books includes consideration of building up new words from known words or parts of words. A plentiful introduction of words of similar families or of similar structure is also a factor in recognition— a pupil may recognise *tall* as simply an extension of *all*, and *into* as a combination of two words he already knows.

Known syllables in a new word often give the clue to its recognition. Hence very useful exercises in developing powers of word recognition are making small words from large words and vice versa, and word building of syllables into new words (*an, man, sand*).

Every word has a distinct visual pattern produced by its length and the nature of its component letters.

For example,   all

one

eye

ate

are all of different pattern, although of the same length.

[1] *The Teaching of Reading and Writing*, by William S. Gray (Unesco and Evans Bros., London, 1956), p. 64, also see Chapter II—'Nature of the Reading Process in Various Languages'.

But it is not as easy to distinguish them from each other as it is to distinguish them from longer words, such as,

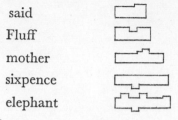

said

Fluff

mother

sixpence

elephant

Words in this latter group differ from each other both in length and in the number and position of the projecting letters of which they are composed. In word recognition more use is made of the letters with ascenders or descenders than of those without, as is demonstrated in the following example, in which the first specimen is more easily read than the second.

(*a*) Thx pxxdxxtxxx xf pxppxt plxyx txkxx thx xdxx dxxxlxpxd xx thx pxxxxdxxg xhxptxx x xtxgx fxxthxx.

(*b*) x xurxxer exaxoraxion is xo xisxrixuxe xaxers anx craxons so xxax a xacxxrounx can xe maxe.

(A further elaboration is to distribute papers and crayons so that a background can be made.)

It would seem that recognition of a word is based on a combination of the total shape of the word, of groups of letters (as in the double *t* in *little*) and of individual letters in it. Obviously these different elements have different values in different words, and they do not always enter into perception in a specific or completely consciously known manner. As M. D. Vernon says :

' Some general form or contour is perceived, with certain dominating letters or parts arising out of it, as the " figure " arises out of the " ground ". The ascending letters seem to play an important part and an alteration of vertical and curved letters may also help in structuralising the form.' [1]

These basic facts of word discrimination are of extreme importance in the teaching of reading, for they have significant bearing on the selection of reading material, on the use of reading methods, on the causes of backwardness in reading, and on the use of effective reading material for backward readers.

Early reading material should contain common words of different visual patterns which will help the young reader in his difficult task of discrimination. If the material is over-loaded with small words of similar pattern, such as, *an*, *as*, *on*, *no*, *or*, *it*, *at*, *if*, *of*, *for*, *by*, *was*, *saw*, *are*, *am*, *hat*, *hit*, *boy*, *big*, *day*, the means of word recognition is decreased and the possibility of confusion is very greatly increased. All teachers are aware of the inability of less able pupils to distinguish *on*, *no* ; *of*, *for* ; *was*, *saw* ; *on*, *in* ; *boy*, *big* ; *day*, *dig*. Yet many of these same backward readers can frequently recognise words like *Fluff*, *mother*, *little* and *elephant*. It is in this aspect that the material of the average phonic reading book not infrequently presents unnecessary difficulties for pupils. For example, material such as the following :

> The pig with a wig did a jig in the bog,
>
> The fox saw a hen in the pen,

although of regular phonic form, loses not a little of its advantage in this respect through the similarity of the visual patterns of the words employed,[2] so that some pupils read *pig* as *big*, *bog* as *boy* or *big*. This is a disadvantage apart from the obvious limitation imposed by the meaningless nature of the sentences.

---

[1] *The Experimental Study of Reading*, by M. D. Vernon (Cambridge University Press, 1931), p. 118

[2] This is not meant as an indictment of the phonic method of teaching reading, for it is recognised that without phonic knowledge of the right kind at the right time many children will not make satisfactory progress in reading. The advantages and disadvantages of various methods of teaching reading are considered fully in Chapter IV.

PERCEPTUAL EFFICIENCY

Saying and Hearing Words

Finally reference should be made to an important perceptual attitude that a pupil needs to develop in the early stages of learning to read, namely the attitude of *looking at words from left to right in a consistent and concentrated manner*. Normally this aspect of perception is part of the function of making eye movements across a page from left to right, and is aided in its stabilisation by the fact that we write across a page from left to right, but most young children require some assistance in concentrating on the beginnings of words when they commence learning to read. Teachers will frequently ask children to put their fingers on the first letter or letters—

' Yes, it starts with *b*.'

or ' This is *sh*, like *sh*op that we had yesterday.'

' Put your finger on *p*.'

In helping the young reader to establish the starting points of new words, the teacher should use the sound rather than the name of the beginning letter or letters—thus the sound *b* rather than *bee* (the name of the letter) ; *sh* rather than *s* (ess) and *h* (aitch). By this means children are sensitised to the functional sounds with which words begin, not in an analytic way but as part of the pattern of the word as a whole. These functional sounds are, moreover, in accord with the words as they hear them in everyday speech. The use of the simple game of ' I spy with my little eye something beginning with . . .' is a means of strengthening, in a natural way, the child's perception of initial parts of words.

Aids such as pointing to initial letters or using markers are at this stage a useful prop, provided we take care to dissuade children from their use when they are clearly no longer required.

Not infrequently the inability of some pupils to make an

adequate perceptual attack on words from left to right, is due to one of three causal conditions. These are :

(a) a general physical immaturity which underlies their disinclination to look at words in a systematic way ;

(b) a personality maladjustment, or emotional upset, which may be the real cause of their perceptual weakness ;

(c) an uncorrected, organic defect in vision which prevents them from focusing with concentration on word patterns.

Results of research show that visual defects may interfere with perceptual efficiency but there is by no means an absolute relationship between visual acuity and reading ability.

Eames found that there was a correlation of ·46 between visual acuity and speed of word recognition.[1] In other words, weakness in the physiological mechanism of sight will interfere with the normal perception of words only in a limited number of children.

A review of research results would seem to indicate that the position is still as I stated it in 1948, namely that 'while visual factors are significant causal factors in reading disability, they are not as frequent as one would be led to infer from a consideration of the fact that reading is primarily dependent upon visual perception '.[2] However, the significant point for parents and teachers is that every case of reading disability should be examined by a medically qualified eye specialist.

In all cases of perceptual inaccuracy teachers should endeavour to determine the real root of the condition, for in the face of actual disability or immaturity, training may only result in partial progress. It is important for teachers to realise that children will not be attracted to studying words

[1] Quoted in *Review of Educational Research* (American Research Association, April 1940), p. 109

[2] *Backwardness in the Basic Subjects*, by F. J. Schonell, 4th ed. (Oliver & Boyd), p. 170

B

unless they have been strongly motivated to do so—hence the importance of using words that appeal to them strongly and relate to their everyday experiences. The use of pictures in this context is obvious, so that the picture dictionary has its place at this stage.

But in addition, recent research shows that there is a relationship between personality adjustment and perceptual efficiency. The unstable or insecure child finds it difficult to attend to words at both the visual and the auditory levels. For example, Meyer reports that the Rorschach records of two groups of nineteen retarded readers and nineteen normal readers matched for Terman I.Q. and chronological age, were differentiated by the accuracy and clarity of form perception.[1] There is undoubtedly a relationship between a child's attention span and his concentration in perception and his degree of personality adjustment. I have continuously noted that disturbed children, for whom insecurity is a factor in their poor reading attainment, frequently display ineffective perceptual habits in looking at words. It is fair to say that our interpretation of ineffective visual perceptual habits is now largely in terms of personality maladjustment together with ineffective training, rather than specific mental weakness.

The significance of this for the teacher is that the teaching of reading always has its emotional as well as its intellectual side. Those children who show weakness in looking at words from left to right may also be helped by experiencing success, by encouragement and by decreasing insecurity or frustration in their lives.

Passing now from visual to auditory aspects of word recognition, we may note that saying and hearing words are essential factors in their later recognition. Although the nature and extent of the child's speech itself are important

[1] See 'Some Relationships between Rorschach Scores in Kindergarten and Reading in Primary Grades', by G. Meyer, *Journal of Projective Techniques*, 17th December 1953, reported in *J. Educ. Res.*, No. 48, February 1955; also, 'Personality Adjustment to Reading Success and Failure', by A. H. Solomon, *Clinical Studies in Reading II*, *Supp. Ed. Monographs* 77 (University of Cambridge Press, 1953).

in the early stages of reading instruction, yet it is the more vital subtlety of the auditory elements of the words themselves that is gradually assimilated (very largely unconsciously) by the pupils through saying and hearing. Thus the pupil unconsciously understands that the word-sound PAT is derived from P-AT, and at a later stage he will be ready to realise (again unconsciously to a large degree) that it is like *s-at*, *th-at*, and *c-at-ch*. But in the beginning this knowledge is assimilated as an indirect and unconscious background for later usage.

Most children are not ready, either intellectually or experientially in British schools, at 5+ years, for an analytic-synthetic sound approach to reading. But at the same time much of the speech of the child, the saying of rhymes and other experiences of the preparatory reading stage are valuable indirect aids to the later phonic work which should be part of an intelligent reading scheme. It is because the hearing-saying aspect of word recognition is so essential in learning to read that young pupils should be permitted to say aloud or half aloud their reading material as long as they have the need for this aid.

Meaning of Words

Inasmuch as early reading material should be set against the child's own vocabulary and language patterns, associated with his experiences, it follows that constant use in speech of the words and phrases in his first reading book will enhance his possible recognition of them later. In fact, some teachers base their early reading programme on well-known nursery rhymes. Although at first the child simply ' reads ' the phrase or sentence because he has memorised it by heart, yet it does not take long for the strength of the sound-meaning association combined with introduction to the visual form of the phrases to trigger off really effective recognition of the material. Many of us know of young children who learn to read by working backwards, so to speak, in this way. They

are given a simple book—one sentence to each picture page—
which is read aloud twice or three times to them. They
memorise the story and can ' read ' (repeat) it with fair
accuracy of sequence by looking at the pictures on successive
pages. Having then been shown the actual words and phrases
on the particular pages, they fit meaning and sound of words
to their visual patterns and positions on the pages. Several
of my young friends have learned to read in this way before
going to school. Books such as the *Before We Read*[1] series
have been the basis of this indirect reading instruction.

The relevant point here, however, is not the pre-school
achievement of a few bright children but the extreme importance of sound and meaning of words in word recognition.
There is undeniable evidence to show that a strong use of
saying and hearing words is of inestimable benefit to children
in developing adequate powers of word recognition in the
early stages of their instruction. For this reason dramatisation
of reading material has very useful supplementary value.

But effectiveness of hearing and saying words as a factor
in word recognition is much dependent upon the degree of
meaning that words have for the learner.

Recent psychological studies of reading have tended to
emphasise the paramount value of meaningful material in both
the preliminary and the instructional stages of learning to
read. Words must mean ideas, not be merely mechanical
patterns. Unless a pupil has familiarity with the meaning and
pronunciation of a word, there is little chance of his assimilating
it with any permanence into his reading vocabulary. Actual
learning and later retention of words are intimately bound up
with their meaning and pronunciation.

Here we may note that the words which young children
learn incidentally are those most meaningful to them. For
example, one 5-year-old could always read ICE CREAM wherever the word appeared. Furthermore, of the material in an

[1] *Before We Read*, by D. Fletcher, R. Bakewell, J. Taylor, T. Ingleby (Oliver
& Boyd)

introductory or pre-primer reading book, the words which pupils most quickly learn to read are those most meaningful to them ; words with least meaning are last to be assimilated into the reading vocabulary. The better and wider the background of the pupil's understood language the greater is his chance of success in learning to read, irrespective of other conditions. Hence, learning to read must be preceded and accompanied by a background of language experiences obtained through home and school. Stories must be told and read, pictures must be shown and books provided so that a variety of talk about everyday situations will produce a wide vocabulary of common words. In this direction the school should plan boldly. Activities for the 5- to 6-year-old stages should aim at building up that necessary background of language experience so vital to later work in reading, while vocabulary extension and direct contact with word patterns, which appear in the pupils' reading material, should arise from the centres of interest of the 6- to 7-year-old pupils. The keynote of the curriculum should be a constant attempt to expand vocabulary through language activities and real experiences, for the ideas produced by words are essential to normal attitudes towards word recognition.

Conversely, of course, planned reading material for the first stages of reading from printed material should be related to the child's vocabulary. One study of the vocabularies of Scottish children [1] revealed the extent to which quite long words commonly occur in the speaking vocabularies of young children. Words such as *always, another, auntie, because, clothes, engine, finger, flower, nothing, penny, people, pictures, porridge, potatoes, pudding, sleeping, something, trousers, writing* were very common. A comparison of the common words listed in this study with the vocabularies of certain infant readers [2] suggests that a considerable number of words common to the child's

[1] *The Vocabularies of Scottish Five Year Old Children*, by A. C. and P. E. Vernon. Draft Copyright, 1943. The Scottish Council for Research in Education.

[2] *Word Counts of Infant Readers*, by A. C. and P. E. Vernon. Draft Copyright, 1940. The Scottish Council for Research in Education.

vocabulary are omitted, i.e. the material in some infant readers is not sufficiently based on child usage, and adult usage influences the content unduly.

KINAESTHETIC AID

Finally, the part contributed by *writing or tracing of words* towards their later recognition in reading should be carefully considered. As a supplementary means of revealing to pupils the function of words as indicators of real situations, and of acquainting them with varieties of word patterns, writing and tracing are essential experiences. Often the young child, having made or drawn a house or a harbour, a shop or a ship, a fort or a farm, wishes to label parts of his model or his drawing —usually in the first instance it is merely to give a name to his total effort. Thus Malcolm would frequently come from his garden sandpen or his playroom with requests such as, ' Will you write ship ? ' or ' How do you write (or spell) fort ? ' These words would then be written on his drawings or copied by him on to separate labels of wood or cardboard and then put in conspicuous places on the models.

It is not too much to say that a considerable amount of early experience with word forms and word ideas can come through the drawing/writing or play/writing situations in a natural and therefore effective manner. The feel of the word to the child as he traces or writes it is of great value in cementing the visual and the auditory aspects of the words into a meaningful whole. With young children word recognition may be consolidated through tracing and writing. The somewhat slower child who is still a little uncertain of new words, may be helped considerably by workbook exercises which include tracing and writing (see *Happy Venture Introductory Workbook* and *Workbook One* [1]). The kinaesthetic process has the effect of producing maximum concentration of attention, at a rate of perception and in a sequence that is needed to impress the word form on the child's mind. Presentation of the visual pattern is

[1] *Happy Venture Workbooks*, by F. J. Schonell (Oliver & Boyd)

often too fleeting or insufficiently pointed. Moreover, as workbook exercises in tracing and writing reveal, the young reader's attack on the perception of words, particularly in developing a systematic left to right perception, is considerably strengthened.

It is probably for this reason that supplementary tracing/ writing methods of teaching have been so successful with older, backward scholars. The additional aid obtained through the kinaesthetic channel often compensates for some degree of weakness in auditory or visual impressions. As I have shown in *Backwardness in the Basic Subjects*,[1] tracing and writing have a general training value when allied with the usual careful control and selection of vocabulary suited to older backward children, and a specific value in eliminating confusion of similar letters such as *b* and *d*, or transposition of letters and reversals of short words. The movement or kinaesthetic impressions of words are no less important than the visual or the auditory impressions in learning to read.

[1] *Backwardness in the Basic Subjects*, by F. J. Schonell, 4th ed. (Oliver & Boyd)

CHAPTER II

FACTORS IN READING ABILITY

From the discussion in Chapter I, of conditions influencing the basis of reading, i.e. word recognition, it is possible to enumerate the factors involved in reading ability. They may be listed as follows :

   (1) General maturity
   (2) Level of general intelligence
   (3) Abilities of visual and auditory recognition and discrimination of word patterns
   (4) Environmental factors in reading ability
   (5) Emotional attitudes of interest, individual application and confidence.

These five sets of factors, mental and environmental, act interdependently to produce the composite power of reading ability. We may then consider briefly the nature of each and the manner in which it operates to make its proportionate contribution to the complete ability of being able to read.

(1) *General Maturity*

We may define degree of general maturity as the level of growth reached by a pupil as assessed by development in a number of different directions in relation to chronological age. We may therefore think of any 5-year-old as having capacity to grow (*a*) physically (*b*) intellectually (*c*) socially and (*d*) emotionally. Obviously development in each of these four fields is uneven in most children ; there is often a difference in the levels reached in the four areas. Sometimes, of course, there is development beyond the norm, so that some 5-year-olds are taller and heavier than their peers and physiologically in other ways slightly advanced ; they are advanced intellectually, their social behaviour is superior to that of most of their friends and they show stable emotional attitudes. At the other end of the scale are children, whom we all know, who are physically and mentally subnormal and socially retarded. The pattern of growth is very much an individual matter and hence to lump together measures of different kinds and to call the product general maturity has severe limitations. But nevertheless it is a serviceable concept for use in educational and psychological work, provided we are continuously careful to note the many separate deviations that it may blur.

Increasingly during the past two decades, general maturity has been stressed as a factor in reading ability. This has been due to the attention that has been drawn to the relation between immaturity and reading failure leading to the post-ponement of formal reading in many school systems and to the introduction of programmes of preparatory reading or reading readiness, of varying quality and length. Of course, the concept is not new. In the late twenties Morphett and Washburne drew attention to the fact that reading should be postponed ' until a child has attained a mental age of 6 years 6 months '. Although subsequent research has modified this statement considerably in terms of particular conditions that prevail in regard to other factors that determine reading ability, yet it did point the way to a careful consideration of the level of maturity reached by young children when they first enter school. It caused teachers to wait before launching all children on the same formal task for which some were not at that point sufficiently well equipped to succeed.

More and more studies have piled up evidence showing that if children are physically or mentally or experientially immature, then we are predisposing many of them to failure in early reading instruction if we do not first do something about their particular immaturity. With some children time for growth is all that is needed, with others it is a matter of training together with opportunity for growth. Supporting evidence is now strong. For example, T. H. Eames, in studying the effects of visual defects, general physical conditions and disease, established a definite correlation between lowered physical powers and reading retardation.[1] Some prematurely born children tended to show visual defects which persisted through childhood to the detriment of progress in reading.

Olson [2] and his co-workers, following their researches in the University of Michigan, have developed this idea of reading achievement being a function of general maturity, and conversely of reading failure being a derivative of immaturity. Their argument is that the criterion of reading achievement is more closely related to ' organismic age ' which is a compound of measurements of height, weight, dentition, strength of grip, ossification of wrist bones, mental growth and school achievement, than to mental age. With this we would agree, for mental age is only one component in reading ability—vocabulary development, environmental background, motivation, physical maturity, particularly of vision and hearing, mental maturity and emotional stability, are all involved in producing reading achievement.

Anderson and Hughes [3] have shown from a study of matched groups of boys and girls in first grade that success in reading at this early stage is a function of total development. Children who are normal or advanced in general maturity succeed ; those who are retarded, particularly physically, tend to fail in reading.

While we would agree that reading is a function of total development, it would seem to us that to regard the compounded resultant of the above measures as synonymous with

[1] Reported in *Review of Educational Research*, April 1949 (American Educational Research Assn., Washington), pp. 107-13

[2] See ' Reading as a Function of Total Growth of the Child ', by W. C. Olson in *Reading and Pupil Development*, Supp. Education Monographs No. 51 (U.C.P., 1940). Those wishing to follow this line of thought further will find a useful exposition of the idea in *The Psychology of Teaching Reading*, by I. H. Anderson and W. F. Dearborn (Ronald Press Coy., N.Y., 1952), pp. 4-49. Reference should also be made to *Child Development*, by W. C. Olson (D. C. Heath & Co., 2nd ed., 1959).

[3] *The Relationship between Learning to Read and Growth as a Whole*, by I. H. Anderson and B. O. Hughes, Sch. of Educ. Bulletin, Univ. Michigan, 1955

total development or total growth, is an over simplification of the issue. This theory minimises the all-pervading influence on reading ability of the child's verbal background, of his home experiences, including emotional attitudes towards school and reading, and his emotional stability, including his degree of security. There are plenty of examples at each end of the scale of children who are less than average height, weight, dentition, ossification of wrist bones, for their age, but who read quite well and conversely, of children who are completely normal in what would be termed organismic age, but who fail to progress in reading.

Olson and his colleagues relate the more rapid physical maturation of girls as compared with boys to the reading superiority of girls as evidence of the close relationship between total growth and verbal achievement, but I do not think that these sex differences can be so simply explained.

Undoubtedly we have been well served by research workers who would ask us to pause and consider the maturity of each child before we dub him a failure in the reading field. But we should also be careful that the theory of total growth in relation to reading ability does not oversimplify the matter and have a dampening effect on some of the excellent training which is afforded to slow learners in reading. When all is said and done, we cannot always be sure when a child moves forward in reading how much is due to training and how much to increased maturity in certain functions necessary for reading. We *do* know that training in certain verbal activities can alter materially the scores in standardised tests which are often used in estimating level of maturity in certain fields.

We know there are children who may be retarded in their school work because of a certain lopsidedness in social or physical growth which, when righted, enables them to function on all cylinders together, so to speak.

In examining the philosophy that reading ability is a function of total growth, i.e. that maturity leads to success and immaturity to failure, we should pause, as I indicated in the opening paragraphs of this section, to dissect general growth or degree of general maturity into its component parts, in respect of each child. Sometimes children can succeed in reading in spite of limitations in growth, physical or mental. I have had scores of children of I.Q.s in the band 80 to 90 who, while coming from poor homes and having certain physical limitations, have nevertheless learned to read sufficiently well to use the skill effectively. Child progress in terms of overall explanations or total concepts must always be examined at the separate component level and in terms of each and every individual pupil.

(2) *Level of General Intelligence*

General intelligence is that all-round mental power which shows itself as an ability to see relationships between items of knowledge and then to apply these relationships to new situations. Level of general intelligence is one of the factors closely conditioning success in reading—obviously more intimately connected with power of understanding accurately and quickly what is read than with the level of word recognition. And while reading comprehension is to some extent dependent upon quick and accurate word recognition, both are examples of the perception and application of relationships. Thus the *mental age* of a child will be one of the determinants of the level and accuracy of his power of word recognition and of comprehension, while his *intelligence quotient* may indicate the speed of learning that can be expected from him. But the relationship between what we call general intelligence (itself a complex, composite ability) and reading ability is not easy to disentangle. All measures of intelligence involve varying degrees of verbal ability, whether they be understanding the oral or the written word. In other words, reading ability and intelligence have much in common, and we should be careful in our examination of the relationship to realise their reciprocal functioning. While measures of intelligence may be a guide in planning reading instruction, and in terms of expectancy of result, yet we should provide for each pupil's reading needs with something of an open mind. There are not a few intelligent children who fail to make normal progress in reading, and numerous examples of rather dull pupils who can read quite fluently.

All of these exceptions to the correlation between intelligence and reading ability can be explained by factors (1), (3), (4) and (5) of the above classification. Nevertheless the mental age and the intelligence quotient are guides of considerable value to (a) the age at which formal reading lessons should be started with children, (b) the amount of progress that should be expected from them, and (c) the nature of the reading material that should be used with them. Mental age and intelligence quotient, along with vocabulary level, and social and emotional development, will be factors in determining reading readiness. In the past too little notice has been taken of mental age in the teaching of reading, and many pupils 5 to 6 chronologically, but only 4 to 5 mentally, have been doomed to failure by a too early start with the more formal aspects of reading. For really dull pupils it is not too much to say that indirect and preparatory stages of reading should be continued for as much as two years, i.e. until the children are at least 7 years of age. The consensus of results from educational research indicates that for normal pupils the more formal approach to reading should not begin before a mental age of about 6 is reached, but of course there will be many exceptions to this guide, particularly where other conditions are favourable.

(3) Abilities of Visual and Auditory Recognition and Discrimination of Word Patterns

In addition to general intellectual power, ability in reading requires normal powers of perception in respect to the visual and the auditory patterns of words. These aptitudes, partly inborn, partly acquired, embrace firstly an ability to discriminate and to remember the visual patterns of words, and secondly an ability to associate sound units of words with the correct groups of letters—partly a breaking-down and partly a building-up process. Obviously, efficiency in these abilities is to some extent dependent upon normal powers of sight and hearing. Defects in either of these senses can cause acute reading deficiencies. But normal perceptual powers in the visual and auditory fields of word patterns mean more than normal sensory equipment. These particular perceptual abilities represent *a mental power which matures at different rates in different children.* This is evident from the cases of pupils whose intelligence, sensory powers, language background and emotional attitudes are normal, but who exhibit gross reading disability in either the visual or the auditory perceptual fields.

These abilities are, in some degree, acquired, and one of the conditions which influences their development is early language experience.

Thus the discrimination of visual patterns of words can be aided by the nature of the reading approach, the material used and the form and layout of the print. A sensible approach which provides the pupil with contrasting visual patterns of words helps the growth of this discriminatory power and obviates early confusion which is likely to inhibit its development. It is clear, too, that early reading material which does not engender confidence through a relatively light burden of new words with adequate repetition might also prevent growth of normal visual perceptual power. (This, of course, excludes the preparatory reading stages when pupils are given liberal help in reading *any* sentences they dictate or associate with their play or projects.)

Research results suggest that we can do much in training perceptual powers ; methods which enable children to detect similarities and differences between words, which increase their powers of word analysis and word study, all improve efficiency in perception of words. At the same time while the training element in visual perception seems to be a powerful one, yet in work with backward readers it is repeatedly demonstrated that some are not able to benefit from the training offered.   Factors of maturation, both of a general and a special kind, retard the progress of such children.   Undoubtedly some of them have not yet matured in the mental functions which underlie the ability to recognise and discriminate between visual word patterns of different kinds.   For the teacher this poses a difficult problem, for there is always the danger that training before the pupil is ready for it will do harm, and yet to leave the child without aid may have an equally adverse effect both emotionally and educationally.   The solution lies in planning remedial work of a broadly based kind which includes experiences that will lead not only to growth in ideas, vocabulary and sentence structure but also to knowledge of word forms.   We cannot afford not to give some experience of some simple word forms, however indirect this may be.   Perhaps the key aim is to remove the threat of failure for the child.

The nature of the print itself can aid visual perception. In the first introduction to a printed book the lines should be short, the type should not be less than 24 point and should resemble as nearly as possible the print script that the child is acquainted with in his writing.   This can be achieved by use of a 24 point Gill Sans type, for example :

Dora fell with the cat.

The dog runs to Mother.[1]

In the first half of the first reading book one-line sentences are advisable ; to begin with, the child is confused if he has to carry on the meaning to a second line.

For later reading books the lines should gradually lengthen and the print should gradually decrease to 18 or 16 point, but finally should not be less than 14 point.

[1] Taken from *Happy Venture Readers*, Introductory Book, by F. J. Schonell and F. I. Serjeant (Oliver & Boyd), p. 15

For example :

High in the house is a swing for the monkeys.[1]

"Stop, stop!" cried the clowns as they ran quickly after the ponies.[2]

Bold, clear type of correct size with adequate spacing between the words and between the lines is essential for correct discrimination of visual patterns of words. If the reader is at all doubtful of this, let him present a number of pupils, between the ages of 6+ and 8+, with typewritten material to read, and then present similar material printed in suitable 18 point type. The increase in rapidity and accuracy of word recognition, particularly with the average and slow readers, is most marked. It is not only the size of the print that makes a difference, but the spacing between the letters, the words and the lines.

The question of spacing brings us to another important finding in the psychology of reading. Photographs of the eyes during reading show that the process consists of a series of eye movements and eye pauses. Nothing is read while the eyes are in motion, but only during the momentary pauses. The number and length of these pauses depends on the age of the reader and the difficulty of the material. Children make more movements and pauses in reading a line than do adults, and there is always a great increase in eye movements as the reading material increases in difficulty for particular reading ages. Thus, reading material designed for 9-year-olds given to a pupil of reading age 7 greatly accentuates the amount of eye movement and the number of pauses in trying to recognise the difficult words. Hence the extreme importance

[1] (18 point). *Happy Venture Readers*, Book Two, p. 45
[2] (14 point). *Happy Venture Readers*, Book Four, p. 39

of suitable reading material for children of differing *reading ages*—an objective that can only be achieved by effective sectional, group and individual reading within classes.

During each eye pause the reader fully recognises two or three words in the material being read, and partially recognises a word or two on either side. The amount properly recognised at one pause is called the *span of recognition*, thus :

When they | got down, | they went | to see the small | elephant.

The partial recognition on either side of the span of recognition serves two purposes ; it helps the child to recognise the next words and it aids his comprehension of what is being read.

If too many difficult words are introduced into the line of print, the span of recognition is unnecessarily narrowed, and as a result the ease and speed of reading, together with the amount of what is understood, are seriously hampered.

Thus, whereas the last example is suitable reading material for a reading age of 6 to $6\frac{1}{2}$, the following would be too difficult:

One crane was unloading
cases of butter from Australia.

(reading age 7 to $7\frac{1}{2}$).

Such material would seriously impede normal development of eye-span and accurate understanding. When material has to be 'worried out' almost word by word, it is obvious that little can be understood of its content.[1]

One final point is the influence of the arrangement of the printed material on the development of normal eye-span.

---

[1] In early reading books there should not be more than an average of two to three new words per page.

C

Plenty of eye space around the lines, and words arranged in possible ' eye units ', aid speedy recognition. Thus :

The children had tea.

"Now," said Dora,
"let us play in a ring."

"Please hold my hand, Dora," said May.

"Hold my hand, Jack," said Dick.[1]

Here the arrangement of the material into useful recognition units and the spacing at the beginnings and ends of the lines make for rapid, clear perception and hence for more effective eye movements.

Ability to associate sounds of letters or groups of letters with their correct visual forms and to blend the sounds into a complete word is, like power of visual discrimination, an aptitude partly inborn, partly acquired.[2] There is evidence to show that ability to distinguish the visual patterns of words is easier than analysis and synthesis of their auditory components. Both aptitudes mature at different rates in different children, but the power of visual differentiation matures the earlier. It is easier for the child to discriminate between the visual patterns of *Dick* and *Mother*, *this* and *which*, than it is for him to make a sound analysis of these words. At the same time

---

[1] Taken from *Happy Venture Readers*, Book Two, p. 25
[2] For a full description of this specific factor see *Backwardness in the Basic Subjects*, by F. J. Schonell, 4th ed. (Oliver and Boyd), Chapter IX.

as the child's reading vocabulary begins to increase he needs the specific power of sound analysis to help him with many new words—discrimination and memory of visual patterns is not sufficient. Thus he tackles numerous new words by a combined visual-auditory approach ; one can see this operating time and time again in the reading of pupils aged 7 to 8 years. For example, they meet the word *London* and quietly say *L-on-don*, at first calling it *London* (o as in *cot* not o as in *won*) and then rectifying any initial error in pronunciation. This analysis and synthesis occurs frequently with longer and newer words once the child has achieved a certain facility in reading.

Examples of words thus analysed into approximate phonic units that I have recently noted with one pupil of mental age $7\frac{1}{2}$ to 8 years are : *church, wanted, kinds, lemonade, sentences, dotted, tomorrow.*

(4) *Environmental Factors in Reading Ability*

Fourthly, we come to essential environmental factors in reading ability, namely language background and extent of experiences—the former dependent to a large extent on the latter. Although the school does and can do much in the matter of language background and general experiences with which speech and vocabulary are so intimately entwined in their growth, yet this element in reading ability is a concomitant of home conditions. There is now substantial research evidence establishing the close relationship between reading and social factors. But home background is a wide and embracing term and includes influences of an emotional as well as a material kind, influences subtle as well as direct in their effects. When discussing this aspect of reading ability we should be clear about what we actually mean.

Most observers would agree that home background can include :

(*a*) economic conditions such as relate to income of the family, size of home, sufficiency and regularity of meals, sleep, etc. ;

(b) opportunities for play and for social experiences of different kinds—these, of course, are linked with the growth of concepts and vocabulary ;

(c) nature and amount of speech and language patterns of children particularly as they are influenced by the talk of their parents ;

(d) attitudes towards reading and writing, the amount of reading done in the home and the availability of books of varying levels of difficulty ;

(e) quality of family life in terms of inter-parental relationships as they influence the child's security and personality growth generally.

All of these are related in some measure to reading ability, though research shows that the relationship with (a) is almost negligible, except in extreme cases of physical deprivation.

A Scottish investigation established a clear relationship between socio-economic status and reading attainment of children of 5 to 8 years, but found considerable overlapping between one socio-economic level and another. While the differences were attributable largely to differences in the intelligence of the children, they drew attention to differences in the language backgrounds between children of good and poor socio-economic levels.[1] Other studies have unravelled the more intimate relationships between home background and reading, particularly as they relate to reading readiness. Differences in vocabulary have been clearly demonstrated. Children from good home backgrounds have larger meaning vocabularies than those from homes where opportunity for verbal growth is restricted. Growth in patterns of sentence structure differs between children from favourable and unfavourable home backgrounds. It is stated that the average child entering school at 5+ has a vocabulary of 2,000 words, but we still need absolute proof of this particular number. Vernon's sampling

[1] *Studies in Reading, Vol. II*—' Socio-Economic Status and Reading Ability', by V. M. McLaren, Scottish Council for Educational Research, Vol. XXXIV, 1950 (University of London Press), see particularly pp. 19-53.

of the vocabularies of 200 children between the ages of $4\frac{1}{2}$ and $5\frac{1}{2}$ collected during the playtime of the children showed how great is the range of words used in everyday situations by different children—varying from 30 to as many as 1,000 different words.[1] While these numbers were not, of course, the total vocabularies of the children, they did represent a sampling of what the pupils used in a functional situation and hence were probably an index of total vocabularies, with, of course, exceptions in the case of quiet, introverted children.

Effect of Adverse Emotional Conditions

While research has generally revealed that pupils with rich informational backgrounds and high verbal opportunities make more rapid progress in reading than those whose backgrounds are meagre, yet it would seem that these conditions are also linked with the kind of emotional relationships between parents and children that exist within the family unit. Sheldon and Carrillo[2] showed that superior reading ability was associated with (a) the number of books in the home ; (b) educational level of the parents ; (c) favourable attitudes of the child to school. Conversely there is ample evidence to show that disability in reading is very frequently associated with adverse emotional conditions within the family, such as those of overt parental hostility, parental rejection, neurotic conditions, separation of parents.

In a survey of reading backwardness and retardation in an English town involving 1,106 boys and 1,130 girls between the ages of 11 and 12, no less than 27 per cent of the backward readers had adverse home backgrounds.[3]

Perhaps one of the most reliable recent investigations of

[1] *Studies in Reading*, Vol. II, S.C.E.R. Publication No. XXVI (University of London Press), pp. 93-124

[2] 'Relation of Parents, Home, and Certain Developmental Characteristics to Children's Reading Ability', by W. D. Sheldon and O. L. N. Carrillo, *Elem. Sch. J.* 52, January 1952

[3] 'Backwardness and Retardation in Reading in Middlesbrough Survey', 1953, *Times Educational Supplement*, November 1953, London

the relationship of reading to home background has been carried out by Richardson.[1] He surveyed the reading attainments of 569 boys and 540 girls distributed in three schools of good, average and poor social neighbourhoods. He then selected from these schools 97 normal readers and 97 backward readers who were matched for age, intelligence, sex, nationality and physical fitness.

Richardson showed in the first part of his investigation that,

(a) better readers tended to come from economically more fortunate homes (see comments above) ;

(b) there is a marked difference in favour of the better readers in terms of educational background of parents;

(c) stability of family background and mental health of the parents favoured the successful readers ;

(d) there is no significant difference between readers and non-readers in terms of size of family, size of house in relation to number in family.

That part of Richardson's research dealing with experiential background strikingly underlined the importance of verbal opportunity in the home in relation to reading ability. He examined such factors as :

(a) number of books owned by the child ;

(b) extent to which the parents encouraged the child to read and attempted to expand his experiences by reading to him and telling him stories ;

(c) library membership ;

(d) radio listening ;

(e) range of experiences outside the home ;

(f) hobbies and interests ;

(g) constructive and educational toys in the home ;

(h) neighbourhood friends.

Difference between the groups was tested statistically.

[1] *Causes of Reading Retardation in the Primary School,* by J. A. Richardson, Ph.D. Thesis, University of Queensland, 1957

As Richardson says of the successful readers, ' the evidence seems quite definite that a far larger proportion of their parents are concerned to guide and encourage them in ways which are generally accounted advantageous from the viewpoint of school learning. They appear as a group to have richer, fuller lives, both as judged by provision made for them in their homes and in the range of their contacts outside.' [1]

In some homes from which the backward readers came the children had not a single picture or story book of their own before coming to school, nor had they any of the usual story telling or learning of nursery rhymes.

But it is perhaps in regard to the quality and cohesiveness of the family as a unit that the evidence is so revealing in its influence on progress in reading. Assessments of family life made by a psychologist and a qualified social worker in regard to the families of normal readers and backward readers related to :

    (a) cohesiveness of the family ;
    (b) affectional relationships between the child and other members of the family ;
    (c) parental concern for the child's welfare ;
    (d) discipline in the home ;
    (e) cultural level of the home ;
    (f) encouragement of independence ;
    (g) present security in the home.

There is obviously some overlap between these items which all make their contribution to item (g) and which in reality represent the total situation in terms of family stability for the child. In every item mentioned above the comparison favours the successful reader, in some cases decisively, as determined by statistical checks.

This aspect of the research was also supplemented by information about the family circumstances during the first five years of the child's life (changes of family environment, separation from parents, traumatic experiences). Richardson's observations [1] are ' there is no question in my mind that

[1] J. A. Richardson, *op. cit.*

the disparity between the groups suggested by the figures represents the true picture and that very many more of the retarded than of the successful children were brought up during the formative pre-school years in families which experienced stresses and upheavals which at times threatened or undermined the security and happiness of its members'.

Reviewing then the nature of the foregoing information from various sources, we may summarise the research findings as indicating that environmental and family conditions of the child may influence his progress in reading in two broad directions :

(a) in terms of the language background and associated experiences of a verbal and general kind that serve as a foundation and continuing support for learning to read—such conditions including not only experiences of a concrete kind but attitudes towards reading and school learning as well ;

(b) in terms of the quality of the home life and its influence on the child's security and hence on his ability to apply himself to his school tasks.

Although some of the influences here discussed overlap one with the other and although no clear cut causal relationship with reading ability is established, yet the nature of the relationship is too strong to be overlooked. We know there are children who succeed in reading in spite of adverse home conditions but, as I have said elsewhere, it is often the particular combination of conditions that loads the dice against the failing child. For the child who succeeds it is often the supernormal quality of his intelligence that offsets poor home background, but for the dull child or the child handicapped by some weakness, who requires every additional aid he can obtain to offset his handicap, then adverse home conditions often just tip the scales against him.

Finally, what is crystal clear and incontrovertible is that a variety of experiences, trips and visits, books and pictures, stories told and questions answered are all contributors to the development of reading ability, for they furnish that background of spoken language so vital to an adequate meaning vocabulary. A child finds it easier to read words he has used frequently in his everyday life, and he finds it easier to understand reading material which deals with activities he himself has experienced. A background pregnant with meaning and experience provides clues to the nature of word patterns and enables pupils to make maximum use of context in word recognition.

(5) *Emotional Attitudes of Interest, Individual Application and Confidence*

We have long observed the effect of failure in reading on personality adjustment, but the influence of personality maladjustment on reading achievement and the converse, namely the effect of positive emotional conditions on effort and progress in reading are not so widely recognised or accepted. And yet ability in reading as with other school skills is just as sensitive to positive and negative emotional attitudes. The vital need is to make clear to all concerned the significance of emotional and personality factors in promoting or inhibiting progress in reading. We know that the child learns best when he is eager to try and when he is interested. Some school methods produce these attitudes, others result in certain children developing a feeling of failure and frustration. Some parents, too, show a sensible attitude towards the child's reading problems by widening his experiences, praising his efforts, and not expecting unduly high standards in the early stages. Others do the opposite by limiting the child's opportunities, robbing him of confidence, or pushing him along too fast, ultimately into the abyss of confusion.

Evidence of this is provided every day by the backward readers who attend remedial centres or educational clinics. Some of these children need extensive therapeutic help before remedial teaching can even commence. Others need opportunities for emotional expression parallel with their specific

instruction in reading. In fact, those working with cases of
reading failure are almost inclined to regard every case as one of
personality disturbance as well as poor reading achievement.
Richardson's comparison of ninety-seven poor readers with
ninety-seven good readers clearly showed the part that emotional factors play in reading ability. Very many more of the
backward readers, as compared with the successful group,
varied from normality as regards personality adjustment.
Apart from differences in confidence, persistence and self-
assertion, there was a marked dissimilarity between the two
groups in regard to fears, mainly centering around the school
or the home. Such information obtained, and checked by
the usual statistical measures, was also supplemented by
studies of the groups by means of projection tests (Murray's
Thematic Apperception Test).

Studies of backward readers would suggest that for a considerable proportion of the children, emotional instability
and insecurity are the major conditions, with school failure just
one symptom of that condition or a precipitating factor in it.

The relationship between adverse personality conditions
amongst good readers (97) and poor readers (97) is very well
exemplified by Richardson's figures :

Adverse Family Conditions	*Good Readers*	*Backward Readers*
Major Factor . .	9·2	51·5
Minor Factor . .	15·5	25·8
Personality Maladjustment		
Major Factor . .	7·2	56·7
Minor Factor . .	15·5	18·6

The way in which the possible effects of adverse emotional
conditions may be overcome is perhaps best illustrated by an
actual case. Janet R., aged $10\frac{5}{12}$ at the time of the examination, had a non-verbal I.Q. of 95 and a Terman Merrill
I.Q. of 113.

'Developmental health history was very poor. She
had been subject to respiratory troubles from an early age,

poliomyelitis necessitating hospitalisation at $3\frac{1}{2}$; severe glandular fever at $5\frac{1}{2}$ years which meant her missing four months' schooling ; and subsequent frequent ailments and irregular school attendance. Additionally, diagnostic tests indicated weakness in the visual perception of words and a tendency to reversals. Despite these difficulties, she was well up to her age and grade level in all aspects of reading and in spelling and was a well-integrated personality. The explanation lay in an exceptionally good home situation. The parents were both well-adjusted, stable people. They had recognised the possible effects of the girl's traumatic experiences in infancy and met temporary behaviour difficulties following separation at $3\frac{1}{2}$ years with consistent patience and understanding. The girl's physical limitations were recognised but not stressed. She had been encouraged to take up compensatory activities—she was a keen stamp collector and an active member of a Brownie troop. Intra-family relationships were good. The parents had successfully avoided the temptation to overprotect their child and had encouraged her to independence in every way. On the educational side, the parents had helped her right from the start by providing and encouraging her to read simple books, appropriate to her level of maturity. During her periods of enforced absence from school they had maintained contact with the teachers and covered at home the work she was missing. In Grade V she ranked 10th out of 43 children despite having missed over one-third of her total possible school attendance.'[1]

Maladjustment and Retardation

It is now fairly clear that good home conditions and stable intra-family relationships may offset considerably a child's difficulties of a physical, emotional or educational kind, and

[1] Taken from *Causes of Reading Retardation in the Primary School*, by J. A. Richardson, Ph.D. Thesis, University of Queensland, 1957, pp. 230-31

hence may result in almost normal learning conditions. On the other hand, adverse home conditions resulting in insecurity may so disturb the conditions underlying successful learning that the child falls behind to the point of severe retardation. How, it may be asked, does this condition come about ? Maladjustment and retardation are twin products of the denial to young children of two major psychological needs, both vital and far-reaching in their effect on the personality growth of children. In the first place young children need security and affection for their effective mental growth. If the child is secure in the love of his parents, then and only then can his emotional life develop normally. This psychological nutrient enables him to apply his physical and intellectual powers with confidence, persistence and initiative. It is insecurity which robs the young child of successful self-expression and a sense of achievement. These two needs, security and satisfactory self-expression, are reciprocal in their action and tend to supplement each other.

The significance for school learning of security and provision for self-expression, through play, companionship and adequate materials, is obvious. In the first place, when the child is insecure his mind is so taken up with his frustration that he is unable to apply himself to the task in hand. This is best illustrated by a case of an intelligent boy of nine, backward in reading and spelling, who attended our remedial centre for the best part of a year, during which he made not the slightest improvement. Why? Because any remedial teaching was quite ineffective in the face of the problem with which the child was wrestling, namely that produced by a continuing conflict in his mind about his parents, who were trying to make up their minds whether they would separate or continue to live together.

In the second place, as I have shown earlier, when there is deprivation of opportunity and frustration in self-expression and achievement, the child may either withdraw his efforts and retreat to become passive, inert and seemingly stupid or direct the force of his frustration towards rebellion and misbehaviour.

Significance of Emotional Factors for Teachers

What then is the full significance of this information to teachers planning a reading programme for pupils between the ages of 5 and 7 ? There are, I believe, three guiding principles to be observed :

(1) There must be an adequate preparatory or readiness period which is not only broadly educational in its nature but compensatory and therapeutic in its effect. All kinds of activities and purposeful play, linking with projects of a creative and constructive kind, should characterise the early stage of reading. In this way we can both discover and help to treat some of those children for whom insecurity or frustration may be a barrier to school learning. Activity situations involving other children will soon reveal the children who cannot concentrate, who cannot persist with a job, who cannot co-operate and who need individual help.

(2) There should be a close bond between home and school so that teachers get to know the parents and family situations, so far as this is possible with forty or fifty young charges to guide all day and every day of the school week. However, here the head teacher can help with that small group of maladjusted and unprepared children. It would benefit Education Authorities to have attached to groups of infant schools, a trained woman social worker, who knows something of infant methods. She could do much within the home to prevent the failure of some children.[1]

[1] See, for example, *The Young School Failure*, by Miriam Highfield (Oliver & Boyd, 1948).

(3) Finally, the school might well seek the help of its psychological service or its remedial education centre to help with the readjustment of potential failures in the early stages of school life.[1]

To sum up, then, the context of this chapter on ability in reading, we have revealed the complexity of the reading process, with the main factors in it, each of an interacting kind. We have shown that factors emotional, as well as intellectual, enter into progress in reading, and have established the fact that the home background, both in its material and its psychological provision, can profoundly augment or interfere with the preparation of the child for reading and his subsequent efforts in reading lessons.

Parental attitudes and reading approaches which sustain interest, preserve confidence and foster the pupil's power of application and persistence, make no mean contribution to progress in reading.

There is the need for teaching methods to allow for gradual maturation in several directions if success in reading is to be achieved. Thus it would seem that the nature of learning to read, and the varying rates of development of different children in the factors producing reading ability, make it imperative that there should be a properly planned preparatory period in learning to read. A detailed consideration of this preparatory reading stage will constitute the next chapter.

[1] See 'Personality Patterns of Retarded Readers', by G. Spache, 1957 *J. of Educ. Res.* 50, pp. 462-9.

CHAPTER III

PREPARATORY PERIOD
IN LEARNING TO READ

MOST children come to school eager to learn to read, but too many of them lose this initial enthusiasm through early failure and discouragement. Why is this so? The question can be largely answered in one sentence—because insufficient care is devoted to creating the correct type and amount of preparatory background for learning to read. As was shown in the previous chapter, reading is a complex process. Ability in it depends upon five major factors, each of which is characterised by a very wide range of development.

As has already been intimated, these factors act interdependently, so that a particular child may reveal all five characteristics highly developed and hence may be most favourably equipped for learning to read. A mature, highly intelligent child, with a stable personality, whose perceptual powers are excellent and whose experiences and language background are exceptionally wide, usually learns to read irrespective of method or of the teacher's endeavours. But it will be apparent that there may be children who are ill-equipped in every one of the five named factors, or, if not in every one, then in at least two or three separate essentials. Imagine the pre-reading handicaps of dull children who come from very poor homes and who already show certain unfavourable emotional attitudes. What calamitous maladjustment must ensue from a too early start in formal reading (with its all too pointed, yet unavoidable, objective evaluations) with these children. With such a picture in mind it is impossible *that anyone should doubt the wisdom of a preparatory readiness programme in learning to read.* This is all the more urgent since, in British schools, children enter at the age of

5+ years. Evidence from my own researches shows that some entrants to infant classes are nearer 4+, and a few 3+, years in intellectual, experiential, verbal and/or emotional equipment.

There is now a wealth of evidence not only in research journals, but available from many teachers, that a preparatory or readiness programme has both preventive and constructive values for children first entering school. Over the past decades we have seen that readiness activities are necessary for *all* children if they are to be helped to adjust to school, to gain those essential attitudes and that foundation knowledge necessary for success in reading. The evidence is conclusive that the introduction of readiness programmes has reduced early reading failure, but more than that, it has enabled young children to develop qualities that stand them in good stead later in their primary school course.[1]

There is no doubt that some young children can be taught to read as soon as they enter school and there are Scottish and English reports to substantiate this, but few educationists or enlightened teachers of reading would support the proposal that children should undertake a formal reading programme as soon as they enter school. Children lose considerably by not having a wise, broad preparation period, and although the loss might not show itself in the first year, there are obvious disadvantages later. A later start seems to favour the development of effective attitudes towards reading, growth in knowledge of sentence patterns and in breadth of reading interests.

Readiness Programmes must be Broad

The term ' readiness ' has come to mean a number of different things.

Firstly, it may mean the pupil's level of maturation in regard to the factors which underlie reading ability.

---

[1] See, for example, the findings of Miss D. E. M. Gardner in *Testing Results in the Infant School* (Methuen, 1948).

Secondly, it may mean a programme of activities designed to bridge the gap from home to school, and to enable children to develop attitudes and to assimilate vocabulary and ideas that will subserve their later reading instruction.

Thirdly, it may mean training in particular skills related to reading, such as noting the differences between word shapes, looking at words and pictures, following a sequence of pictures, and so on, such as are contained in reading readiness books.

From the outset I would like to emphasise that a readiness programme must be broad in its objectives and must cater for the very wide range of abilities and backgrounds found amongst new entrants to school. A reading readiness programme is really only one aspect of a wider provision for fitting children to the job of school learning. Provision for reading readiness must include a wide variety of activities that involve self-expression, the use of language, listening to stories, handling books, working in groups, developing concentration, training in attention and a host of other experiences that will all help the pupil to work not only by himself but with others, not only at reading but at other school subjects as well.

A reading readiness period would be seriously limited in its usefulness if it involved only exercises from so-called readiness books, together with a few desultory discussions and some rather narrow preparation for the reading books the children were later to use. In brief, *a preparatory or readiness period must improve pupil adjustment and develop attitudes as well as give practice in related verbal activities.*

Readiness programmes are not readily accepted by all who are involved in teaching children to read. While a few of those who do not adopt this approach are to be found amongst head teachers of primary schools to which infant classes are attached, or in small rural schools, yet the strongest indirect opposition often comes from parents. The now small and decreasing amount of teacher opposition is often based on ignorance which could be eliminated by arranging for all

D

training college students who propose to teach in primary schools to have a short course on methods of teaching reading at the infant school level, with visits to see classes of children in action. Head teachers and others may well be converted through refresher courses which include demonstrations.[1] Teachers in charge of small country schools should be led to see that many of the activities of the preparatory period fit in well with the demands on them for allocating assignments to some pupils in certain classes or sections while they themselves are engaged in instructing others. Many of the activities of a good readiness programme involve the development of independent habits of working so necessary in the small rural school.

With parents who expect their children to begin reading books soon after they enter school, there is the need for information pamphlets and school Open Days through which to explain how vital is the preparation stage in order to ensure that *all* children will be ready for reading of the more formal and accepted kind. But, of course, the best argument is that reading readiness activities constitute the teaching of reading in its best form. Children are not only adjusting and getting ready, but they are adding to their vocabularies and, moreover, learning to read many words and phrases that they will later need in their books. Whatever the argument or method used to inform parents, it is important to take specific steps to counter parent pressure in regard to early steps in reading instruction.

Specific Objectives

The specific activities and objectives of a reading readiness period should therefore include :

1. varied use of language for increasing concepts, vocabulary and knowledge of sentence patterns—stories, discussions centering round classroom activities ;

2. listening to stories to improve attention ;

---

[1] Morris (*op. cit.* p. 148) found that 75 per cent of head teachers in primary schools believed in reading readiness—this is no doubt due to refresher courses.

3. asking questions to develop the desire for understanding ;
4. free activities with self-chosen play material to develop that sense of purpose, concentration and persistence so necessary in learning to read ;
5. rhymes and songs to develop a sense of sound ;
6. drawing and tracing to aid in the understanding of ideas and recognition of word patterns ;
7. projects to develop a train of ideas, expand vocabulary and increase knowledge ;
8. participation in group work to develop co-operation and initiative ;
9. participation in group activities which involve following teacher instructions ;
10. becoming acquainted with books through opportunities to handle picture books connected with everyday activities or centering round a project.

The methods by which these objectives may be achieved are discussed in detail in later sections, and we might well conclude this section by emphasising the fact that the readiness or preparatory stage of reading is not something distinct and apart ; it is simply an early stage of reading instruction and should be considered as such.

Pupils as Individuals

It is imperative to consider our infant school pupils during their 5- to 6-year stage as being fitted out experientially and emotionally for the more serious demands of the 6- to 7-year period. Provision for adequate maturation must be the key-note of the training in this first year—some dull pupils may even need a longer period for maturation, perhaps to 7+ or even 8+ years. Now, in this respect, it is important to consider each pupil from an individual viewpoint. This can be accomplished by using some such guide as the reading readiness chart represented on pages 52 and 53.

READING READINESS CHART[1]

SURNAME ....

CHRISTIAN NAME(S) ....

Date of Birth		
Day	Month	Year

DATE............... ACTUAL AGE.............years...........months

1. MENTAL LEVEL[2]

(i) Remarks based on class observations

(ii) Supplementary data (if used)

Intelligence quotient............... Mental age............

Remarks :

2. READING READINESS ABILITIES[2]

(i) Remarks based on class observations

(ii) Reading Readiness Test Results (or results from use of a Reading Readiness Book)

SCALE FOR SECTIONS 3, 4, 5, 6 AND 7

(a) much above average   (c) average   (e) much below average

(b) above average   (d) below average

---

3. ESTIMATE OF EXPERIENTIAL BACKGROUND[2]

(a)   (b)   (c)   (d)   (e)

Remarks :

[1] The actual card, which is published by Oliver & Boyd, has of course considerably more space for remarks and other entries.

[2] See 'Notes on the Reading Readiness Chart', pp. 54-9.

4. EXTENT AND QUALITY OF PLAY WITH OTHER
   CHILDREN
   (*a*)　　　(*b*)　　　(*c*)　　　(*d*)　　　(*e*)
   Remarks :

5. (i) ABILITY TO LISTEN TO WHAT IS READ
   (*a*)　　　(*b*)　　　(*c*)　　　(*d*)　　　(*e*)
   Remarks :

   (ii) ABILITY TO ATTEND TO INSTRUCTIONS
   (*a*)　　　(*b*)　　　(*c*)　　　(*d*)　　　(*e*)
   Remarks :

6. EXTENT OF VOCABULARY AND TALK WITH OTHERS
   (*a*)　　　(*b*)　　　(*c*)　　　(*d*)　　　(*e*)
   Remarks :

7. ATTITUDE TOWARDS BOOKS AND PRINTED WORDS
   (including a desire to learn to read)
   (*a*)　　　(*b*)　　　(*c*)　　　(*d*)　　　(*e*)
   Remarks :

8. SOCIAL AND EMOTIONAL ATTITUDES[1]

9. PHYSICAL EQUIPMENT

	Normal	Below normal
(i) Vision		
(ii) Hearing		
(iii) Speech (accuracy)		
(iv) Physical state (energy)		

   Measures taken in respect to any defect :

10. RECOMMENDATIONS AS RESULT OF SECTIONS
    1 TO 9

11. FURTHER PROGRESS

[1] See 'Notes on the Reading Readiness Chart', p. 56.

While it is now accepted educational practice to give all pupils a period of reading preparation, we should use this as a diagnostic stage also, so that we know at the end of the time those pupils who still require further readiness activities.

There are four main fields in which we should look for readiness. These are :

(1) mental or intellectual level ;
(2) experiential background including speech and verbal level ;
(3) social and emotional attitudes, including both individual attitudes and ability to play and co-operate with other children ;
(4) physical conditions.

(1) *Mental or Intellectual Level*

This may be determined from the child's reactions in class as shown in such situations as his ability,

(a) to understand a story and retell its main incidents in the correct sequence ;
(b) to carry out simple instructions demanded of him ;
(c) to look at and interpret pictures ;
(d) to recall a sentence or digits dictated to him ;
(e) to know the meanings of simple words.

But is is also useful if a mental age, as determined by an acceptable intelligence test, is also available for indicating readiness. The best test for use with children of this age is either the *Stanford Binet Intelligence Test*[1] or the *Wechsler Intelligence Scale for Children (WISC)*[2] but both these are individual tests requiring previous training for their effective administration. The *Moray House Picture Test*,[3] which is a non-verbal group test, may be used, but we need to be most cautious

---

[1] See manual for the third revision (Houghton Mifflin, 1960).
[2] By David Wechsler (Williams & Wilkins Co., Baltimore)
[3] *Moray House Picture Intelligence Test*, by M. A. Mellone (University of London Press)

in the use of its results inasmuch as some children who fail to understand the oral instructions may obtain scores lower than their real intellectual level (on the other hand understanding oral instructions is one measure of intelligence and some who fail in the test do so because their poor level of mental development prevents them from understanding what is required of them).[1] Any result from an intelligence test should simply be regarded as one item in predicting reading readiness—the correlations with reading results are usually about ·5. No tests should be given until the child has had several months in school.

(2) *Experiential Background and Verbal Level*

Some estimate of this is perhaps the most important single item in assessing reading readiness, for we are dealing with the very stuff on which successful reading is based, namely extent of ideas, vocabulary and sentence patterns. While reading readiness tests may yield some information on this item, yet we should, during the preparatory period, endeavour to assess the child's vocabulary knowledge and his ability to participate in speech situations, to ask and answer questions, to relate stories told to him, and to react in an interested way to picture books, particularly in attending to details of pictures.

During discussion periods the teacher will in turn deal with home situations that involve names of articles and their uses, shopping, routine personal activities and articles associated with them. Facts about the social environment—tradespeople, animals, the postman, vehicles, and so on—will enter into the talks, as will simple concepts of space, time, size, number and colour. All of these situations will give the teacher a chance to estimate the levels of general verbal and informational development of her children.

Knowledge of vocabulary, extent of speech, ability to listen, attend and understand in oral situations, together with attitude towards books and name labels, will give a teacher the best indication of whether a child is ready for reading.

[1] Equally, some children score higher I.Q.s on this test than they do with an individual test.

(3) *Social and Emotional Attitudes*

Although teachers are occasionally inclined to overlook emotional attitudes as factors in reading readiness, research over the past decade (see Chapter II) has clearly established their importance in determining early progress in reading. For the teacher in the classroom, evidence of these factors will be available from the various activities in which children engage. She will soon be able to name those children who find it difficult to listen continuously, who cannot settle to self-chosen play, who give up tasks quickly, who do not join in effectively with others but who stand aside in a passive, introverted way or who take a delight in interfering with the play of others. As Miss Alderson and Miss Simpson revealed so clearly in their account of the daily free play period in their infant school at Doncaster, these children soon show up if situations are provided for free activities.[1] Under the old classroom conditions of 'sit in your place, do this, don't talk', independence of action and group efforts did not enter and the adverse psychological conditions of such children were masked or hidden. They are now quickly revealed in the modern activity approach, which, while it is so effectively educative for most children, can be both diagnostic and, later, therapeutic for those needing special help.

Emotional attitudes of independence, interest, persistence and self-confidence which are revealed in any preparatory stage of reading are essentials to success in reading. Along with these go attitudes towards books and the printed word. Teachers should endeavour to make some kind of assessment in each of these characteristics of the young learner.

(4) *Physical Conditions*

Here, as I have shown in earlier chapters, there is the need to discover whether a child is physically fitted for commencing

[1] See *Creative Play in the Infant School*, by D. Alderson and D. Simpson (Pitman & Co., 1950).

reading or whether he requires some attention to make him physically effective for the task of learning to read.

The most obvious conditions that the teacher should note are :

(*a*) *the child's vision*

> Is he able to attend to books ?
> Does he screw up his eyes or complain of sore eyes or headaches

It is a useful precaution for all young children to have their eyes tested when they enter school.

(*b*) *the child's hearing* [1]

> Does he keep his mouth open frequently ?
> Does he misunderstand questions or ask for words to be repeated ? (This, of course, is also done by dull children.) It may be necessary to send a child for an audiometric test.
> Is he inclined to be timid or reserved ?

Some children with hearing defects are inclined to be withdrawn and somewhat suspicious of others, mainly because they cannot grasp all that is going on.

(*c*) *the child's speech*

> Is the child's speech clear or is there an impediment ?
> Does he confuse sounds like *f* and *th*, *d* and *t* ?

Speech handicaps are sometimes linked with hearing defects. Occasionally baby speech tends to persist, but this usually disappears in a normal social atmosphere. Where there is a speech defect then a child should undergo a special examination which might need to be followed by speech therapy.

---

[1] Teachers may find the *Stycar Hearing Tests*, published by the National Foundation for Educational Research, useful for screening purposes with young children and retardates.

(d) the child's physical state

Note should be made of the physical state of each child. While information on this may be gathered during visits of members of the School Medical Service yet teachers may themselves discover those children who obviously are not functioning at par. The general signs are irritability, an inability to settle at a task, shown in restlessness or lassitude, and a tendency to fatigue. Anaemic children and those who have insufficient sleep are unable to attend and to concentrate. I have shown in *Backwardness in the Basic Subjects* that a proportion of school failures come from the listless pupils, who tire easily and who not infrequently suffer from a succession of catarrhal colds or common infections. The attention of visiting health workers or school nurses might well be drawn to these children.

ASSESSMENT OF READING READINESS
Notes on the Reading Readiness Chart

(1) *Mental Level.* This may be judged mainly from the child's behaviour, taking into consideration points mentioned on page 54. It is by no means imperative to use an intelligence test, scores of which do not correlate highly with later reading achievement. Moreover, many children of 5+ in their first months at school are not sufficiently well adjusted to do a group test.

(2) *Reading Readiness Abilities.* These may be noted during the readiness period, but the teacher will be aided in her assessment by use of results from a reading readiness book.[1] In addition to its training value a reading readiness book has diagnostic value, particularly for those immature children

---

[1] For example, *Happy Venture Reading Fun*, by F. J. Schonell (Oliver & Boyd, 1961)

who will need an extended preparatory reading stage. The main points to look for will be :

(*a*) the child's ability to follow oral instructions ;

(*b*) the child's ability to make some recognition of words, such as his own name, labels of common objects round the room, names of characters in the book he will first use (e.g. Nip, Dick, Fluff, Dora) ;

(*c*) ability to follow the sequence of incidents in a pictorial representation of a story ;

(*d*) identification of pictures of common objects ;

(*e*) seeing likenesses and similarities in words and phrases;

(*f*) being able to follow and interpret simple stories read aloud.

There will be some overlap here between abilities listed under (1) *Mental Level*, and those elements used for making an assessment under (2).

(3) *Experiential Background.* This is meant to cover an assessment of the kind of experiential background, particularly in regard to general information, extent of knowledge outside the home and level of sentence structure attained. It relates fairly closely to the kind of home background which the child has, not economic background, but quality of stimulus and interest provided by the parents and others.

(4) *Social and Emotional Attitudes.* An estimate of these will be based on classroom observation of the child at his play/work and his playing/working with others. Perhaps the most important elements for the teacher to note are :

(i) ability to settle to a task and persist with it ;

(ii) the child's degree of security as evidenced by attitude towards teachers and children, and in various situations demanding independence ;

(iii) ability to co-operate and play with others ;

(iv) any special behaviour difficulties, such as bullying, temper tantrums, untruthfulness, undue self-display ;

(v) any undue tendency towards withdrawal, timidity, undue fear, infantile regression.

Reading Readiness Tests

In Britain and British Commonwealth countries there is a very limited use of reading readiness tests, although they are used in varying degrees in different States of the U.S.A., but in this respect it should be remembered that in most British Commonwealth countries children enter school at 5+, whereas in an appreciable number of U.S.A. States they do not start until 6+. British teachers prefer to make use of their reading readiness stage not only for preparation but for diagnosis as well and, moreover, to let their pupils become well oriented to school situations before any tests are given. However, it may well be that simple, well-tried readiness tests suited to the 5+ child might yield useful information in regard to early training for reading.

On the other hand as more and more schools make provision for a reading readiness period of sufficient length to reveal those children who are not fitted to proceed to formal reading at the end of such a period, then reading readiness tests are to a large extent being rendered redundant.

While reading readiness tests vary considerably in their content, the types of exercise they employ fall into two main groups :

    (*a*) exercises based on aspects of the reading process, but not dealing with words, e.g. identifying pictures of common objects, selecting the missing item in the drawing of a common object ;

    (*b*) exercises that employ words, phrases or sentences which the testee has to match, find differences in, or otherwise use or interpret in some way.

Some are unrelated to any series of reading books ; in others the second type of exercise is based on words and phrases in the pre-primers or primers of a particular series. More specifically the tests consist of these types of exercises :

    (*a*) finding similarities or differences between pairs of pictures of objects, animals, geometric forms, etc. ;

(*b*) following instructions ;

(*c*) detecting missing parts of pictures of common objects or designs ;

(*d*) picture vocabulary tests ; identification of pictures of common objects or concepts ;

(*e*) relating words, phrases or sentences to pictures ;

(*f*) finding differences or similarities in letters, words and phrases ;

(*g*) rhyming of words ;

(*h*) working out the sequence of events in a series of pictures which tell a story ;

(*i*) recalling the ideas in a story.

Results of experimental studies with readiness tests do not yield very promising correlation coefficients in terms of their prognostic values, usually of the order of ·4 to ·6 according to the nature of the sub-test. The more the material in the readiness test deals with words and phrases, matching them or finding differences between them, which is really the essence of reading, then the higher is the correlation. But there is something tautological about this approach, which virtually means that if the pupil shows he has developed word recognition in the readiness test, then he will succeed in word recognition in his formal reading material.

A compromise that has both diagnostic and preparatory value is to give children exercises such as are contained in readiness books as a small part of their general preparatory programme. In this way the teacher may gain the best of both approaches—readiness book results are then used as part of the wider and more careful observation of children in a variety of functional situations.

The chart on page 52 has value not only for the material it yields about the children and the basis it provides for correct grouping later, but also because it brings more vividly before the mind of head teacher and class teacher alike the complexity of maturation needed for normal progress in reading. It shows that chronological age is much less important than mental age in determining readiness for reading ; it shows that other factors besides either chronological or mental age exert an important influence. It emphasises the need to provide preparatory experiences of a wide and integrated kind which will enable consolidation to go on slowly and unconsciously through the first year at school.

How is this background achieved ? What kinds of experiences should we provide for its effective development ?

PRE-READING EXPERIENCES

The preliminary background for reading must be built up by providing the children with experiences that will lead to comparatively rich and varied language development. Their spoken language must be wide enough to cover many of the common words and ideas that they will later meet in a printed form. Without such a background of spoken language there is a chance that the printed symbols will have only an artificial and arbitrary meaning for some pupils. Furthermore, the indirect experiences of the pupils with books, pictures and printed words in different situations should be such as to create the correct attitude towards reading. The printed word must 'tell something' to the child ; it must unfold information that he likes to hear, that provides pleasure and incentive for him.

The preparatory reading stage may be divided into two periods :

(a) that between 3+ and 5 years, spent either entirely at home or partly at home and partly in a nursery (kindergarten) class or school ;

(b) that between 5 and 6 years of age, spent in an infant class.

In both periods play will be the most profitable activity for the development of language. In the former period a variety of materials and toys should be provided so that situations will develop which demand the use of language.

Naturally such situations are more likely to arise in a well-ordered nursery (kindergarten) class. Here the pupil will have the added incentive to talk and to indulge in dramatic play through constant contact with other children. This early play period is regarded by many psychologists as indispensable to the pupil's later application in school activities. Certainly it enables the child to try out his emotional self and gradually to stabilise himself through expression of his emotions in a variety of situations. Charlotte Bühler [1] has produced evidence that the pupils who fail in their play, either through some environmental limitation or from some early emotional maladjustment, are not infrequently the ones destined to become failures in school.

In this period, too, the use of picture books and pictures with simple captions will do much to mould the initial stages of an understanding attitude towards books.[2] Particularly useful are the child's attempts at drawing and painting for clarifying his conceptions of everyday experiences—a considerable amount of speech often derives spontaneously from the child's artistic efforts, which represent a desire to show what he knows rather than what he sees.

But just as valuable as the play of the 3 to 5 period is the contact with understanding adults. The young child is doubly fortunate if he finds these in both his school and his home. It is in this way that the much discussed only child often makes up very much more by this contact than he loses in the lack of child companionship. Intelligent parents—and contacts with other interesting adults—can produce most amazing vocabulary development in young children, and it is not an exaggeration to say that normally intelligent children under such conditions may often, in vocabulary, be two or three years ahead of other children of the same age in a less

---

[1] See *Birth to Maturity*, by C. Bühler (Routledge).

[2] The various materials and associated play situations for this stage are admirably described in *The Child under Eight*, ed. by F. I. Serjeant (Gresham Publishing Co.), Vols. i-iv ; and also in *Learning and Teaching in the Infant School*, by E. G. Hume (Longman & Co.), Chapter II.

fortunate environment. The constant and varied discussion that naturally arises in many one-child families provides for unlimited vocabulary development on the part of the child.

Even more useful than the informal discussion with adults are the stories read and told to children. Here, of course, nursery classes can make provision for all children. A considerable amount of speech and questioning can arise naturally from story situations.

Although by far the greater amount of the preparation for reading in this first period (3 to 5 years) is general in nature and entirely incidental, yet there are occasions upon which children can be helped to discriminate their own name from others. There are times, too, when they request one to write the name of a favourite friend or animal, or to provide a name or a title for their constructive efforts. These and other such sporadic examples should be fostered, for in them lie the very beginnings of successful word recognition.

PREPARATORY STAGE (SECOND PERIOD, AGE 5-6 YEARS)

Perhaps one of the most natural and most effective ways of introducing pupils to the reading situation in this second preparatory stage is through their growing interest in drawing and painting.[1] At 5+ the child is beginning to use his brush, crayon or pencil with sufficient co-ordination to show what he knows about everyday situations and activities. Usually he wishes to talk about his drawings, and this natural connection between speech and action may be used to start a real interest in writing and reading.

For pupils at this age a simple drawing book can be made by sewing into a semi-stiff paper cover a number of paper

[1] Some of the ideas in this section I owe to the co-operation of Miss F. I. Serjeant, formerly Lecturer in Infant Method, Goldsmiths' College, University of London. Miss Serjeant's insistence upon the psychological need for an adequate period of preparation in the pre-reading period, based on use of the pupil's everyday interests, made a useful contribution to the teaching of reading in British schools.

butts (4 inches long and 1 inch wide) to which blank drawing pages can be pasted.

DAPHNE'S

BOOK

The pupil draws, in colours, anything he likes (usually something relating to home, play, or everyday experiences) and then the teacher, at the pupil's direction, prints a number of sentences on the opposite page. A specimen of a page from Malcolm's book (at age 5½ years) is given on pages 74-75.

The teacher reads the sentences back to the pupil, who then tries to repeat them with very liberal help. *No standard is fixed and no attempt at formal correctness is made in this work, but indirectly a meaningful reading situation is created.* Later the pupil may trace over the sentences with a crayon or a thick black pencil, a prelude to a further step of copying sentences. In this way writing and reading situations are naturally linked. Sometimes the pupil cuts out and pastes into his book pictures about which rhymes may be written. What has been printed by the teacher has maximum meaning and interest for the pupils—essential requisites in learning to read.

Constructive and Make-Believe Play

In addition to drawing and painting, pupils of 5+ should be allowed to pursue individual interests[1] connected with

[1] Further suggestions on the preparatory stage are given in the *Happy Venture Teacher's Manual*, 1959, pp. 33-42.

E

making things and arranging materials. A variety of odds and ends such as wood (e.g. suitably sawn to represent the hulls of boats, or in various shaped blocks), clay, cloth, boxes of all sizes, paste and paints should be provided. Pupils may be given a little guidance in this work, but for the most part they will follow individual desires and make something which satisfies them—it is only with pasting, pinning, nailing or painting that some assistance may be required. Together with making things, children like arranging materials such as boxes (to make ' play ' boats, houses, lifts, forts), small animals (to put in farmyards or zoos), soldiers, trucks, guns (to set out in encampments), tiny aeroplanes, hangars, searchlights (to arrange in aerodromes), small ships (to arrange in harbours or on voyages), trains, trucks (to arrange on lines or in lines).

Associated with all these activities there is considerable talk and some questioning. More advanced pupils often require labels to be printed so that they can place them on what they have constructed or what they have arranged. All this individual or small group work is a natural preparation for a group study or centre of interest which may be successfully planned with 5½- to 7-year-olds.

Book Corner or Library Table

Simple supplementary reading devices [1] for this preparatory period should be given a place in the daily time-table. Thus a library table on which are coloured pictures with simple captions, good picture books which the children will want read to them, and collections of cards bearing pictures and rhymes will contribute towards satisfactory reading readiness.

It is important that children should handle books and be attracted to the pictures. If possible, there should be some group work in which children follow the teacher while she reads a very simple story, pointing not only to the pictures

[1] For further discussion of activities associated with this stage of reading, see the *Happy Venture Teachers' Manual*, by F. J. Schonell (Oliver & Boyd).

but to the print.[1] In time pupils will be able to select particular books for story reading time—all of this is part of the
process of interesting children in, and orienting them towards,
the time when they will use their first reading cards and books.

Nature Charts, Reading Charts, News Sheets

The keeping of a nature calendar, a weather chart, a news
sheet, all provide opportunity for contact with meaningful
printed material relating to the pupils' own experiences, e.g.

Monday	wet		Monday	Fed the tadpoles
Tuesday	fine, cold		Tuesday	Tom brought a newt
Wednesday	fine, windy		Wednesday	Went into the woods
Thursday	dull		Thursday	
Friday	cold		Friday	

Pupils of 5½ can be led to keep simple charts such as the
above.

Reading charts or news sheets are an excellent way of
developing an interest in reading and of preparing children for
the first steps in word recognition and in gaining a meaningful
attitude towards reading. Events at home or in school are
taken as the basis for discussion. Simple sentences are placed
on the blackboard from dictation by selected pupils. These
are later used with appropriate illustrations or drawings by
the children to compile a reading sheet on an ordinary sheet of
semi-stiff manilla.

Teachers should be careful in compiling these to use only
very short sentences, three to five words in length, very boldly
printed. The selection and repetition of words might follow
the principles that characterise the compilation of a first book

[1] Sets of *Before We Read* books (Oliver & Boyd) are excellent for this. The
series consists of various sets of books each underlining a different background
approach ; thus *Ann's Toys* (4 books) *John's Toys* (4 books), *Animal Books* (photographs of animals with large clear captions), *Interest Books*, (photographs of
children engaged in various activities with appropriate captions), *Round and About
Books, Town Books, Helen Books, Red Squirrel Books.*

in a reading series.[1] Three sentences on a chart would be sufficient.

A development of this is the compilation of group reading charts with groups of ten or twelve children in the class, during which activity work the teacher manages adroitly to use a considerable number of the same words from chart to chart. While the key or topic words associated with, say, ' My Birthday ', or ' Bonfire Night ' are different, there are many others from chart to chart that have something in common. It is amazing how much of these charts children can memorise, later actually recognising particular titles or words, and at a still later stage actually reading some of the sentences.

A useful individual chart is, ' This is me ' or ' My Chart ', consisting of personal information together with drawings by each pupil. Nursery rhyme sheets with appropriate pictures may also be helpful at this stage.[2]

Need for Exercises in Matching, Noting Similarities and Differences in Pictures and Words in the Readiness Programme

Experience with preparatory reading programmes reveals that there is a real need for specific exercises, such as those shown opposite, leading up to reading, in addition to the general verbal and experiential activities that characterise most readiness periods. These exercises should come later in the programme after attitudes have been established and ideas, sentence patterns, speech vocabulary and information have been expanded. The exercises, which are discussed in the section on readiness books, might include:

(*a*) those which have as their basis *matching* of pictures of objects, and *detecting differences* between pairs of pictures, later introducing words in relation to pictures. The primary colours might well be included in the exercises.

[1] Teachers will find a full discussion on vocabulary and sentences construction in early reading books in the *Happy Venture Teacher's Manual*, pp. 14-22.

[2] For detailed considerations of these and other devices, see *The Child under Eight*, ed. by F. I Serjeant (Gresham Publishing Company) pp. 10-27.

The above are smaller black-and-white versions of exercises taken from *Reading Fun* (the reading readiness book for *Happy Venture*) by F. J. Schonell (Oliver & Boyd, 1961).

(b) *listening to sounds* of words, at first in nursery rhymes, later in sentences based on the first book of the reading series, e.g. :

> Fluff is my cat
> She is fat.
> Here is Dick.
> He has a stick

This is merely a method of training children to listen to sounds of similar endings, but the same idea may be applied to beginning letters of words. ' Listen, these words start with the same sound ' :

' Dick, Dora,
Yes, they both start with *D*.
Doll, dog ; yes, they both start with *d*.
Mother, me ; yes, they both start with *m*.
Now listen, which *two* words start with the same sound ?
cat, cap, boat.' (repeat)

Such exercises, interspersed with intervals of ' I spy with my little eye, something beginning with . . .', and the supplying of the end words of nursery rhymes, all add zest to the preparatory period, and also lay a foundation for the pupil in his handling of words in the reading book. It should be remembered that young children do not recognise each word simply as a separate, stark visual pattern ; often they say or half say words to themselves and the combination of meaning and sound values triggers off that sense of the familiar to them by setting the word against its speech background.

Additional Aids

Further verbal activities would include dramatisation, the use of labels associated with common objects in the room, or associating the names of fruits, vegetables, seasons, etc., with their printed symbols. Activity cards are useful with older and more able pupils, e.g. :

> Clap your hands.
> Shut the door.

Nursery rhyme cards with appropriate pictures are also helpful at this age.

Finally, reference might be made to the use of devices which enable the child to concentrate on the composition of individual words and in this respect Swiss and French educationists have urged the use of printing sets and typewriters in the teaching of reading. Certainly printing sets are useful with older backward children, and tachistoscopic methods, the exposure of words one at a time in the slit of a tachistoscope, have been known to improve word recognition with slow readers,[1] but these would seem to be devices for use at a later stage in reading, and for the failing pupils.

READING READINESS BOOKS

I have indicated earlier that the readiness period should provide for specific exercises as well as general verbal experiences; in other words it should provide for training as well as maturation. In this respect reading readiness books with a variety of exercises which lead up to reading, and which may include some of the words and phrases that children will later experience in their first reading book or reading cards, have a part to play at this stage. These exercises not only have novelty but they introduce children to handling a book and in so doing develop attention to printed material. The books certainly provide discussion, and they give practice to pupils in following pictures, patterns and words from left to right. Readiness books may be made the medium of consolidating information about common objects, colours and word meanings.

How far exercises which purport to develop visual or auditory discrimination have a close relationship with reading,

---

[1] For a summary of tachistoscopic experiments, see *Visual Perceptual Abilities and Early Reading Progress*, by Jean T. Goins (University of Chicago Press, 1958).

or really develop these aspects of the reading process, has never been satisfactorily tested experimentally. But for other reasons they certainly have a place in the readiness period. Children like them and they give the child a sense of purpose as he handles a book and uses a pencil. Readiness books which contain an introduction to the characters in a reading series, help also to make the transition from the oral to the printed word easier.

Group Study or Centre of Interest

A sound reading programme aims at teaching pupils to read in a way that is meaningful and satisfying. Actual contact with printed symbols should be preceded by and accompanied by experiences which really interest children and which ensure that they understand what they read. The idea should be constantly kept in mind that children will recognise words more easily if the material to be read represents pleasant actions and experiences with which they are familiar. Thus reading material should be intimately related to the children's lives. To achieve these various aims the obvious method of approach is to relate early reading matter to a group study or centre of interest in which all pupils are interested and in which all can participate.

Practically every child is interested in building a house, and if a suitable space in the classroom is available this is an activity which can be linked with much meaningful reading.[1]

According to the age of the pupils there will be proportionate limitations to their building efforts ; pupils of 6+ are much more effective in planning and in making continuous efforts than pupils of 5+ years. If possible, younger children may be aided by providing large cardboard boxes, which can be slit along certain sides to provide a house with ceilings and rooms, and then various aspects of decoration may be pursued from that point. But what is enjoyed best is the building of a

[1] Other studies suitable for the $5\frac{1}{2}$- to 7-year period are making shops of different kinds, preparing for and giving a party, etc.

This is a story of the
highway patrol highway
patrol are police   But they
were different unifoms.   There was
once a man who commited crime one
day he went up some bank steps
and when he was nearly at the
top of them he disguised him self
with a mask he said hand over
the money so they had to give
him the money and he had
to pass a gurd to get to
farnsworth he said let me throo
the gurd said whate a minute
but the man shot the gurd and
the highway patrol shot the man
that shot the gurd that serves
him right dosent it do you think so
I do.

The engine is going
to Scotland.
The coal is in the truck.
The coal is going to
Scotland.

(Malcolm had twice been by train to Scotland)

One moring morning Prudence Kitten
was coming down stairs when
she heard someone singing at
the gate that must be
Alexander water rat. Prudence
walked along the path
good morning miss Prudence

I have got a letter
from your sister Primrose
she says we will be
coming to tea will four o'clock
do prudence said go and
tell her
Primrose married a sailor
called Nelson.

house from the beginning, so to speak. For this purpose the teacher provides a couple of clothes horses, or trestles with laths to form the walls of the rooms. Then all pupils paint patterns or pictures on large sheets of paper which are pinned on to the frame of the walls. All-over patterns may be made by older pupils to form quite attractive walls.

Talk about the home and those who live in it may keep pace with the building of it. Reading sheets may be prepared by the teacher using simple words and dealing with the interesting aspects of the home as they develop. Thus, initial talks may centre round Mother and Father and about a boy and a girl named Dick and Dora who live in the home.

The first reading sheet may show :

> Mother lives in this home.
> Father lives in this home.
> Dick lives in this home.
> Dora lives in this home.

In further talks the pupils may suggest that Dick has a dog and Dora a cat. The pupils may then make a drawing of Dick's dog and Dora's cat. The names of Nip and Fluff may be selected for these animals. A further stage in the compilation of the reading sheets may include :

> Dick has a dog.
> Dora has a cat.
> Dick's dog is called Nip.
> Dora's cat is called Fluff.

The teacher may read these sentences through to the class and then the class read them through with her. In addition some of the brighter pupils may be encouraged to read the sentences individually. Here again there is no formal teaching as such. Some pupils learn some words, whilst brighter ones may even assimilate quite a number of common words.

The next step in the building of the house is the attractive one of interior furnishing and decoration. Boxes are used to make a table, chairs and cupboards. This involves some sawing, hammering and painting by the boys. At the same time the girls may be encouraged to sew with brightly coloured wools or beads dish-cloths to make curtains for the windows and cupboards.

Then some pupils make table-cloths from paper, cut out in patterns or coloured with crayons or paints, while others make coloured table-mats from stiff paper.

The making of utensils—cups, saucers, plates—is usually a fascinating part of the study, and here papier mâché is suitable ; it can be hardened and covered with white paper upon which simple patterns may be painted. Knives, forks and spoons are cut from stiff paper or cardboard. Imitation foods may be prepared by mixing flour and salt (three parts flour to one part salt) and then allowing pupils to mould loaves of bread, cakes, eggs, fruit, etc. The salt causes these to dry hard, after which they may be painted or covered with coloured paper or tinsel such as is found around chocolate biscuits.

In addition it is possible to develop all kinds of interior decoration such as construction of vases (from flour and salt covered with brightly coloured paper), drawing pictures, illustrating stories told by the teacher, and making toys (balls, tops, cars, boats) to be placed in or near the home.

A useful preparation for word recognition is the use of labels both on the various parts of the house and on its contents. These are of inestimable help later, as in the more systematic stage of learning to read the pupils will be reading about their activities connected with the home, and many of these words will appear in the printed material.

Coincident with the building and decorating of the home and the making of articles for it, the teacher may continue stories about the activities within the home by its different occupants. She will relate what Nip can do—beg for a bone, play with a ball, play with Dora and Dick—and she will encourage pupils to discuss what Fluff does—where she sleeps, what she eats, and all about her kittens. Stories will be told about Dora and her doll Jane, Dick and Dora, Nip and Fluff, about skipping and jumping, and about visits to the shops.[1]

Only a few of the incidents connected with building and furnishing the home and occasional stories told by the teacher will be used for the reading sheets [2]—not a little of the material will be for extending experiences and increasing vocabulary preparatory to the more intensive teaching of reading.

At the same time the more able children (mental age 6+ onwards) can make good use of the reading sheets to assimilate common words, many of which will appear in their first readers.

Supplementary to the reading sheets are the reading books which the pupils can prepare for themselves. These are similar to those described in an earlier section, but deal specifically with the group study and the people (Mother, Father, Dick, Dora, Nip and Fluff) connected with it.

Older pupils of 6+ may be expected to make use of work books. These contain cyclostyled sheets, previously prepared by the teacher, and consisting of simple sentences relating to the group study. The sentences are formed of words which will appear in the first reader and they all involve drawing, colouring, cutting-out and pasting. Examples of pages from a teacher-made workbook are given in Appendix III.

Other exercises which can be used to extend the reading value of the group study are

(*a*) matching cards,

(*b*) copying sentences from the blackboard.

(*a*) Cards such as those provided in the Happy Venture Card Material (Oliver and Boyd) may be used, and sets of

---

[1] This discussion will form an excellent background of meaning and vocabulary when pupils are introduced to Introductory Book (*Fluff and Nip*) and Book One (*Playtime*) of the *Happy Venture Readers*.

[2] The amount of material used by the teacher for reading sheets or for the pupils' workbooks, the level of construction in the group study and the amount of word recognition and assimilation will depend much upon the age and calibre of the children. Varying standards and varying contributions will be expected from different children within the same age group.

words given to each pupil. The simple sentences on the card are then matched by the pupils from the separate words.[1]

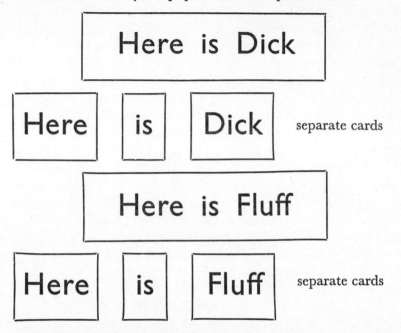

(b) More able pupils of 6+ who have made some progress with writing may be allowed to copy a sentence relating to the group study from the blackboard.

RESULTS OF THE PREPARATORY STAGE

The results of this preparatory reading period between the ages of $5\frac{1}{2}$ and 6 years, or beyond 6+ for some pupils, should have been firstly to provide the pupil with the necessary experiences and to stimulate his talk so that he will acquire a vocabulary helpful in his understanding of the printed words. Secondly, this period should arrange experiences intimately associated with the child's life which can form the basis of his reading material. If he has made the things,

[1] The Happy Venture Card Material provides graded material for matching words, phrases and sentences found in the *Happy Venture Readers* (Oliver and Boyd).

talked about the experiences and seen words associated with the activities and objects on which his first reading books are based, he is likely to succeed in the all-important task of learning to read. Finally, with respect to this period, and as a preparation for the second, more formal aspect of learning to read, teachers should note that little is achieved by forcing pupils to read. Some of them will make little apparent progress between the ages of 5 and 6, then in the 6+ stage they will forge ahead with rapid strides. In this preparatory period give them all kinds of opportunities for achieving the necessary verbal background and the right attitude towards words, but do not set rigid standards. The consolidating period between 5+ and 6 or 6+ is often not measurable ; its effect is often delayed, but there is little doubt of its value from 6+ onwards for those children who are fortunate enough to have had it.[1]

[1] An excellent supplementary chapter to this is Chapter VI of D. H. Russell's very readable book, *Children Learn to Read* (Ginn).

CHAPTER IV

A PSYCHOLOGICAL ANALYSIS OF READING METHODS

FROM the flexible preparatory reading stage described in the last chapter we now pass to the more systematic reading lessons which should take place in an intensive way with pupils of *mental* age 6+ onwards. Naturally not all pupils in a group will be ready for the more formal introduction to a reading book, and for those not ready a continuation of methods such as those outlined in the last chapter is probably the best procedure. For the others the problem of method needs consideration, and this seems a suitable point at which to consider methods of teaching reading as such. Briefly, we can enumerate three methods of teaching reading :

    (i) the phonic method
    (ii) the word whole or look-and-say method,
    (iii) the sentence method.

Not all educationists would agree with this simple tripartite classification of reading methods. In the first place I have left out the old, outmoded alphabetic method, by which our grandparents learned to read, namely learning one's A, B, C and then simply spelling out the words—of course other aids were employed, particularly word building, and children learned to read often because they noticed differences in shapes of words, and in spite of the basic alphabetic approach.

In a recent admirable survey of the teaching of reading,[1] particularly as it relates to work in different countries, Gray has drawn attention to a classification, with a *historical basis,*

---

[1] *The Teaching of Reading and Writing,* by W. S. Gray (Unesco and Evans Bros., 1956). Students of reading might read Chapter V in this interesting book.

noting that earlier methods were very specialised while later ones have tended to be much more eclectic. His list is :

(a) *Alphabetic Method*
Names of letters—a spelling method.

(b) *Phonic Method*
Sounds of letters—a sounding method, more effective with a regular or phonic language.

(c) *Syllabic Method*
Key unit is the syllable—syllables are learned and then combined as in the teaching of certain Asian languages, also Spanish and Portuguese. It has been found useful in literacy campaigns involving teaching reading to adults, but the method may lead to confusion, particularly as the syllables taught increase in number.

(d) *Word Method*
This is basically the word whole or look-and-say method which is now used in conjunction with other methods.

(e) *Sentence Method*
This starts with the sentence as a unit, but really becomes a sentence/word whole method, for the study of words is vital to its development.

(f) *Story Method*
This starts with a story in the beginning and breaks down to sentences and words later.

In discussing methods I do not consider the activity method a separate method as such, but as an approach to reading whereby an accepted sentence/look-and-say combination is used to teach children to read, per medium of material which is compiled round the children's activities or projects. Nor can the supplementary impressions, gained by children through writing and tracing words, vital as they are for many children, be termed a method. The kinaesthetic approach is simply a means of consolidating visual and auditory impressions of words.

Although we may consider the phonic method, the word whole method and the sentence method as separate methods, it is not very often that we find only one method used for a continuous period to teach pupils to read—perhaps the only example would be a thoroughgoing phonic method. Actually the main interest lies in the answer to the question, ' Which method is used in commencing to teach reading ? ', for most enlightened teachers make their reading method (after a time) a combination of all three methods.

(i) *The Phonic Method*

This is an analytic method which aims at providing pupils with the sounds of the various letters of the alphabet. By various picture and letter association devices the pupils are taught that

a says a	as in *apple*		
b ,, b	,, ,, *bat*		
c ,, c	,, ,, *cat*	and so on.	

Then they are given regular words to read.

Only one sound is given for each letter, so that the scheme is weak in the first place because it provides only twenty-six sounds out of the sixty-odd sounds which the twenty-six letters of the alphabet may represent.[1] For example, *a* may be

---

[1] There have been attempts, happily now no longer used, to provide phonic alphabets, in which the variations in sound of the vowels, the silent letters and the several sounds of some consonants have been indicated by particular marks on the letters themselves. Of such a kind was the Hayes phonoscript method. In Hayes phonoscript primers special distinguishing marks were put on the various variations of the vowels and consonants. Thus :

> *a* as in *cat* was printed without any mark,
> *a* as in *all* had a mark in the middle of the letter,
> *a* as in *cage* had a mark at the base of the letter.

Then there would be lines of print giving practice in these modifications of the sounds, e.g.

> Paul has a pet cat.
> Paul's train is all bent. He will weep. (*ee* and *e* would have distinguishing
> Let me tell Sam.   marks.)
> Pip is a gentle little pet.
> It has a cage.

All final letters which were not sounded had a ' silence ' mark. See *Phonoscript Primer*, by Alfred E. Hayes (G. P. Putnam and Sons Ltd., London, 1922).

sounded as in *cat*, *all*, *ate*, *arm* or *any*. Using only one sound form of each letter limits to some extent the reading material that can be used in first reading books. Irregular words (*here*, *one*, *Mother*) must be omitted or else learnt as word wholes. Furthermore, words containing the vowels must be of the five taught forms—*a* as in *cat*, *e* as in *wet*, *i* as in *bit*, *o* as in *cot*, *u* as in *cut*. Obviously these limitations make the reading material largely artificial. Thus in one phonic reader we find :

> The red hen is in the pen.
> The pig in a wig did a jig.
> The wig fell in a bog.

Such material is not related to the pupil's interests, activities and everyday experiences, and can have little real attraction for them. No preliminary background of vocabulary and understanding is created by the advocates of this method.

Another disadvantage of the limitation in word forms available for phonic readers is that too many two- and three-letter words are used. As a result of this, pupils are not only deprived of the most important means of learning words, namely, through contrast of their visual patterns, but confusion of words of similar length (*on*, *no; as*, *in; is*, *so; if*, *of*, *for; was*, *saw; am*, *an*) is thereby produced. There is insufficient use of longer common everyday words like *Mother*, *bring*, *this*, *play*, *father*, to form contrasts to words like *on*, *is*, *at*, *to*, which should be very sparingly introduced at properly spaced intervals into early reading material. Moreover, numbers of small words with artificial association destroy the story element which means so much to young pupils.

Psychological research confirms the opinion that for many pupils the phonic method is too analytic—they do not really understand what they are doing, and not a few of them are mentally unable to associate sounds with symbols and then to analyse and blend these as they find them in words. Dolch and Bloomster[1] provide evidence that few children with

---

[1] E. W. Dolch and M. Bloomster, ' Phonic Readiness ', *Elementary School Journal* (1937), xxxviii, pp. 201-5

F

mental ages below 7 show ability in phonic analysis, even where there has been systematic instruction.

Research and classroom evidence show that the phonic method is an artificial mechanical approach, which is beyond the ability of some children—they cannot intelligently make extensive use of the breaking down/building up method of tackling new words. Perhaps the matter is best summed up by head teachers of infant schools who took part in a recent action experiment preparatory to a change-over from a formal phonic method using the usual, dull, unattractive books to the newer, sentence/word whole approach, using well-illustrated books, which deal with material related to children's interests and which employ vocabulary control :

> ' These children find the task of learning to read so much easier than under the phonic method. There is no strain. At no time, as yet, have the children seemed to be striving to do something beyond their ability. From little faces there has been an absence of frowns and worried looks that plead, " What is it all about ; why can't I do it ? " ' [1]

Another head teacher in a large infant school participating in the experiment, reports of the new sentence method and the new material :

> ' The words are of varying lengths and are readily recognised through this difference in appearance. The words in the present readers (i.e. phonic readers) are all the same length and can only be distinguished *by the use of phonics, which at this stage are a meaningless jumble to most children.*' [1]

A further disadvantage of the accompanying analysis and synthesis of the phonic method is that it tends to slow down learning by word wholes, and hence interferes with

---

[1] *An Investigation of Methods of Teaching Reading in Infants' Schools*, p. 15, Bulletin No. 9, Research and Guidance Branch, Education Department, Queensland, 1955

the idea of grasping words, phrases and sentences as meaningful reading units. This is particularly so where drills on groups of similar phonic words are excessive. With some children sounding becomes an end in itself, and in consequence both normal eye movements and understanding of what is read are unnecessarily impeded.

In the experiment referred to above the most marked difference between the children taught by the phonic method with phonic material and those taught by sentence method/ look-and-say, with material based on everyday interests, was an increase in fluency and understanding of what they read.

One advantage of the phonic method is that it gives the pupil more power in tackling *certain new* words, not, as is claimed, a method of tackling *many* new words, for irregular words must be learnt as wholes ; variations from the learnt vowel and consonant sounds occasion difficulty to all but the bright pupils. However, this confidence produced in pupils by the use of simple controlled material in the initial stages is not to be underestimated. My own experience is that I would rather see children of below-average intelligence using a phonic method than an ultra-modern ' experience ' or ' project ' method where the material is simply ' groaning ' with a too heavy vocabulary burden which does not give the pupils a chance to learn gradually a selected number of new words. Such a method is all project and little reading. Actually neither method is the most effective with the duller section of the class.

It is obvious from the foregoing remarks that the phonic method for *beginning* reading is not the most suitable approach. This fact is being increasingly recognised by intelligent teachers. But it is also just as sure that at a certain stage in the pupil's reading he requires some phonic training, particularly to supplement his attack on words, and as a basis for his spelling. To this point I shall return later in the chapter when the place of phonic training in a sensible reading programme is discussed in detail.

Some teachers, while following a phonic method, use the word whole method in conjunction with it. Irregular words are put at the top of each reading page and pupils learn these before commencing the lesson. This does reduce the artificiality of the reading material, but on the whole the method labours under the various disadvantages previously outlined.

(ii) *The Word Whole or Look-and-Say Method*

As the name implies, this method of teaching reading commences with a unit larger than the letter or sound, namely, the word. To a degree this method is psychologically sound, for it starts with large meaningful units which the child understands as ' telling him something ' and which provides for easier discrimination through length and shape of differing word patterns (see Chapter I). The method is sound in so far as words like *run, jump, dog* may assume for a young child the nature of a complete language unit, i.e. the word may be equivalent to the true unit, a sentence, for the above words may mean ' See me run ', ' I can jump ', ' Here is my dog '. In this respect much more meaningful material is employed early in this method of teaching reading than in the phonic method. Furthermore, words are soon expanded into sentences. Some teachers introduce the word whole method through an extensive use of pictures. Cards are prepared which have a picture illustrating the word or revealing its meaning with the word printed underneath.

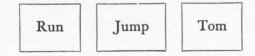

Then the next development is short sentences :

Run to Tom.
Jump to Tom.
Tom jumps.
Tom runs.

A limitation of the method is that it does not always rest on that secure foundation of pre-reading preparation which characterises the sentence method. Pupils are sometimes deprived too long of the very real aid of contextual clues as conveyed by the sentence, and therefore a too long initial introduction through words alone may set up a considerable amount of guessing. However, progressive teachers, who make full use of pictures and activity work and who soon merge words into sentences, obtain striking success with this method. My own experience is that *the word whole method of commencing reading, particularly when concrete words adaptable to illustrations are used, is the best method to use with the duller 25 per cent of the class.* A small vocabulary based on the children's interests can be built up very quickly.

(iii) *The Sentence Method*

In the sentence method of teaching reading the sentence is regarded as the unit to which the pupil is introduced. In its early form the sentence method was artificial and psychologically unsound—the sentences used were unrelated to children's interests and activities and were too long and difficult. Not a few pupils were destined to failure when the early material was of this type :

The round moon is shining on the silvery water.

Pupils were acquainted with the sentence through a short story and a picture. Further sentences and pictures about unrelated topics, followed by sentence matching or word matching, often completed the confusion of the poorer members of the class.

Some of the most backward readers I have had to examine have been rather dull children who had been taught by this artificial kind of sentence method. This form of sentence method has happily disappeared, and in recent years the method has been linked with the real experiences of the children. As a result the sentences have been real and natural. Moreover, sound textbooks have limited the sentences to three or four words in the initial stages. To begin with, short sentences like these are used :

Here is Dick.

Here is Nip.

Then two or three sentences about Dick and Nip may follow, and next a simple story of four or six lines embodying some incident. Later sentences lengthen to seven or eight words, repetition being used to help the development of word discrimination.

On page 101 is reproduced a page from a textbook based on a scientifically planned sentence method approach, with small vocabulary burden and illustrations of maximum assistance to the pupils.

The great value of the sentence method lies in the help it offers to the pupil from the context and from the continuity of meaning that can be embodied in the material. Although sentences appear as the units, all pupils have had some association with many of the words used during the preparatory stage (see Chapter III), because the method is based on child experiences and activities, and hence makes use of everyday words that the child uses in those activities. It is not restricted in its words or material, and its selection of these is psychologically sound for it is based on child development. In the centre of interest previously outlined many pupils have had experience of words like *Dick, Jack, Mother, dog, tea, home, shop, toy*, which later come into the early reading books.

In both word whole and sentence methods the names of the letters are learnt through a sensibly related writing-reading programme.

Parallel with the first attempts at reading from cards or a book there is a certain amount of word matching, making sentences from sets of cardboard words, and sentence matching. This together with workbook exercises makes the approach to the printed sentences in the books a much easier matter. Where new words per page are controlled, and hence where repetition is adequate, it is possible for pupils to see printed on the blackboard the new words in the next page or pages they have to read. Moreover, they can, if necessary, write the new words before attempting the next page in the reading book. This may not be necessary for many pupils, but is a great aid to the less able readers. Finally, most teachers of the sentence method allow for some phonic training when a usable vocabulary has been mastered through the combined effects of meaning, and of visual and kinaesthetic impressions.

RESEARCH COMPARISONS OF VARIOUS METHODS

Over the decades of the present century numerous attempts have been made to compare various methods of teaching reading, but all such attempts, while demonstrating that a particular method has particular values in developing some aspect of reading for some children—word recognition, fluency, ability to tackle new words, interest, comprehension and so on—have revealed marked limitations. This general finding has been due to the fact that there are many variables influencing growth in reading, an appreciable number of which, in many experiments, have not been taken into account. Furthermore, while it has been possible to measure objectively certain aspects of reading, some of the important variables of a subjective kind such as interest in reading, pupil application, confidence, improvement in oral and written language patterns and so on, have not been measurable. Gray has given a useful summary of these experiments in *The Teaching of Reading and Writing*,[1] while other accounts have appeared in the successive three-yearly reviews of investigations in reading in the *Journal of Educational Research* [2] and the *Review of Educational Research.*[3]

In general, research studies have served to show not that any particular method, effectively used, has complete superiority

---

[1] *The Teaching of Reading and Writing*, by W. S. Gray (Unesco & Evans Bros.), Chapter IV, 1956
[2] Published by Dembar Publications, Box 737, Madison 3, Wisconsin, for the Educational Research Association, Bloomington, Illinois
[3] Published by the American Educational Research Assn., 1201 Sixteenth Street, Washington, 6

in every aspect of reading over any other method, but that *each method or major aspect of reading instruction that has been developed over the decades makes its own contribution to the teaching of reading.* Now this only holds good provided that factors of age, intelligence, motivation, books used and language background of the pupils are favourable. An old-fashioned, dull as ditchwater, phonic method in which unnatural, uninteresting material is used, is definitely inferior to other methods. Similarly, an activity method, employing material with a very heavy vocabulary burden, is completely unsuitable for dull children.

This all points to the need for an eclectic approach to instruction in early reading, and to the need for educationists and teachers to see that reading programmes are not narrowly conceived, but that they take note of accepted findings in regard to the *particular contribution that different approaches to the teaching of reading can make for particular groups of children.* The task of teaching children to read is too vital to their educational progress and to their personality growth to permit the narrow philosophies that characterise those who attack the sentence/word whole approach to reading instruction, now widely used so successfully in so many countries.

ESSENTIALS OF AN EFFECTIVE READING PROGRAMME

Here we might interpose [1] a note on the general principles that should guide an effective reading programme. They are :

(1) pupils should be *ready to learn to read*—(reading readiness programme) ;

(2) the material used in the early stage should be *scientifically prepared* ;

(3) material should be so planned to give *success to every child* ;

[1] For a discussion of these principles see pp. 6-12 *Happy Venture Teacher's Manual,* by F. J. Schonell (Oliver & Boyd).

(4) material should develop in pupils *strong powers of word recognition* ;

(5) reading should have as its major aim *the development of comprehension* ;

(6) there should be adequate supplementary books and material to *introduce activity and arouse interest* ;

(7) children should *commence their instruction in reading with a sentence/word whole method,* and this should be supplemented by advantages from a combination of methods ;

(8) phonic work should *not commence until the pupil has mastered a sight vocabulary* of about 50 words ;

(9) books and material should be modern in *production and presentation* ;

(10) method and materials should allow children *to proceed a their own rate.*

Finally, we might conclude this section by stating the proven points that come from research in regard to the respective merits of different methods.

(*a*) Research and classroom practice have conclusively shown that it is better to commence the teaching of reading by a sentence/look-and-say method in order to enable children to develop (i) the right perceptual attitude towards words and (ii) the meaningful attitude towards reading as a new activity.

(*b*) Pupils taught by a sentence/word whole method develop greater fluency in reading than if taught by other methods.

(*c*) Some phonic teaching is necessary at a later stage as a means of attacking larger words and as a basis for spelling of common words.

(*d*) Activity methods develop maximum interest for children but without the supplementary use of carefully compiled books with a controlled vocabulary may lead to failure and confusion amongst the less able 40 per cent of the class. Activity methods seem to show some superiority in regard to children's attainments at a later stage in other verbal subjects (e.g. written English).[1]

(e) Sentence/word whole methods arouse better interest in children, compared with phonic approaches, as shown by the amount of supplementary reading done by pupils.

The research on activity programmes and informal methods of teaching reading is inconclusive except for the above points, and it would seem that a thorough going activity method, unaided by a systematic approach, has some distinct limitations for some children.

SUMMARY

The three methods of teaching reading are the phonic, the word whole (look-and-say) and the sentence methods.

The *Phonic Method* starts with letters and sounds which are used to form regular words and then sentences of a somewhat unreal, artificial form.

The *Whole Word Method* starts with meaningful words which are assimilated through pictures and actions and are soon used in sentences.

The *Sentence Method* is the complete opposite of the phonic method, for it starts with the large unit, the sentence, from which develops a study of the words of which it is composed, and finally, much later, a study of some of the letters or combinations of letters and sounds which make up the words.

The sentence method approach usually rests upon an organised, preparatory reading period involving all kinds of discussions and verbal activities and usually including group studies or centres of interest in which some of the common words occur.

Many teachers use a combination of methods such as

[1] See 'A Modern Systematic versus an Opportunistic Method of Teaching Reading, an Experimental Study', by A. I. Gates, assisted by M. I. Batchelor and J. Betner, *Teachers' College Record*, Vol. XXXII, April 1926.

phonic/word whole or sentence/word whole. The essential point is that children should not begin to learn reading by an analytic phonic method, but should begin with words or simple sentences.

MODERN DEVELOPMENTS IN THE TEACHING OF READING

For the guidance of those concerned in the teaching of reading it will be beneficial to catalogue briefly the modern developments in reading instruction which are psychologically sound. These make the teaching of reading more effective and are characteristic of the best reading schemes.

(1) *The Use of a Systematically Developed Preparatory Reading Period or Reading Readiness Programme*

This has been discussed fully in Chapter III and includes general activities as well as specific training.

(2) *The Use of Everyday Experiences as a Basis for Reading Material*

The psychological value of using the interests, the activities and the experiences of children, and information about children in other lands as progressive reading material has now been firmly established. What the child does and says, what he has himself seen and experienced through play, projects and stories, is so vitalised for him that when he meets these ideas embodied in the printed words he has an excellent chance of understanding what they mean. As has been shown in Chapters I to III, one of the most important factors in teaching children to read is to see that they are in possession of the ideas conveyed by phrases and sentences. We must ensure this by selecting from their experiences (where the environment is satisfactory) or by providing them with these experiences through talk and properly planned play. Unless this part of reading is satisfactorily accomplished, not a few children are bound to be confused and discouraged in their early introduction to printed words.

The use of experience or activity material, however, does not mean that the story element should be missing. My own opinion, substantiated by those of teachers, is that children like a mixture of both. They like to read about doing and making by other children, about their goings and comings in and out of home and school, about their pets ; but they also like some real stories with strong action. The interest created and the contextual value of a story are aids to reading—there are plenty of instances of pupils not recognising a word in an isolated form, but reading it at once when it is embedded with other words in an interesting story.

Nevertheless, a reading programme which gives pupils all stories and folk tales and omits entirely the experiential or activity material limits its possible success, particularly in the early stages of learning to read. Similarly, texts which keep too long to the everyday material and do not introduce stories soon enough are correspondingly impoverished. The correct scale of proportion appears to follow these steps :

(a) Keep to activities in the immediate experiences of the pupils when they begin reading, for the reality, simplicity and immediacy of their contacts aid recognition and understanding.

(b) Lengthen the printed material relating to the topics and introduce a story element. .

(c) Extend the experiences to be dealt with beyond the home—to the shops, the streets, the zoo, the parks.

(d) Increase the amount of story content considerably.

(e) Include with stage (d) a certain amount of wider experience from other parts of the pupils' own country—visits to the seaside, to a port (to see ships, docks, etc.), to a farm, to an orchard, to a fishing village, to a mine, etc.

(f) Include information about children in other lands— main details of their lives and occupations through stories.

An example of this progression from a modern series of reading texts [1] as worked out in the various books is as follows :

Introductory Book—The main characters in the book are introduced by short sentences relating to such child activities as running, jumping, climbing and playing ball.

At this stage the very small amounts of reading matter are preceded and filled out by the teacher's story, before the actual reading matter is taken.

Book One—The number of sentences per page is extended and the story element is increased. Games with pets—the cat, the kittens and the dog—are recounted, while more activities such as skipping, playing cricket, bathing the doll, visiting a shop to buy toys are described.

Book Two—In this book stories are longer and bring in other animals and pets like horses, rabbits, the hen and her chicks. More incidents in the children's lives are introduced and the range of experiences extends to the park, the pond, the zoo, the fields (flying kites).

Book Three—At this stage the reading matter, which covers a wider range of activities in the life of the pupils, includes topics like going to school, a visit to a railway station to see an engine, shopping, baking, preparing for a party, fun at the party, a visit to a fire station. Stories occupy half of the book and are of the type, ' The Tar Baby ', ' The Little Coal Truck '.

Book Four—In this book, although the everyday life of children still forms part of the reading material, the experiences have extended beyond the immediate vicinity of home and school. Thus the train journey, holidays at the seaside, visits to the circus, the merry-go-round, the day at the docks, all parallel the development of the interests of somewhat older children. Furthermore, the stories now tend to become longer, fifteen or even nineteen pages, with also a slight introduction to other lands, for example, Australia and India.

---

[1] *Happy Venture Readers*, a series of five books (Oliver and Boyd). The five Happy Venture Playbooks are closely integrated with these Readers (see p. 105).

Modern reading texts endeavour to provide material relating to continuing centres of interest, and to maintain some continuity in the principal characters from book to book.

Finally, in the selection of material for the early reading books, there should be recognition of the ready response of children to rhythm, and ample opportunity should be provided for dramatisation. This last aspect is considerably facilitated if books contain a generous measure of direct speech.

(3) *The Use of a Controlled Vocabulary*

One of the most significant modern advances in the teaching of reading has been the use of a controlled vocabulary of common words in early reading books and the consequent repetition of words used.

In the past some texts, particularly those exclusively using stories, have revealed a pronounced shortcoming in the matter of vocabulary control. For example, one series starts with 44 new words in the first book and then jumps to 218 new words in the next book. Because the vocabulary is so heavy and there are too many new words per page, many children are forced to proceed extremely slowly—some cannot proceed at all. Many of the less able ones need drilling repeatedly on the same page, and with the weakest pupils this results in memory reading. Even when the pupils have mastered a page with 12 or 16 new words upon it they are greatly discouraged to find that there are just as many new words they do not know upon the next page. Not only is training in adequate word recognition thereby neglected, but the pupils are discouraged by the difficulty of the task. *The only way to provide for progress for all pupils is by grading the reading material.*[1] If we agree to teach by the sentence method *it is essential that the vocabulary burden of the material in the early books should be adequately controlled.* The number of new words per page should be limited, and full provision should be made for

[1] Grading of material in arithmetic, both as regards the numbers and the difficulties of the various phases of a process, is a firmly established principle, but we seem to be much slower in adopting a similar fundamental in the more important subject of reading.

repetition of old words, so that maximum use can be made of learning through discrimination of visual patterns of words. Each page of reading material should, in the initial stages, present not more than 2 to 4 new words embedded in known material. Later, as both stories and sentences lengthen, pupils can manage up to 5 or 6 new words on a page, provided the average throughout is not more than 3 to 4 new words per page. Below, for example, is an analysis of the vocabulary burden of a modern series of readers.

HAPPY VENTURE READERS	Approximate Number of Running Words	Total Number of New Words	Number of Pages in Book
Introductory Book, *Fluff and Nip* . . .	550	44	27
Book One, *Playtime* . .	1,310	62	33
Book Two, *Our Friends* .	2,744	103	49
Book Three, *Growing Up* .	5,500	210	86
Book Four, *Holiday Time* .	12,740	384	118

In the typed draft of one of the publications by the Scottish Council for Research in Education, namely, *Word Counts of Infant Readers*, the following was the analysis of the first two (or three) books of four different Infant Series :

Series A—
    Introductory . . 40
    Book I . . 244
    Book II . . 418
              702

Series B—
    Books A and B . 95
    Book I . . . 202
    Book II . . . 440
              737

Series C—
    Book I . . . 214
    Book Ia . . . 244
    Book II . . . 564
              1022

Series D—
    Book I . . . 140
    Book II . . . 326
              466

In the Happy Venture Readers the vocabulary content, i.e. of different words used in each book, runs as shown above, 44, 62, 103, 210, 384, in the five books respectively. This gradation gives every child a chance to make progress, and brighter children get on more quickly to new books. A too heavy vocabulary burden slows up children to the point of disappointment and confusion, with consequent loss of confidence and dislike of reading.

Psychological research shows that a most important factor in reading instruction is the initial attitude set up by the pupil. If success can be registered early, then the pupil will persist in further efforts. With a sentence method, success is best ensured by interesting material and by repetition of new words. A very light vocabulary burden in the early stages enables pupils to assimilate words as they appear and reappear on succeeding pages. For example, in the above series, the Introductory Book uses only 44 different words spread over 27 pages and making up a total of 550 running words, i.e. the repetitions of the 44 different words vary between 8 and 15 for each word.

The only reading material on the first page of this book is :

' Here is Dick ' (picture).
' Here is Nip ' (picture).

The words ' here is ' are repeated on that page and the pictures help the pupil to identify Dick and his dog, Nip. Then the next page introduces

' Here is Dora.'
' Here is Fluff.'

There is repetition of ' Here is ', and pictures aid in recognition of Dora and her cat, Fluff.

On page 3 ' Here is ' again appears. ' Nip ' appears twice.

On page 5 ' is ' appears twice, ' Dick ' three times, ' Dora ' once and ' Nip ' twice.

The new words are ' run ' and ' to '.

Dora will wash Jane.
    She is a rag doll,
    so Dora can wash her.

Dora has a line by the tree.

May sits on a seat to see
    Dora wash the doll.

" Bow-wow, bow-wow,"
    said Nip.
    " You will not wash me."

In this way the pupil is given confidence in his recognition of words, while the adequate repetition allows gradual assimilation to take place without the soul-destroying drill on each page. A child thus reads a book relatively quickly, while bright children can read the first three books (27, 33 and 49 pages respectively) with such speed that great zest is added to the reading lesson—the idea of starting a new book is of paramount importance to young readers. Completing one book quickly and passing to the next develops a sense of power and accomplishment.

In each book the new words that appear on each page as the book progresses are printed against the page number at the back of the book. For example, here is a section of the word list of Book One (page 40).

Page 2	basket	Page 4	stop
	for		her
3	little	5	he
	kitten		on
	Fluff's		bad

This is of inestimable value to the teacher who can take preparatory and revision work on the new words either from the blackboard or from the word list itself.

The carrying on of the vocabulary from book to book is another essential feature of modern reading texts. For example, the 44 words in the Introductory Book of the above series are used in the next book, Book One, and similarly the 103 new words of Book Two, as well as being adequately repeated in the book, are embedded throughout in the 106 words from the first two books. Thus natural, continued acquaintance with early material is maintained.

Careful grading of reading material not only ensures success for all pupils of varying intellectual calibres and verbal backgrounds, but it makes provision for group work for the different sections that inevitably occur in reading classes. The short books with their adequate control of the material

G

are perfectly suited to groups of different reading levels within the one class.

(4) *The Use of Properly Prepared Additional Books for Supplementary Reading Parallel to the Basic Readers and Involving the same Vocabulary or a Slightly Advanced Vocabulary*

Progressive reading programmes have, amongst other improvements, conclusively demonstrated the use of carefully prepared supplementary reading books to consolidate the reading progress made by each pupil with the basic books. This, of course, is an exemplification of a sound teaching and psychological principle, namely that we should revise and consolidate in various ways what has been gained in our initial teaching, if this is to pass into permanent possession of the pupil.

Mastering a reading vocabulary requires constant application on the part of pupils, and constant assistance from teachers, and it is in this respect that teachers can do so much by supplying consolidating material at just the right points. In the past this consolidating and revising of material has not been provided in reading schemes, and teachers have been faced with taking slower readers over the same book and introducing better readers to other books not properly graded.

The modern approach introduces two forms of supplementary reading material : [1]

(*a*) a series of *graded books* which are geared in vocabulary load to each basic reader, so that each group of additional books has, in the main, *the same vocabulary* as the corresponding basic book ;

(*b*) *parallel readers* which while they contain some new words, have much of their vocabulary in common with the basic books.

[1] Details of these as they relate to the *Happy Venture Reading Scheme* are given on pp. 68-72 in the *Happy Venture Teacher's Manual*, by Fred J. Schonell (Oliver & Boyd).

(a) *Additional Graded Books with the same Vocabulary as the* Corresponding *Basic Book*

These books are used after each basic reader has been read in order to consolidate the vocabulary of the basic reader. For example, in the Happy Venture Scheme there are five little books (called Library Books), each of ten pages, and each based only on the vocabulary of 44 words of the basic Introductory Book. Similarly there are five Library Books based entirely on the vocabulary of basic Book One.

The provision of this kind of revision material, with the old words set in a new context and a new story, is not only of great value to the teacher for individual and group work, but of inestimable psychological value to the pupil. Quick pupils read each small book with the great thrill of completing another book, while the dull or slow-learning children gain all the assistance and consequent satisfaction of going over the basic book vocabulary, of which they are uncertain, in an entirely different setting.

There is little doubt that this method of supplying children with revision material of this kind, is both pedagogically and psychologically a distinct advance on older practices.

(b) *Parallel Readers*

Recent advances in reading stress the fact that children learn to read best when plied with carefully graded material of the right kind at the appropriate point in their reading instruction. Word drills are only incidental to the teaching of reading. For this reason it has been accepted practice to provide children with a graded set of reading books parallel to the basic readers. While each of these books contains some of the vocabulary of the parallel basic books, they also introduce a minimum of new words, but at an easier or lighter rate than in the basic books. For example, the Happy Venture Scheme, in common with other modern schemes, has a set of such parallel readers, called Playbooks. The vocabulary burden of each of these is so much lighter than its corresponding basic reader that children of average reading attainment can read it in about half the time they take over the basic book. These parallel books achieve a triple purpose of consolidating some of the vocabulary of the basic books, expanding the child's word recognition by introducing *some* new words, usually not more than 1 to 2 per page, and adding zest and interest to reading by the provision of new stories. They represent an advance in reading skill, not only in word recognition, but in comprehension and in reading interests.

To illustrate from the Happy Venture Scheme, vocabulary of the first two parallel readers is as follows :

	Basic Readers	*Playbooks*
Introductory Book	44 new words	18 new words
		17 derivatives
		based on words in Introductory basic reader
Book One . .	62 new words	37 new words
		33 derivatives
		based on words in Introductory Reader, Reader 1 and Playbook 1

This relationship between basic reader and parallel reader should characterise any reading scheme.

(5) *The Value of Illustrations*

There is not as yet sufficient realisation of the vital value of illustrations in the teaching of reading. Too often books contain insufficient pictures or are lacking in illustrations of real teaching and artistic worth. When learning to read the pupils obtain almost as much aid in recognising words from the right kind of illustration as they do from the various other cues.

Rudisil made a study of the responses of children to five types of illustration in books for children.   These included coloured and uncoloured photographs, coloured drawing ('realistic in form and in colour'), outline drawing ('realistic in form but outlined in colour without regard for realistic effect') and the coloured drawing ('conventionalised in form, decorative but unrealistic in colour').   Gray, in an excellent summary of reading investigations for 1951-52,[1] reports that the following conclusions emerged from the study.

(a) 'In looking at a picture, a child apparently seeks first to recognise its content.'

(b) 'Any picture (assuming a certain content) proves satisfying to the child in proportion to its success in making that content appear real or life-like.   Whether it is coloured or uncoloured is less important than the appearance of realism.'

No doubt these conclusions would vary in degree with the age of the children, but they are a salutary knock to those artists who would try to be clever and precocious with illustrations for children.   Vigour, action, realism with potent content value in relation to the text, should be the basic principles underlying illustrations for young children.

There should be but a small amount of print in early books, with plenty of bold, clear pictures specifically portraying the ideas of the printed material.   Artists who really understand book illustrations for children, who are capable of painting pictures which interest children and who have the right concept of form, pattern and colour suited to the child's aesthetic-educational mind, are few in number.

On page 119 is a specimen of clear, bold illustration with a minimum of print.

---

[1] 'Children's Preferences for Colour versus other Qualities in Illustrations', by Mabel Rudisil, El. Sch. J. LII, April 1952, pp. 444-5 ; reported in J. of Ed. Research, pp. 401-37, 'Summary of Reading Investigations', July 1951 to June 1952, by W. S. Gray

(6) *Use of Specially Prepared Teaching Aids*

One further development of modern reading programmes is found in the published reading aids now available to teachers of reading in infant classes. Happily the time is passing when infant teachers were expected not only to teach fifty young pupils, but also to prepare all supplementary teaching material. Although many Education Authorities do recognise this need at the infant school stage, yet there are still some who might well be more generous in their grants for this purpose.

Adequate supplies of teaching aids make the task of the infant teacher much more effective, not only in terms of teaching technique, but also in time and energy made available to help children who need individual attention.

Although teachers will still wish to, and do, make some teaching aids, in the main the properly prepared, printed aid is usually more effective. There is plenty of scope for imagination and variety in the ways in which the material may be used. Teaching aids increasingly used in modern teaching programmes now include :

1. *Readiness Books*[1] (discussed earlier).
2. *Wall Pictures* [1] or *Charts* showing pictures of incidents and characters contained in the early basic books of a series. These large charts, which teachers can use with a whole class, are invaluable for discussion involving development of vocabulary and sentence patterns, so vital to the beginning stage of reading.
3. *Flash Cards of Words and Phrases.*[1] These are used both for teaching and for revision as the pupils progress through the first two books of a series. Single word cards may also be used for tachistoscopic exposures.
4. *Workbooks.*[1] Useful as a teaching aid in conjunction with each basic book as it is taught—an exceedingly helpful supplementary teaching device with slow

[1] The *Happy Venture Reading Scheme* includes these special teaching aids.

learners. Workbooks aid in both the teaching of and the testing of a basic reading book.

5. *Filmstrips* [1] for the readiness period and for exposure of words and sentences for revision purposes.

6. *Card Material*,[1] containing matching exercises, vocabulary study and comprehension exercises.

7. *Picture Dictionary*. For some children a picture dictionary is a useful adjunct to developing word recognition. It is often a most effective supplementary device with slow-learning pupils.

8. *Lotto* or *Wordo Cards*, for playing group games which have as their aim the improvement and speeding up of word recognition.

(7) *The Place and Use of Phonic Training in the Teaching of Reading*

As has been previously stated, there is now general agreement that phonic analysis of words by pupils should be postponed until they have (*a*) acquired a certain vocabulary through sight methods and (*b*) reached a certain *mental* age. When pupils have acquired a reading vocabulary of from 70 to 100 words they are able to read very simple material fairly fluently and they have formed an aptitude for the discrimination of the visual patterns of words. In addition they have formed the right attitude, namely reading by phrases or groups of words, so that an understanding of what is read is being developed ; reading is not limited to saying words. At this stage some pupils may need the help of phonic training to further their reading ability.

Because of the recognised limitations of phonic analysis as an approach to reading (see pages 84 to 88), some teachers and educators have gone too far and have entirely discarded the use of phonics in the teaching of reading at any stage. This is psychologically unsound and indicates an extremist

[1] *The Happy Venture Reading Scheme* includes these special teaching aids.

attitude based on ignorance—ignorance of the place and function of phonic analysis.

When a pupil assimilates a word into his reading vocabulary he should be able to,

(a) recognise it by its visual pattern,
(b) pronounce it correctly,
(c) understand its meaning.

In a few cases pupils have reached (a) and (b) without (c) ; but this is not usual, as so much of the reading material in enlightened textbooks deals with common words within the speaking vocabulary of the pupils.

Now what is the exact function of phonic analysis in respect to these three capacities ? It can be best explained thus : if the pupil, on experiencing a new word in his reading (i.e. one of which he does not know the printed pattern), has previously heard the word and knows its meaning and pronunciation, then a phonic analysis of the word will bring it to his mind and he will be able to read it, particularly if the context is also helpful. But it should be noted that the aid provided by the phonic analysis is only supplementary to the cues of recognition of words through hearing and meaning. If, on the other hand, the word is an entirely unknown one (i.e. it is not known in respect to (a), (b) or (c) above), then it is doubtful, except with the brightest pupils, whether phonic analysis will help—the pupils may sound the word, but not get beyond that stage. This suggests three points :

(i) the limitations of phonic analysis,
(ii) the value of context in word recognition,
(iii) the value of verbal background in reading.

Without (ii) and (iii) phonic analysis cannot be very effective. Its chief value lies in enabling pupils to arrive at the correct pronunciation, which will bring into their mind ' the total knowing ' of the word as it appears in front of them in print. At this point in the teaching of reading many pupils are helped by this supplementary device of word recognition.

Certain points, however, should be observed in the development of phonic analysis. With many children there is the need to produce a certain sensitivity to sounds in words before they can be expected to associate sounds with corresponding letters. This they do through extension of their meaning vocabulary, through hearing many words and through repeated reading of the words acquired in initial reading lessons. All children should be helped with the intriguing game, ' I Spy ' :

> ' I spy with my little eye
> Something whose name begins with b ' (sounding it phonetically).

Different letters can be exercised on different days. This, together with increased experience of words, will fit the pupil *at about a mental age of* 6 *to* 6½ *years* to be introduced to the connection between certain sounds and their printed symbols.

Slower and less intelligent pupils may need rhyming exercises and help through picture-word-sound association.

Another important point is that *phonics should always be used in close relationship to the material being read.* The study of lists of unrelated phonic words is to be deprecated. The best principle upon which to proceed is to associate the phonic work with the material the pupil is reading or likely to read in the near future. This practice does not aim at developing a hypothetical phonic ability, but at providing a help for pupils to recognise the words they are meeting day by day.[1]

Generally it is useful to approach phonic work in a play spirit. The teacher may ask pupils to look at the first letter of the word and then at the remaining unit (e.g. b-at). Suggestions for other words may be taken from the children. Later an introduction to long vowels may be given.[2]

---

[1] In the *Happy Venture Readers*, lists of common phonic families are given at the end of the second book in the series, and these words provide a direct preparation for reading the material in that book and in the two succeeding books.

[2] Further suggestions on the teaching of phonics are given in the *Happy Venture Teacher's Manual*, pp. 56-60.

In conclusion it should be remembered that phonic work should be given to the pupils only when it is required. It should be functional—that is, closely related to the actual reading material, and should not be taken before a vocabulary of sight words has been assimilated, a background of meaning developed and a sensitivity to letter sounds (in words themselves) created.

CHAPTER V

ORGANISATION OF READING IN INFANT CLASSES

THE organisation for reading in the infant department or classes may be considered as catering for pupils between the ages of 5 + and 7 + years. It cannot be too strongly emphasised that there should not be any attempt to teach reading formally to children under the age of 5 +, and with most pupils of 5 + years the early instruction should be largely of an incidental or preparatory kind. *All pupils under 5 years of age, irrespective of their intellectual brightness, should not be provided for in a formal scheme of reading.* Naturally, these under-fives will take part in all kinds of games, see pictures, handle books, trace names, hear stories, talk about experiences and classroom doings, and engage in varied activities that will be an indirect preparation —and in the case of class projects and centres of interest a direct preparation—for actual reading lessons later on. The tendency to force bright children under 5, and to go beyond the experience and intellectual power of the duller pupils is, I believe, a real danger of the nursery class attached to an infant department, unless the headmistress is an understanding person with a knowledge of child psychology and a full realisation of the psychological requirements of the under-fives. Many pupils would make greater progress in reading if there were no formal teaching in reading until 6 years of age.[1] Obviously, an aim such as this presupposes that the 5 to 6 period will embrace a very rich, extensive and varied preparatory reading programme.

[1] And as Miss Gardner shows, pupils taught by early informal method would gain in personality development and in later powers of persistence, intelligent application and understanding. See *Testing Results in the Infant School*, by D. E. M. Gardner (Methuen, 1948).

Bearing in mind this basic principle of not forcing the young child beyond his intellectual and experiential level, we may pass to the second major aim, namely, that of making our organisation sufficiently flexible to provide for the varied range of intellectual abilities of our pupils and to cater for the varying rates of progress displayed by them. This involves knowing our pupils well, and it is here that for each pupil at the age of approximately $5\frac{1}{2}+$ years the information obtained by means of the chart in Chapter III, pages 52 and 53, is useful for grouping and organising within the classes in the initial stages of a reading scheme.

Thirdly, a carefully considered reading scheme embraces a mixture of individual and group methods, with perhaps more emphasis on group than on individual teaching. Although the individual consideration in matters of coaching and in material to be used must guide us at all stages of teaching reading, it is my experience, and with this many headmistresses and class teachers agree, that children learning to read seem to make greater progress when in a group, even if the group is small, say, only three or four children. Moreover, grouping does not preclude liberal individual help. The communal, ' help each other ' spirit, with mild competition and rivalry (providing the confidence of all members of the group is sustained), has a most stimulating effect upon powers of application and the desire to learn. Most young children learn almost as much from their colleagues as they do from their elders, if the environment is one of maximum opportunity.

As the mechanics of reading are mastered at different rates by different children there will be greater need to suit material to individual reading ages.

Fourthly, the well-planned reading scheme with a combination of word whole and sentence methods in the initial period may be said to proceed by four stages.

Stage I may, according to the intellectual calibre and language background of the children in the school, follow, *from 5 to $5\frac{1}{2}$ years of age*, either of two lines.

(*a*) With pupils who are not very bright and who come from rather poor homes, culturally, it is probably advisable to base the whole of the first stage (for the weakest ones up to 5¾ years) almost entirely on projects or centres of interest. No books will be used, but liberal numbers of pictures and posters, associated with the projects and with words and phrases to explain them, will be employed. Written notices about the incidents and activities connected with the developing project will help these children to become familiar with words as meaning something, and will lay the foundation indirectly for word recognition and word discrimination. The aim should be to associate spoken and written words in a natural and impelling, yet not too objective manner. Games involving words to extend the pupil's vocabulary, news sheets about the children's activities—'All about Us', 'Our Weather Chart', 'Our House'—will occupy the last three months of this stage.

There would, of course, be obvious advantages in allowing these slower children to work through a reading readiness book. The exercises, while having preparatory value, would also indicate to the teacher those pupils who might join a more advanced reading group.

(*b*) With pupils who are bright and who come from homes where the general language and cultural influences are good, the ground covered in Stage I will be somewhat greater and progress will be speedier. For example, children will learn with greater speed to recognise the names of their friends and the names of other children written on the blackboard. Names of animals and of children entering into stories and into the making of the toy house will be assimilated. Another strong aid to learning at this stage is the use of stand-up figures and names of the chief characters in the early books of the reading series[1] that the children will use. Many of the bright

---

[1] Philip & Tacey Ltd., Fulham High Street, Fulham, London, S.W.6, produce such stand-up figures for certain reading schemes, including *Happy Venture*.

children will be able to read such words as Fluff, Nip, Dora, Dick, Tosh, and Mac, and simple sentences (printed as notices in appropriate positions) like,

> This is Nip.
> This is Nip's house.
> The door is green.
> This is a window.
> The window is red.
> Nip is a dog.
> Fluff is a cat.

These pupils might also do the exercises in a reading readiness book and use could be made of reading charts and filmstrips connected with a reading series. It is essential to provide plenty of discussion centering round the characters and incidents in the first reading book which pupils will use in their early lessons. The more effectively the ground is covered in terms of ideas, words, phrases and sentence structure directly connected with the first reading book, the better chance will the pupils have of succeeding in their first attempts at reading from cards or a book.

These brighter groups of pupils are usually ready to commence with a very simple reading book relatively quickly during this stage. Thus they may be started with such readers as *Fluff and Nip*, Introductory Book of Happy Venture Readers (Oliver and Boyd), *John and Mary*, John and Mary Readers, *Mac and Tosh*, Mac and Tosh Readers (Schofield & Sims).

While it is not advisable to hurry a child on to a book too soon—initial failure with books and a consequent dislike of reading must be avoided—many children like to feel that they can read from a book and they derive considerable stimulus from their first book. First books should be very simple and very short, and should contain a minimum of material with a maximum use of pictures. If possible, introductory books should be used containing material, the words and phrases of which the children have to some extent experienced in their preliminary activities. The steps in Stage I dealing with the introductory book are as follows.

(i) The pupils learn, or have learnt, or revise the names of the characters in the book. For example, in the Introductory Book of the Happy Venture Readers, these names would be Dick, Nip, Dora, Fluff, Jane, Mother and Jack. This revision might well be done by means of the first Happy Venture Filmstrip. Activities connected with the colouring and perhaps cutting out of characters in the Happy Venture Colouring Book will also supplement this part.[1]

A story is then told about the first page—this may be entitled ' Dick and his dog Nip '. The children are told about Dick and about Nip, about the way in which Nip plays with Dick, and so on. A similar story can be told about Dora, her cat Fluff, and her doll Jane, and in subsequent pages further incidents dealing with these characters are recounted.

(ii) When the story about the first two pages has been told to the section of pupils commencing the book, the children gather round the teacher and the pictures are discussed. The teacher then reads the sentences several times until the children can associate the sentence with the picture, either the whole sentence or just certain words. *In these early stages the teacher should not aim at absolute accuracy.* Assimilation of words proceeds slowly, and teachers should not hurry or worry children if they do not know some of the same words on subsequent pages. Association with the words in slightly different contextual settings over a period of time brings a gradual and constant increase in reading vocabulary. There appear to be, with all young children, quite long periods of subconscious consolidation. Provided there is continuous consistent association with the words, and *mental effort on the part of the pupil,* progress will be made. From this it is obvious that the short frequent lessons are preferable to long ones and that the pupil's interest or power of application and concentration must be

---

[1] Details of the use of the Happy Venture Filmstrips and the Happy Venture Colouring Book are given in the *Happy Venture Teacher's Manual* (Oliver & Boyd).

operating during the lessons. I emphasise this latter point, because there are some who would allow children simply to 'float along', turning away or choosing some other activity when they meet difficulties. There is a midway course between the two extremes of *laissez-faire* and the driving, drilling, worrying methods of the 'bad old days'. The child should be encouraged to go at his own pace, with time allowed for consolidation, but he must be trying, he must be putting forth mental effort.[1]

For consolidation of each page the teacher might well use the carefully ordered revision provided by a workbook, or inset frames with pieces for matching word or phrase to picture, or word to word (see opposite page 124), or jigsaw puzzles.[2]

(iii) In the third aspect of this first stage a number of different groups of pupils will be similarly started with books, and they will be encouraged to read the few pages to the teacher and to one another under guidance.

Stage II—This stage involves the entire class, which is now working in groups still with a combination of look-and-say and sentence methods. The weakest members of the more backward group, or groups, will require extra matching of word and phrase cards. An example of word-picture, sentence-picture matching cards together with simple comprehension questions is that provided by the Happy Venture Card Material.[3] As pupils complete their first book they will be given an opportunity to consolidate its vocabulary by reading the simple supplementary books that correspond to the basic

[1] It is interesting to note that some of the intelligent children who fail in reading are those whose temperament or emotional attitudes interfere with their attempts to apply themselves with concentration and persistence to the job of discriminating and remembering word patterns. This is particularly so with pampered children whose initiative and independence have been undermined by having too much done for them. See *Backwardness in the Basic Subjects*, 4th ed., pp. 201-2.

[2] Philip & Tacey Ltd., Fulham High Street, Fulham, London, S.W.6, produce jigsaw puzzles for certain reading schemes, including *Happy Venture*.

[3] For details of use, see *Happy Venture Teacher's Manual*, pp. 79-91.

Here is Dick.

Here is Nip.

readers (in the case of the Happy Venture Reading Scheme these will be Library Books 1 to 5).

Some groups may have started on the second book of a modern reading series in which initial books are small in size and light in vocabulary burden. Thus in the Happy Venture Readers the more progressive groups of pupils will be working from Book One (*Playtime*), that is, the second book in the series, or from the first book of the supplementary parallel series, namely Playbook One (*Hide and Seek*), while other groups will be using the Introductory Book (*Fluff and Nip*). New words will be written on the blackboard as each group deals with successive pages in different parts of either the Introductory Book or Book One. Here controlled vocabulary reading books have a distinct advantage over those which have not been compiled on a scientifically selected and controlled vocabulary. A teacher using an uncontrolled type of reader is unaware of the new words on each page. As she takes pupils through the successive pages of initial books it is somewhat of a ' hit and miss ' affair, but with the *controlled vocabulary reader* the number of new words per page is limited to two or three, and the teacher can write these on the blackboard or arrange for pupils to trace them from their writing pads. Thus, in taking a group of pupils with page 21 of Introductory Book (*Fluff and Nip*) the teacher knows from the word list given at the end of the book (page 28) that the only two *new* words on the page are *Jack* and *bring*. Or again, with a group of brighter pupils, who in this stage are commencing to read pages 13 and 14 of Book One (*Playtime*), the new words listed in the word list on page 40 are :

> page 13 : jump, do, jumps
> page 14 : kittens, up

While it is the teacher's duty to try to anticipate word difficulties and to prevent failure, elaborate word drills are to be avoided. When the reading material is scientifically constructed with proper attention to vocabulary burden,

H

word drills are limited—all that is required is careful preliminary attention to the few words appearing on the pages about to be read. It is obvious that at this stage pupils are beginning to reveal quite different rates of reading progress, and hence organisation should provide for this. Use books which suit particular groups, and allow pupils to change from group to group as their rate of progress indicates. Thus a pupil who is making rapid progress may be promoted quickly from a group still reading Introductory Book to one using Book One, or conversely a child who has not been able to maintain progress on Book One may be given a supplementary book of Introductory Book level—this obviates the disappointment of going back to a book already ' read '. Some individual work based on the reading material (suggestions for these are given in Appendix III) can be given to certain children. Matching, colouring, completing sentences, answering riddles, telling whether statements are true, etc., will all help to develop vocabulary and will afford useful preliminary training for silent reading. Workbook exercises [1] prepared on sets of cards can easily be made by teachers along the lines suggested in Appendix III.

WORD RECOGNITION EXERCISES FOR WEAKER SECTION OF CHILDREN

While the aim should be to employ word drills sparingly for the reason that most children are more effectively taught to read by using attractive, suitably graded, continuous material, yet there will be some pupils at all stages of instruction, who require repeated presentation of words to ensure their mastery. Results of remedial teaching with backward readers have now firmly established the principle of providing practice with separate words and phrases, particularly those containing elements which the child finds it difficult to consolidate in his reading vocabulary. While certain exercises

---

[1] Publication of the workbooks, one to accompany each of the Happy Venture basic readers, will start in 1960.

are given in Appendix III, and the Happy Venture Work-books will give teachers material for others, yet it might help to suggest a few additional devices that involve a minimum of preparation and produce a maximum of quick practice.

(1) *A simple tachistoscope or word-phrase exposure device* for presenting words or phrases singly, without any conflicting stimuli, has proved useful in stabilising and speeding up the recognition of words or phrases. A tachistoscope can be made by the teacher from a piece of 3-ply wood having a slit for the exposure of the material, which is printed on a strip to be pulled down through a gate on either side of the slot, for exposure of the words or phrases. Alternatively, words may be presented through the slit on separate cards, with a shutter to reveal them each time.

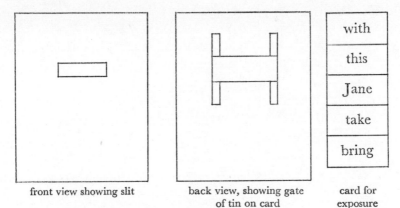

| front view showing slit | back view, showing gate of tin on card | card for exposure |

(2) It is useful to note the words of which a child is un-certain and then to require him to keep an individual list of these. These words may be used for tachistoscope exercises for the backward group.

After each six or eight pages of a book have been read, the teacher might check each pupil's knowledge of all new words as they have appeared in the book, up to that point, by testing his word recognition from the word list of new words at the end of the book. Children may then be asked to write several times, words of which they are uncertain, and to transfer them to their individual word lists.

(3) Words which children do not readily recognise may be embodied in new phrases and used in the tachistoscope.

(4) Word and phrase recognition in relation to pictures is a useful form of drill. A series of pictures related to the book being read is prepared, each with an envelope containing six words or phrases. Children have to place the words or phrases on the appropriate parts of the picture. A variant of this is to require children to place the cardboard or wooden pieces on which words are printed, into grooves or insets on a 3-ply picture base. (See illustration opposite.)

(5) Matching games of various kinds may be effectively used to speed up word recognition. For example, in one game each player in a group has a base card on which there are printed nine words.

run	Fluff	here
see	Mother	dol
stop	this	Jane

Although about half the words are common to all base cards, very few base cards of nine words are exactly the same as any other. The children are then issued with an envelope containing nine separate word cards, and shown how to arrange their word cards alphabetically ; not all will be able to do this accurately, but it is an excellent exercise in encouraging children to look carefully at the beginning of words. After this preliminary preparation the teacher takes a card from a box, which contains all the words on all the base cards, and she reads it three times to the children. If they also have such a word card they place it over the one on their base card. The

Frame and wooden tiles for matching word to picture and word to word

By courtesy of Mrs E. Hall, Oldham

Photographer: Mr Geoffrey Newton, Oldham

A book corner where children—readers and non-readers alike—have their interest in books stimulated. (See pages 66 and 185.)

Photograph by courtesy of Mr L. P. F. Miller and the National Book League

winners are the ones who fill their base cards first. It is prefer-able, psychologically, to allow for two or three winners in each game.

(6) Multiple choice exercises similar to those in the work-books provide useful methods of establishing word recognition and discrimination [1] with slow learners.

Stage III—At this stage, that is when most pupils have reached the age of 6+, the work still proceeds in groups with appropriate individual work, but the range of reading ability is so great that each *group* will probably be working from a different book. Although sentence and look-and-say methods are largely used, yet this is the stage at which to introduce some phonic training.

Here two points stand out.

(*a*) All pupils should be given some phonic training. With brighter pupils the amount required will be small because of their larger vocabularies and their superior power of analysing and synthesising the sound elements of words. With these children phonic training will be largely incidental and will proceed rapidly.

(*b*) The phonics taught to all children should be functional phonics, that is, sound analysis of common words which they are reading, rather than some elaborate phonic scheme designed to give children the key to successful reading—a quite erroneous conception of the purpose of phonics. Phonic practice should occupy only a few minutes of each lesson. As far as possible we should apply our phonic teaching to words which come within the meaning vocabulary of the pupils. Teachers should note how quickly pupils are able to deal with the phonic analysis and synthesis of familiar words—that is, familiar in meaning, but not in printed form. With such words many pupils need only the most cursory ' breaking down ' and ' building up '. The hearing of the familiar word, particu-larly if aided by contextual clue, helps the pupil to recognise it quickly once he has analysed it into its constituent elements.

[1] See Happy Venture Workbook One.

For example, I recall from recent work in an infant school how a pupil (age $6\frac{5}{12}$) reading a simple story was able to apply her phonic knowledge quickly to new (but familiar in meaning) words in this way.

> One day when Dick was in the gar-den—garden— he saw a gr-e-at—greet—great light up in the sky.

This pupil, who was bright and had a good meaning vocabulary, was applying the functional phonic training which had been given at this stage. The words used by the teacher for phonic analysis had been taken from their reading books, and although only a certain amount of analysis and synthesis had been done, it enabled the pupil to tackle new words. Thus the *ea* in *great* had not been experienced, and the first attempt at synthesis was *greet* (as in *seat* which had been learnt). The use of intelligence, together with aid from the text, enabled the pupil to make the necessary modification.

Throughout this stage in the teaching of reading the most practical phonic scheme is to base the study of phonic families on the words in the actual book being read and in the books to be read in the immediate future. Such phonic practice does not aim at developing a hypothetical phonic ability, but is a direct teaching of units to help pupils to recognise words they are meeting day by day. The golden rules in the teaching of phonics are :

(*a*) Do not commence phonic practice before pupils are intellectually ready for it—phonic analysis and synthesis require throughout the various steps increasing intellectual ability.

(*b*) Use phonic lists sparingly. Wherever possible link up or use phonic training in relation to continuous reading material. Breaking up and recombining words are only one aid in recognition—we should never neglect the major aid of the cue from continuous meaningful material, arranged in short sentences, and permeated by a story element.

In any phonic scheme the short vowel sounds will obviously be studied first. With bright children most of these groups of words will be taken in their stride. What is most important to all children is to be shown how to attempt an analysis and synthesis of words ; thus acquaintance with the structure of *r-un* and *s-ing* will help the pupil to try *r-un-ning* when he experiences it in his reading material. The introduction to common sound units is of immense value to many pupils ; thus the *-ar* in *c-ar* is the same *-ar* in *st-ar-t*, and if pupils have been introduced to *st* as in *st-op*, *st-ill*, *st-and*, then it is a very easy step to analyse quickly and recombine (almost automatically) the elements of *start*. As the child proceeds with his reading, much of the phonic analysis and synthesis will be done almost unconsciously, and will provide correct, indirect aid in the process of reading. The main thing in phonic teaching is *not* to allow phonic analysis, with its sounding of words, to become anything more than an aid to reading. *It must receive only its correct proportion of attention, yet it is an aid with which nearly all children should be provided.*

The progression of phonic practice might profitably follow, at this stage of reading, that laid down in Book One (second book in the series) of the Happy Venture Readers. Pupils would thus be introduced by a series of steps to graded word families in this way :

Groups of words with these endings

c-*at*	s-*it*	g-*ot*	d-*og*
b-*ig*	c-*an*	l-*ip*	h-*op*
m-*ud*	c-*up*	b-*ed*	w-*et*
l-*eg*	c-*up*	b-*ag*	d-*id*
p-*in*	m-*en*	d-*ug*	
s-*and*	f-*ell*	w-*ill*	m-*ust*
n-*est*	s-*ing*	s-*ick*	b-*ack*
n-*eck*	d-*uck*	b-*all*	f-*ull*

With most of the brighter groups of pupils there need be little actual phonic practice with these groups, but weaker readers may require to go more slowly over these steps and to be introduced to as many common words as possible with these endings. Brighter pupils are always able to make more effective transfer of knowledge than duller ones

The phonic practice, *which occupies only a few minutes of each lesson*, may take the form of rhymes constructed by the teacher from the group of words under consideration,

e.g. -*ot* group (in the first step)—

Spot, Spot	I can say :
fell in the pot	' Rain, rain, go away
and got hot.	And come on Mother's washing day.'

Pupils may be encouraged to give lines or groups of words which rhyme. As the phonic steps progress, so use may be made of well-known nursery rhymes and songs.[1]

At first simple rhymes :

> Pat-a-cake, Pat-a-cake, baker's *man*,
> *Bake* me a *cake* as fast as you *can* ;
> Prick it and pat it and mark it with T,
> And put it in the oven for Tommy and me.

Later longer rhymes such as :

> Wee Willie Winkie
> Runs through the *town*,
> Upstairs and *down*stairs
> In his night *gown*.
> Rapping at the window,
> Crying through the *lock*,
> ' All the children in their beds
> Past eight o'*clock*.'

In later steps pupils are introduced to common consonant combinations, e.g. *ch*, *ck*, *sh*, *st*, *th* ; and long vowels, e.g. *came*, *make*, *white*, *ride*, *line*, may be given.

[1] The teacher will find *Mother Goose's Book of Nursery Rhymes, Songs and Riddles* (Dent) useful sources.

The bulk of the phonic teaching at this stage will be given to groups, and distributed according to the progress being made by the pupils. A little class teaching of certain phonic families may be helpful.

Additional use will be made at this stage of prepared reading cards, which are a natural way of linking reading, English and writing. These cards not only provide facility for extending the vocabularies of the pupils, but they give practice through writing of some words with which pupils might not be quite familiar in their reading.

Stage IV—At this stage all pupils should be able to read a simple book with a certain amount of fluency and comprehension, so that individual reading books from various series can be introduced.

Parallel with this development there will be the need to acquaint pupils with other consonant combinations such as *-nk, -ng, -ar* ; and with common consonant and vowel digraphs such as *wh* and *ee*.

Here, too, familiarity with phonic families may come through nursery rhymes or through puzzles. All practice will be short and incidental, never detracting from the main objective of encouraging and allowing pupils to read continuous material from appropriate books.

Supplementary Reading Material

Considerable use may now be made of graded supplementary reading books to give further practice for children who have progressed well with the class textbooks in use. A stimulus to the reading of simple supplementary books is to allow pupils to keep, on prepared cards, a record of the books read. As at this stage reading comprehension should be developed and tested, it is useful to have very simple exercises based on the supplementary texts in order to direct the reading and, at the same time, to check the results of the reading, much of which will be done in groups. With more advanced children a considerable amount of reading will be done silently, and here again it is advisable to motivate it and to provide ingenious methods of testing.[1]

[1] See *Backwardness in the Basic Subjects*, 4th ed., pp. 248-76, for suggested ways of motivating and testing silent reading ; tests also in *Diagnostic and Attainment Testing*, 4th ed., by F. J. and F. E. Schonell (Oliver & Boyd, 1960) pp. 47-63.

A useful summary of reading devices is to be found in *Reading Aids through the Grades*, Bureau of Publications, Teachers' College, Columbia University, New York City. See pp. 38-9 and pp. 43-50 for exercises designed to aid and test comprehension.

CHAPTER VI

ORGANISATION OF READING IN JUNIOR CLASSES

In junior classes of pupils aged 7+ to 11+ or 12+ years the important objective, particularly with the first and second classes of pupils aged 7+ to 9+, is to ensure continuity of reading instruction from the infant department. The bulk of the pupils promoted from infant classes or departments will have mastered the mechanics of reading, and if suitable graded reading material is available they will continue to make progress. But there will always be from all infant classes a percentage of children, from 15 per cent to as many as 40 per cent in some areas, who are still having difficulty with the mechanics of reading. Occasionally this percentage of backward readers is due to bad teaching, sometimes to environmental conditions, such as absence or continuous change of school, but most often, as I have shown elsewhere,[1] it arises from the fact that these children have not matured at the same rates as their companions either in general intelligence or in the special abilities required in learning to read. It is therefore vital that these groups of children, backward in reading and spelling, should continue to receive instruction similar in kind and in quantity to that of which their friends were able to take full advantage in the infant classes. Unless these children secure this careful attention they either stagnate in verbal attainments or, in some cases, lose the little ground previously gained in their infant groups.

Furthermore, unless they progress in reading, it is likely

---

[1] *Backwardness in the Basic Subjects* (Oliver and Boyd) in Chapter IX. Causes and symptoms of disability in reading are considered in detail, and in particular the differing rates of maturation in special abilities in learning to read are explained and illustrative cases of backward readers are described.

that their personality development and the whole of their instruction in junior classes or junior departments will be marred by their backwardness in reading. Thus organisation of reading in the lower levels of the junior school is a matter of paramount importance—in fact more important than any other subject or activity. It is only by attention to the right methods and materials for these backward readers that we can prevent personality deterioration, which in some cases results in a compensating outlet of delinquency.

There is an intimate connection between mental health and degree of success in learning to read. This relationship is particularly close in pupils between the ages of 7+ and 11+, and not a little of the truancy, misbehaviour and minor delinquencies in junior pupils can be directly traced in part to verbal failure—to backwardness in reading and writing. Furthermore, the right treatment, early, prevents backwardness in reading becoming a barrier to progress in written composition, spelling and even arithmetic, and it obviates later illiteracy in the secondary school, and with some, illiteracy in adult life.

Organisation

What junior schools must realise is that *it is their job to teach reading from beginning stages* (just as much as it is that of the infant school) to the pupils who come from infant classes still very weak in the mechanics of reading. All must realise that it is absolutely necessary for teachers of pupils of 7+, 8+ and 9+ in junior classes to know how to teach reading to non-readers and very backward pupils, that text-books suitable for backward readers should be available, and that for such pupils the time-table should be so organised as to permit two short reading lessons per day.

The problem of catering effectively for all grades of reading attainments amongst pupils of 7+ to 9+ is almost as much a responsibility of the administrator and the training college lecturer as it is one for the school staff. For in the first instance there should be more flexibility allowed between infant and junior classes or departments—the hard and fast age of transfer should not prevail in the cases of a small number of children who, if left for six or nine months longer with infant teachers using infant methods, would profit immensely in their reading instruction. Furthermore, there should be, in lower junior classes, teachers who are not only sympathetic towards modern infant school methods, but who are well informed about methods and materials for teaching reading at infant school levels, and who have had some experience with pupils of 6+ to 7+.[1]

Finally, for that small core of backward readers who present more than usual difficulty even up to the age of 10+ years, Education Committees should provide opportunities for selected teachers to attend a full course (of eight or ten weeks) in diagnostic testing and in remedial teaching methods. Even one such qualified teacher in a junior school could be of inestimable value in diagnosing the difficulties of very backward readers, in planning remedial teaching for them, and in giving general guidance to his or her colleagues upon remedial methods and materials.

PLANNING BY CLASS TEACHERS

There are signs that improved organisation is very slowly coming into being in some of the more progressive areas, but even when this is universal to the education system, it will still be necessary for the class teacher in the junior school to plan his reading instruction scientifically. Briefly, the steps in this planned reading programme are : (1) Use of a graded reading test ; (2) planning of methods and division of groups on the basis of the reading test results ; (3) selection of appropriate materials ; (4) maximum practice in oral

[1] In this respect it is encouraging to see that some training colleges have taken up this problem and now train a body of students capable of teaching over a pupil age range of 5+ to 9+. These students take a course in child psychology, and one dealing with teaching methods and materials applicable to pupils aged 5 to 9. They do some teaching practice in both infant classes and lower junior classes.

and silent reading for particular groups ; (5) testing the progress of selected children.

USE OF GRADED WORD READING TEST

The first step in this scientific planning, the intelligent use of a graded reading test, is probably only necessary as a universal measure for pupils in the first and second classes in junior departments. Inevitably there will always be in classes of pupils of 7+ to 9+ a wide range in reading attainments. Perhaps the one exception to this will be in a large junior school, where the enrolment permits of three streams and where the first year A and second year A classes are sufficiently homogeneous to contain pupils all of whom have no difficulty with the mechanics of reading ; but even in such classes it is my experience that there still exists a fairly wide range in speed and accuracy in silent reading.

In most classes in the lower part of the junior school the range of reading attainments is usually about four years, and not infrequently five or even six years ; that is to say, there are some pupils aged 7, 8 or 9 who have not progressed beyond a 5+ reading level, while there are others who can read almost as well as the average 10-, 11- or 12-year-old pupil. Indeed, if we test an entire age group in the junior school, we invariably find a larger spread in reading ages than this. Recently I tested fifty-nine boys *between the ages of* 10 *and* 11, and their reading ages ranged from the cases of two boys who had only reached reading levels of 5·1 and 5·2 years respectively to a group of six boys whose power of word recognition in reading was 13·1, 13·1, 13·2, 13·4, 13·5, 13·5 years— a range from poorest to best in the entire group, of 8·4 years. The detailed distribution of results is shown on page 135.

As might be expected, these 10-year-old boys were spread throughout four different classes.

Now, it is a simple matter to determine the reading age of each pupil in one's class—information which is invaluable in planning methods, selecting material and checking

Reading Ages	Number of Pupils
5-6	2
6-7	2
7-8	4
8-9	4
9-10	4
10-11	7
11-12	17
12-13	13
13-14	6

the progress of the weaker pupils. In Appendix I (pages 256 and 257) is set out in print, varying in size to suit the ages of the testees, a graded word reading test. The words in this test were selected, after careful preliminary trials and testing with groups of pupils between the ages of 6 and 14+ years, from a much larger body of words. The test thus represents a scientifically selected sample of words, of increasing difficulty, that will give an accurate estimate of a pupil's power of word recognition, which is the basis of his ability to read and understand printed material. Almost all of the test words increase by a known amount of difficulty from one word to the next within each group, and from one group to another. This even increase in difficulty was obtained from the calculation of the percentages of passes made for each word by the pupils in each age group from 6 to 13 years. From these data it was possible to allot ten words, gradually increasing in difficulty, to each age group from 5 to 6 years up to 13 to 14 years.

It is thus apparent that the words which constitute the test provide the teacher with a measuring instrument of carefully selected, scientifically graded units, by use of which he can determine the level a pupil has reached in his power of word recognition. As the detailed instructions show on pages 258 to 263, we aim at discovering the total number of these words that the testee can read. We then calculate his reading age on that basis. So that *reading age for word recognition* is obtained in this way :

$$\frac{\text{the number of words } \textit{correctly } \text{read}}{10} + 5 \text{ years}$$

There are ten words in each age group from 5 years onwards, and five years are added to the score for the pre-testing years. The testing usually takes about five or six minutes per testee, so that at the end of three reading lessons (thirty-five or forty minutes each) the teacher will have a complete list of reading ages of the entire class.

The criticism that the words, not being in a continuous meaningful form (i.e. sentences or paragraphs), are therefore not in a setting familiar to the testees is not a valid one. The form of the test does not disturb testees, and experiments show that even if all words were couched in sentences the actual reading ages obtained would not materially alter. In all probability the high degree of accuracy revealed by the test, not only of relative accuracy from pupil to pupil, but of reliability, might show a slight decline if the sentence form of testing were used.

Extensive use of graded word reading tests shows that this type of test is a most accurate way of estimating the level reached by pupils in the mechanics of reading. Hence teachers are able to use the results from the test for three things, as a basis upon which to divide their classes into sections and groups for reading, as a guide in the selection of reading books, and as a check upon the progress made by backward readers over a given period.

METHODS AND MATERIALS

It is apparent from the range of reading ages which we obtain from testing pupils in lower junior classes that reading cannot be taken simply as a class lesson. Two forms of organisation are possible to meet the problem of the wide variation in levels of reading achievement within the classes. The first is to group pupils in sections in each class according to a small range of reading age, and the second is to organise pupils throughout the school into *reading classes* as nearly homogeneous as possible and then to meet differences in reading that still exist by use of sections within each class.

This latter course means that reading must be taken at the same time every morning for every class, i.e. register class, throughout the school. Although this method has advantages in schools which contain classes with very wide ranges in reading ages, it has the disadvantage of placing children in classes with teachers other than their own class teacher for the most vital activity in the whole curriculum. A compromise which is sometimes adopted is to use this method of cross classification or reading classes only for the first two classes in the junior school, and then to invite class teachers to supplement this by an additional period of reading with their own class. Another method sometimes adopted is to organise a special class for backward readers. These children have two lessons a day in reading—naturally care should be taken not to include in such a class of pupils of ages 7 to 9 years, those children of 11+ or 12+ who might be influenced adversely in self-esteem and confidence by such a grouping.

It is essential that the reading lessons should be planned to give maximum practice with materials suited to the pupils' reading ages. Some will require much oral practice with very simple reading books, while others will be sufficiently advanced to be able to do a considerable amount of motivated silent reading.[1] The most effective organisation for this is a combination of class sections for reading and group reading. The pupils should be divided into two or three sections on the basis of their reading ages, and appropriate textbooks used for each section. With these reading books suited to the range of reading ability in each section it will be possible for

[1] For a detailed consideration of the use of the Graded Word Reading Test and the relation of test results to the use of the graded series *Wide Range Readers*, see 'Reading in the Junior School', F. J. Schonell, *Educational Review*, Feb. 1950.

I

the teacher to do a certain amount of oral reading instruction for the benefit of pupils in each group, while other sections are engaged in individual card work or in silent reading checked by questions and exercises. To obtain still more intensive practice for the weaker members, the class may be divided into even smaller reading units, namely, five or six reading groups. Each group should contain pupils of approximately similar reading ages, and in this way we can still further suit the material to the reading level of the pupils and arrange for more practice for the backward readers.

BACKWARD READERS IN THE PRIMARY SCHOOL

For the really backward readers in the junior school [1] there is the need to select material and methods that will strengthen their powers of word recognition. They should not be expected to deal with a class reading book that is beyond their level of attainment. The few with reading ages as low as 5 to 6 years will constitute a section and they might well use Happy Venture Readers, Books Two and Three, or basic books of a similar level from any word controlled series. Furthermore, these pupils need plenty of supplementary writing of simple words that come into their reading/spelling vocabulary, words such as *here, there, which, what, bring, those, much, many, father, brother*. We have found at our Remedial Education Centres that very backward pupils between the ages of 7 and 10 profit greatly by being taken systematically through the first two groups of common words in the *Essential Spelling List*.[2] This material (Groups I and II), which consists of 852 very common words, carefully graded and grouped according to similarity of structure, constitutes about 70 per cent of those words that these pupils will experience in their remedial reading.

The fact that the words are arranged in structural families

---

[1] This section may be supplemented by appropriate sections from *Backwardness in the Basic Subjects*, 4th ed., by F. J. Schonell (Oliver and Boyd).

[2] *Essential Spelling List*, by F. J. Schonell (Macmillan)

of increasing difficulty—for example, this is the nineteenth set in Group I for pupils of reading/spelling age 7 to 8 :

bite	may	ever
white	way	every
like	away	never

stay   mile   very

and the fact that pupils write each word, as well as merely look at it, is of considerable psychological value in strengthening their weak powers of word recognition. They are assimilating the patterns of words as much by kinaesthetic impressions as by visual means.

In addition they need every help in fusing the words into a functional whole and hence it is through a global approach akin to that of the Belgian educationist, Decroly, that these children are able to assimilate words permanently into their reading, spelling and meaning vocabularies. This functional approach to word study is obtained by combining each set of words such as those above into a short story, and then associating reading, spelling and written exercises with the study of the words in a meaningful context.[1] The following is an example of a story embodying the above set of words, suitable for remedial material for backward readers and spellers at the 7 to 8 reading/spelling age level (but of any chronological age).

The White Rabbit

Once there was a white rabbit who lived about a mile away from a farm. Every night he went to the farm for some turnips. He could not stay away for very long.

He would say to himself, ' I like turnips so much I could eat them for ever and ever. I may never get any more turnips. I must go back for another bite.'

And so he would soon be on his way back again to the

---

[1] Short extracts or stories embodying sets of words in the *Essential Spelling List*, together with exercises, will be found in Books One and Two *Essential Read-Spell Books*, by F. J. and F. E. Schonell (Macmillan, 1961).

farm. But the farmer was very angry. ' I will take all these turnips into the barn,' he said. Next night when rabbit came there was not a turnip left.

In addition to a study of the words singly in their smaller structural families, children are required to do such exercises as these :

Read the story twice.

A. 1. I am white.
I live a mile away from a farm.
I like turnips.
Who am I ?

2. I grow on a farm.
A white rabbit took a bite out of me.
A farmer took me into the barn.
What am I ?

B. Put the right word in each space—very, every, ever never.

1. The white rabbit went to the farm ..... night.
2. He was .... fond of eating turnips.
3. He thought he could eat them for .... and ever.
4. ' I must go back for another bite,' he said, ' because I may ..... get any more turnips '.

Research results show that this triple approach to word study has greater transfer value than simply studying words as separate units. It is both the functional meaningful application of the words, together with the use of impressions gained through studying, reading and writing the words, that enable children to assimilate such words when they have failed to master them at an earlier stage.

It must be remembered that these pupils—two, three or four years behind in reading—who have failed to learn to read during their infant school period, almost invariably have weaknesses of a perceptual, experiential or emotional kind. They need special help and special encouragement in studying words and for them properly planned word study by various means is as necessary as carefully graded reading material suited to their lower levels of attainment. For these backward readers it may be necessary to continue with workbook and word study exercises similar to those discussed in the last chapter.

ADEQUATE SUPPLY OF GRADED BOOKS FOR ALL PUPILS

Most progressive junior schools today realise the importance of plying the pupil of 8+ onwards, who has mastered the mechanics of reading, with plenty of suitably graded reading books. While there are still a few schools that constrict their children unduly by over-detailed study of a single set of class readers, yet happily these grow fewer each year. Most schools now employ parallel sets of readers and also provide supplementary material related to projects or other activities. Class libraries (discussed in the next chapter) are being used increasingly. However, for children between the ages of 7 and 11 we should have a reading programme planned round parallel sets of reading books connected with their projects or interest books, whatever else they read.

While all children will do some oral reading from these books, the amount done as a pupil proceeds through the junior school should decrease and give place to directed silent reading.

This newer approach to reading in the junior school may be illustrated by reference to the *Wide Range Readers*,[1] which consist of parallel sets of books compiled on the basis of reading age, not chronological age. Thus this series provides these books :

Reading Age	Blue Books	Green Books
7 - $7\frac{1}{2}$	I	I
$7\frac{1}{2}$ - 8	II	II
8 - $8\frac{1}{2}$	III	III
$8\frac{1}{2}$ - 9	IV	IV
9 - 10	V	V
10 - 11+	VI	VI

[1] *Wide Range Readers*, by F. J. Schonell and P. Flowerdew (Oliver & Boyd)

In the first place, Blue and Green books are completely interchangeable throughout the series, both being of the same standard at each reading level. Two sets of books provide ample material at each age level without burdening the slower child with an apparently long book.

In the second place reading series compiled in this way make provision for an overlap with the infant school level and hence the first books are geared at a 7 to 7½ reading age level. Because the material is interesting and informative the pupil of average or better ability has no trouble in going relatively quickly through both Blue Book I and Green Book I and so gaining not only in vocabulary, sentence structure and information, but in enjoyment. It cannot be stressed too emphatically that reading is like learning to ride a bicycle. Children gain facility, not by studying it, but by doing it. They gain in fluency and in word recognition, they increase their vocabulary and improve their sentence structure, they add to their knowledge *not* by studying *one* reading book in minute detail but by reading many books. For this reason the modern approach is to provide planned material in plenty for the 7+ to 10+ stage : for example, in the Wide Range series there are ten books to cover these four years. Some children, if given the chance, will have read during class lessons, seven or eight of these books in the first two years, together, of course, with many other suitable books (see Chapter VII).

Some teachers buy sets of ten or twelve books suited to particular age levels, to supplement the parallel class readers. *Increasingly, instruction in reading in the junior school means providing graded material so that the child may proceed at his own pace.* This means that section or group reading is superseding class reading, when every pupil in the class was supposed to proceed lock step, irrespective of his reading age and needs, with the study of a single class reading book. Increasingly, also, for a basis on which to form groups and sections, teachers are using a graded word test or simple silent reading test, such as those described elsewhere in this book.

Some head teachers now test all new entrants from infant schools to junior schools with the Graded Word Reading Test, and a range in reading ages from 5 years 2 months to as much as 10 years 9 months is not infrequently revealed. Obviously such a range demands a flexible approach. Furthermore, it requires not only the use of many books for the good readers but material of suitable level for the poor readers.[1]

But reading books for pupils in junior schools need to be carefully compiled not only as regards selection of vocabulary and choice of sentences, but in the inclusion of material that will interest, challenge and stimulate the curiosity of children to the maximum. For this reason good reading texts for juniors should provide information—geographical, historical, scientific, general—as well as tell a good story. While the young pupil between 8 and 12 years is an inveterate lover of stories, he is also strongly motivated by a widely varying intellectual curiosity which makes him voracious in his tastes and in his search for information. For this reason there is the need to provide class reading material that is a judicious blend of fact and fiction, of story and chronicle. All information should be absolutely accurate, but much of it can be adroitly framed in attractive story form. Most of the facts about Leonardo da Vinci or Newton, about Handel or Helen Keller, about the Great Fire, the Great Trek or the Australian Flying Doctor Service can be given in story form without departing from accuracy of statement.

Choice of Books for Group Reading

Finally, in group reading it is possible to make use of *some* of the short supplementary texts now published. Simple short, graded stories, each constituting a book, are enjoyed by the pupils who have a sense of achievement as they complete

[1] One junior school, typical of many, using a scientifically planned scheme based on a combination of Happy Venture and Wide Range, reports average gains in the reading ages of groups of children at the rate of 1 year 7 months in a period of 10 months and 2 years 5 months in 1 year 10 months. (See *Wide Range in Practice*—obtainable from Oliver and Boyd.)

book after book. Teachers must, however, be most particular about the vocabulary burden for the reading age level of such material that they use for group or silent reading. A service that an Education Department or Committee can render to its teachers is to draw up suitable short lists of supplementary material which have been assessed on a reading age level by a competent reading committee. Such information will enable teachers to purchase sets of ten or twelve books which will supplement class reading books for group reading sessions. This work will no doubt be facilitated at some point by the application of a *simple* readability formula to determine difficulty level of reading material.[1] The readability formulae at present in use are cumbrous and lacking in accuracy and universal applicability, mainly because they neglect to take into consideration sufficiently those subjective elements of style, literary merit and power of telling a story or imparting knowledge that make material dull or interesting, difficult or easy for children. At present, in the assessment of suitability of material for children of different ages and different levels of intelligence, there is no substitute for the really experienced person who knows both children and qualities of reading material. However, in judging whether books will be suitable for different age levels, teachers, while taking into account the very important subjective elements to which I have referred above, might be guided in their assessment by these character-istics of the material.

(a) *The difficulty of the vocabulary used.*

Here bear in mind the difficulty of the ten words which are included in each of the age groups 5 to 6, 6 to 7, 7 to 8, 8 to 9 years, etc., of the Graded Word Reading Test. The words were placed in those age groups because they were read by approximately 45 to 55 per cent of the age group to which they were allotted.

[1] Those who are interested in experimenting with the various readability formulae. (Lorge, Flesch, Dale and Chall, etc.) now available, might consult the three-yearly reviews of reading research by Gray in the *Journal of Educational Research* or those in *Review of Educational Research*.

(*b*) *The nature of the sentences used.*

In the main simple sentences are easier to read than complex ones. Long, involved sentences tend to make the material difficult to read. Readability formulae employ as one measure *the average sentence length in number of words*—sampled of course from a number of pages. We notice that young children find difficulty in dealing with sentences starting with prepositional phrases.

(*c*) *The number of common or uncommon words.*

Earlier we discussed the importance of common words in reading material as a means of facilitating word recognition. While books are a means of improving and extending a child's vocabulary, yet at the same time if there are too many uncommon words, these may slow up the child's interest and his ability to master the material.

In general, therefore, teachers might be guided in their choice of material for particular reading age levels by answers to these questions.

1. *Does it fit in with the interests of the children of the particular age?*

    Older retarded readers still have the interests of children of the same chronological age ; that is why they read books written with, say, 7 to 9 vocabulary but 11- to 14-year-old interests.

2. *Is it attractively written?* (Style, attractive phrasing, dramatic element, etc.)

3. *Do the illustrations fit the text and help to enrich the reader's interpretation?*

4. *Is the print of clear face and adequate size?*

5. *Is the spacing between the words and between the lines adequate or does the page look cramped?*

6. *What is the vocabulary level of the book for the age of pupil?*

7. *Does it contain many uncommon words?*

8. *Is the sentence structure suitable?*

In general for junior school children difficult material has long, involved sentences ; the vocabulary burden is too heavy ; it contains too many words outside the child's own language, and has a heavy loading of polysyllabic words. Parenthetical phrases, clauses and prepositional phrases may increase difficulty for some children.

ORAL READING IN THE JUNIOR SCHOOL AND ITS RELATION TO GROUP READING [1]

Attention has already been drawn to the very wide range of attainments in reading amongst junior school children in every school class, and this naturally points to differences in their reading needs—needs that are not only met by variations in methods and materials.

The old practice of expecting the whole class to use the same class reading book neglected to take note of these differences in reading ages within the class. Under this method pupil after pupil was asked to read aloud a paragraph or even less from the class or grade book while everyone else was expected to follow sentence by sentence, or in the case of very backward readers, word by word, the progress of the oral reading. Every now and then the teacher asked a question about the meaning of a phrase or a word or drew attention to the spelling, grammatical function or derivation of a word, all of which slowed down the actual amount read and interfered with the enjoyment and understanding of the extract as a whole. This over-analytic approach continued page after page, chapter after chapter, for every reading lesson in the week, for children were required to ' know ' the book thoroughly. Many able children had already read the entire book but they still had to take their daily dose of this soul-destroying scrutiny. A few adventurous spirits read other material surreptitiously, casting a glance from time to time at

[1] The actual technique employed in section reading and in group reading in junior classes, with suggestions for remedial material to suit reading ages from 5 to 9 years, is given in detail in *Backwardness in the Basic Subjects*, pp. 237-44.

the teacher and relying on their co-pupil alongside them to ' show them the place ' if called upon to read or answer a question.

Backward readers derived little from the practice because the material was often too difficult for them and the more able pupils read too fast for them to follow or to give attention to difficult words. Moreover, competent readers formed bad habits inasmuch as silent reading being faster than oral reading their development of quick phrase reading was impeded. As a result also of this artificial approach to reading some children tended to carry on longer than was necessary such props as finger pointing and semi-articulation of words and phrases in their efforts to keep to the slow pace of the lesson. It is little wonder that bright children who could read well became inattentive and bored, particularly as they listened to the stumbling efforts of a pupil with a reading age two to three years their inferior.

In other words, neither slow readers nor able readers really obtained effective reading practice from this ' all in together ' method. The effect of the method is well illustrated by the conversation I had with a bright 8½-year-old, with a reading age of 11, who had transferred from a school which provided a plentiful quota of group reading to one that still conducted reading by the ' all in together ' method. One day she said to me :

' I don't like reading any more.'

' Oh,' I said, ' why is that ? I thought it was your favourite lesson.'

' Well,' she said, ' at this school we don't really read ; we just listen to others who can't read trying to read, or we answer questions about words. Sometimes a good reader reads, but I haven't read all the week. We only read four or five pages in a lesson.'

Could there be a more damning indictment of this dull as ditchwater activity ? Yet the amazing thing is that it has lasted so long in many schools—and in fact in some schools in the British Commonwealth it is still accepted practice in junior reading lessons, that is, for children of 8+ upwards.

Now it should not be thought that all oral reading is valueless for children of age 8 and onwards[1]—it is only unsound if it constitutes the total approach with the *one* book as in the ' all in together ' method.

Modern Methods Recognise Individual Differences

As I have indicated earlier, modern methods in reading provide for the range of reading attainments found in every class. Hence they include class sections for reading, group reading, individual reading related to projects, interest books and activities, which encourage the child to dig out information for himself, and on occasions class reading for specific purposes. While oral reading will enter into almost all of these forms of provision for reading in the junior school, there will also be a place for silent reading.

Class Reading

We may use, occasionally, *class reading*, when a story unknown to the pupil is read aloud in class by the better readers, any comments being limited strictly to the meaning of the extract or story as a whole, and designed to help the pupils in their understanding and interpretation of it. In this way a strong audience situation is created, children are trained to listen, and the more able children obtain that practice in careful oral reading with expression that their less able friends obtain in their separate daily section reading.

Or again, a teacher may use a class reading text with the whole class, selecting a poem or a short story as a model through which she wishes to improve phrasing, enunciation and general interpretation of the spoken word. Simple

[1] See *Reading in the Primary School*, by J. M. Morris, National Foundation for Educational Research Pub. no. 12 (Newnes, 1959) p. 97.

dramatic reading, provided we can introduce plenty of characters, is most valuable for this purpose.

Or still again, she may select certain extracts which she uses especially as a basis for word and phrase study. She wishes to reveal to the pupils the niceties in the choice of words, the selection of phrase and the turn of sentence—all of this is a legitimate and most effective use of oral reading, but it is for a particular purpose on a particular occasion.

Oral Reading in Groups

But of course oral reading may be done by *all* children in a school which takes certain lessons in the week as *group reading*. The children, divided into four or five groups of approximately similar reading attainments, form their own reading circles or coteries by moving into different corners, or, in modern schools where desks are easily moved, by arranging a few desks together in a selected spot. Under these conditions every child in a group has a chance to read aloud—children having been warned that they need only read in a quiet voice on account of other groups working near by.

The success of this depends to some extent upon the choice of group leaders to whom exact and careful guidance should be given in conducting a group. All group leaders should see the class teacher conduct a group, and then each one should take his turn as group leader under the supervision of the teacher. During supervision of the work by the teacher most help is given to the less able groups. Oral reading will naturally be the means by which the backward readers reveal their weakness in word recognition, their tendency to omit words, to phrase incorrectly or to neglect the punctuation. For the less able reading group or section most reading instruction will still be in the form of oral reading.

Group reading is more easily conducted with parallel reading texts, like the Wide Range Readers, which have a good supply of books at the lower reading age levels. More able pupils of 10 and 11 years may make use of sets of eight or ten books, which are stored in the reading cupboard or class library, and clearly labelled in terms of difficulty—Group A, Group B, with appropriate colours. For example, there may well be for reading age groups 9 to 11, sets of the excellent Active Readers (Ginn). Some of the titles are :

White Hawk,
  by K. M. Gadd
X Bar Y Ranch,
  by K. M. Gadd

Diamonds in Springbok Valley,
  by Fay King
Powder Monkey,
  by Andrew Wood

Sally Ann: A Tall Ship, by K. M. Gadd

The practice of buying books in sets of eight or ten is increasing in junior schools—guidance for this may be obtained from the list contained in Chapter VIII.

Through group reading five or six times as much practice in reading is given to children than by instruction in classes, and what is more important, it is given with material which enables all children to make progress. Remember that groups should be flexible, with changes made in their composition at appropriate points in the child's progress, or lack of it.

Sections for Reading

Only a proportion of reading lessons need be conducted in this way.

A commoner and more easily managed procedure is to divide the class into three sections each with its book to suit reading levels. While the weakest section (Section C) engages in oral reading with the teacher, the more advanced sections (A and B) undertake silent reading with special assignments and exercises.

There is clear evidence from classes which adopt a combination approach to reading in terms of varying amounts of oral and silent reading conducted in groups or sections or individually, with occasional class lessons, that children make more rapid progress in reading, they read more books, their interest in reading is greater and they develop attitudes towards using books independently both for enjoyment and in their search for information.

CHECKING PROGRESS

Our major aim in the junior school should be to see that all pupils progress in reading. Unless we make this our first objective it is possible for some children to remain in their classes in junior departments month after month and to make little or no progress in this all-important subject. Unless our organisation is such as to permit maximum practice for all pupils with suitable material, then some pupils will ' stagnate verbally', and will pass through the junior period and be transferred to senior classes or secondary schools as non-readers. In spite of all efforts we make to use the most effective methods, to arrange for individual help and practice, and to provide appropriate reading materials, we are occasionally faced at the end of the junior school stage with a small residue of non-readers who, through a combination of circumstances, are as yet illiterates. But this small residue should not be more than 2 per cent—it certainly should not be 8 or even 10 per cent, which is the figure one not infrequently finds in some areas. It is obvious that a secondary school receiving 10 per cent of non-readers and a further 5 or 6 per cent of weaker readers from its contributory junior schools is handicapped from the outset in its objectives of giving suitable post-primary education. It should therefore be the aim of each junior school to check *the progress of its weak readers every six months* in order to see that reading retardation is being reduced to the lowest possible margin.

The Graded Word Reading Test, already used for grading, may be used here. It has been found that this test is extremely free from practice effects, for each word represents a sample of reading material at a particular level of difficulty. As the pupil makes progress so he is able to read an increasing number of words. If the pupil is not making progress in reading, then it does not matter how often he is given the test—his result remains approximately the same.[1] Thus the test may be used to check the progress of the ten or twelve or even twenty weakest readers in the school. With proper organisation of reading lessons and provision of suitable reading books it will be found that in six months some of the pupils will have made remarkable progress ; it is not uncommon to find pupils increase their reading age by as much as eighteen or twenty months in six calendar months. Others will have made average progress, i.e. a gain commensurate with the increase in chronological age, while a few will not have made more than a very slight increase, e.g. from reading age 6·1 to 6·2 or from reading age 6·11 to 7·2. The lack of progress of this last-named group is a challenge to the teacher—obviously these pupils need some additional stimulus ; perhaps a new attack on the subject, with parental co-operation, is required. Perhaps more individual help and additional periods of reading practice are necessary, in which case reading practice during other lessons, the help of older boys or girls, with an extra few minutes here and there from the teacher, might produce the desired improvement. With all such pupils we should look closely at the method we are using—possibly more writing and tracing are required, or it may be that further systematic phonic work would help others. With this very backward group some attempt at a more detailed diagnosis of their condition should be made before continuous failure hardens into frustration and creates emotional barriers which are difficult to dissipate. It is suggested that teachers should read Chapters VII to X in *Backwardness in the Basic Subjects* for an understanding of the lines upon which diagnosis and modification of teaching methods might profitably proceed.

Finally, we should not overlook the far-reaching effect of extending the pupil's speaking and meaning vocabulary

[1] Naturally in giving the test, either initially or at a later retesting, the teacher should not read to the pupil nor teach him the words which he does not know. Retests of groups of children with the graded word test showed a high reliability coefficient, namely, ·96.

in general. The wider we can make his verbal background the better is his chance to progress in reading. The keen class teacher might of course retest her whole class after an interval of nine or twelve months. It is satisfying to see how much progress some pupils have made, while at the same time with other pupils it is a further stimulus to teaching powers and to our skill in adaptation when an objective assessment reveals how little they have profited from instruction.

We should always keep in mind the fact that reading is only a means to an end. Pupils learn to read, at first largely orally and later silently, in order to understand the printed word. The ultimate objective is to understand the ideas, to appreciate the story, or to follow instructions, or to enjoy the beauty of the words or the rhythm, or to gain information from the written words of the author. Thus, as soon as a child has mastered the mechanics of reading, he should be introduced to directed silent reading, increasing in amount as his actual technical skill in reading increases. All kinds of stimuli and motives can be introduced to direct and vitalise the silent reading. These motives are manifold, and vary from the absorbing interest of a story to the sheer delight of understanding the clues in a treasure hunt. It is the teacher's job to make reading as real, meaningful and purposeful as possible. Occasionally, as the pupils progress through the school, it is necessary to check their powers of silent reading. Are they able to understand and use what they are reading? In this respect the sparing and occasional use of a silent reading test [1] may reveal definite difficulties and weakness on the part of some children who may have mastered the mechanics of reading, but who are not yet able to use their newly acquired tool with the fullest effect. The pupils need some help in learning to read silently for a variety of purposes.

[1] Suitable silent reading tests which cover a variety of aspects of silent reading —for detail, for general impression, for inference, for following instructions— available in booklets which can be used and re-used for different classes, are obtainable from Oliver and Boyd : *Silent Reading*, Test A (for ages 7 to 10) ; *Silent Reading*, Test B (for ages 9 to 12).

K

FINAL OBJECTIVES

As our final objective we should remember that the curriculum in the junior school should provide activities and experiences that will cater for personal needs and stimulate a social awareness. To achieve this the reading programme must be at the same time planned yet flexible, directed yet varied—our aim should be to provide all children with as many experiences as possible. The enrichment of language background through oral work connected with activities will be the surest way of aiding our reading programme. For this reason we cannot dissociate the planning of reading from the various centres of interest or environmental studies based on the requirements of the children. Group studies of such topics as ' Our clothes ', ' The story of books ', ' The story of time ', ' How we travel ', ' How people live ', ' The market ', ' The post office ', ' Wheat and bread ', ' The farmer ', ' Shops ', ' The games of boys and girls ', ' Our town ', can give rise to an immense amount of selected, informative reading for pupils of different ages.

Teachers will find that *Projects for the Junior School*, Books 1 to 4 (R. K. and M. I. R. Polkinghorne) contain helpful reading matter for use in conjunction with group studies.

Moreover, the knowledge thus gained and the attitudes thus formed should be of great value to pupils later if we can evolve an enlightened, sensible, realistic curriculum for our post-primary schools.[1]

[1] See *The Social Approach to the Curriculum*, by C. Fletcher (The English New Education Fellowship).

CHAPTER VII

UNDERSTANDING AND INTERPRETATION

ALTHOUGH a considerable proportion of the time devoted to early instruction in reading must of necessity be concerned with the mechanics of reading, that is, developing each pupil's powers of word recognition and his reading vocabulary, yet we must never lose sight of the fact that the ultimate aim of reading instruction is to enable pupils to read silently with adequate speed and to be able to understand and interpret what they read—sometimes to gain information, sometimes purely for pleasure, often for a combination of both.

The ability to understand and interpret the printed symbols on a page is influenced considerably by (*a*) the pupil's intelligence, (*b*) by his vocabulary and level of word recognition, (*c*) by his background of knowledge and experiences and (*d*) by the strength of purpose motivating him to understand. Complementary to this, of course, is the fact that understanding of what is read is dependent on the nature and the difficulty of the material. In the past we have tended to interpret different levels of comprehension in pupils too much in terms of (*a*) and (*b*) and to neglect in our planning the very important influences exerted by (*c*) and (*d*). Although in general the more intelligent child is more effective in understanding what is read, yet there are many exceptions. Certainly a child cannot begin to understand a passage until he can read the words, but effective word recognition does not necessarily mean effective comprehension. There is now sufficient evidence to show that background of knowledge, particularly that gleaned through talks and discussions with adults and supplemented by all kinds of experiences of an active kind—mastering common skills, making things, observation of natural phenomena, visits and excursions—including also experiences of a more passive kind such as those associated with the screen, television and radio, play a powerful part in comprehension and in interpretation.

But even then, in addition to all these, and at times transcending them, is motivation—that impelling force of emotional energy which drives an individual to 'worry out' somehow from material, even in face of limitations of experience, intelligence or literacy, information that he *must* have. Time and again with older backward children, we see this force at work. When the need for information is strong enough their lack of ability disappears, and in a matter of months they can read their self-chosen themes. With one it may be racing cars, with another cricket and cricketers, with a third, bird watching and identification, with a fourth, the breeding and training of racing pigeons, while with a fifth it may be an all-absorbing interest in ships, all of which such topics adroitly handled through 'interest books' with careful vocabulary control, produce the means of success.

But even strong motivation will fail if suitable material is not at hand. The school boy who is passionately devoted to the study of birds or butterflies, or the girl who is intensely interested in wild flowers or shells, will experience something of a setback if no relatively simple reference books are available. Fortunately the last three decades have seen a vast improvement in this direction. For example, for our budding botanist or enthusiastic ornithologist, conchologist or entomologist, there are attractively written series such as the *Romany Books* (University of London Press), the *Lady Bird Books* (Wills & Hepworth), the *Nomad Books* (University of London Press), *Let's Watch the Birds* (Nelson), *Observer Book of British Birds, Butterflies, Flowers, etc.* (Warne) and Ward Lock's *Library of Natural History Books* (Ward Lock). In addition there are interesting books in which the material is provided in story form, such as *Stories of the Wild* (McDougall), the Arthur Ransom Books, various Puffin Story Books and the *The Wild Life Series*, by C. B. Rutley (Macmillan).

Training in Comprehension

Comprehension has different purposes. A consideration of the function of reading in relation to different forms of material immediately suggests that understanding and interpreting differ in purpose in different situations. The boy who so avidly wants to know how to breed and train racing pigeons requires to extract an accurate step-by-step understanding of what he reads so that he can put it into practice, The boy who is reading about racing cars and their drivers is mostly satisfying his curiosity at an enjoyment level, in much the same way as he goes to the cinema. He brings away with him a few facts but it is immaterial whether he remembers them or not, except to recount them to his peers. So with different material in different situations the purpose and level of understanding varies. The pigeon expert is not unlike the student ; he must understand and remember all the facts, the only difference being that some of the facts remembered by the student are worthless and will not stand the test of practical application.

On the other hand the student may at times just *skim certain passages* to glean the main general idea, or he may read an article, a play or a novel to supplement his knowledge or experience in a general way, or from a particular angle. At other times he *must search his material with top level intellectual power to select facts that fit into an argument or a theory.* On still other occasions he must marshal every fact with completeness and closeness, discarding irrelevant issues, if he is to make the *correct inference or arrive at a logical conclusion.*

There will be situations also in which the reader may be seeking to *interpret the deeper and perhaps more sensitive or aesthetic meaning* of the writer or the poet through his choice of words or phrases, his form of imagery or rhythm, or the nature of his plot or the philosophy of his message.

Now while all these various forms of comprehension and interpretation in reading come only through much reading allied at times to writing, it should be the function of the school to help children to make the fullest use of reading in every sense. In other words, it should be a major objective of schools to lead children to effective comprehension and interpretation. While many schools do an excellent job in regard to interpretation in literature lessons, there is a tendency for them to neglect to give specific aid to pupils in the finer points of comprehension and in the formation of effective study skills in other school subjects.

No doubt some of the weakness found in British schools in regard to these aspects of reading instruction lies in the fact that they are not regarded as responsibilities of the school. Too often schools believe that children will develop powers of comprehension and study skills for themselves. While this is probably true of the top thirty or forty per cent of children, it is not true of the majority. The reading needs of the 10-to 14-year-old group, whether they be in the primary school or the first forms of secondary school, are very different from those of younger children and we need to include in our time-table periods when we help older boys and girls to form study habits, to understand what they read and to build up a deep and lasting interest in reading. American research has shown that we can contribute considerably to the improvement of comprehension and the development of study skills by teaching methods of both a direct and an indirect kind.

Start Early

In the direct approach to the teaching of comprehension it is important to implant in the pupil's mind at the beginning the idea that he is seeking meaning, not merely reading words. Hence a reading programme should from the earliest stages include some exercises designed to test the pupil's understanding of what he reads. As we have shown elsewhere these should be varied and should challenge the child's curiosity and his skill. Questions of various kinds may be supplemented by multiple choice selection, by crosswords, by puzzles of the ' Who am I ? ' ' What am I ? ' or the treasure hunt kind. But quite early also comprehension of what is read should be linked with practical activities such as writing freely chosen topics illustrated by drawings, mapping, making things, writing simple letters, preparing an ' interest book '. Initially it is through discussion, through use of workbook material, through cards of exercises based on their reading matter, that young children unravel the meaning of sentences. While easy exercises in the early stages lead children to see that they can use information based on their reading, such testing also enables the teacher to discover pupils who are failing in this aspect of reading.

Speed and Comprehension

While speed of reading is important, it should not be developed at the expense of understanding. At the same time some children, mainly through faulty phrasing, are handicapped by very slow reading. Experimental work with tachistoscopic exposure of material, phrase by phrase, shows that speed may be improved, up to a point, without loss of understanding. However, for teachers the important objective is to train children, directly and indirectly, through motivation and by special techniques, not only to understand what they are given to read but to be able to discover information for themselves. Speed is a minor problem for it has been repeatedly demonstrated by objective tests that newer methods of teaching reading with vocabulary controlled material and with adequate spacing of words and lines, lead to greater fluency.

The relation between speed and comprehension has been the subject of many experiments, and while in the main the children who understand best are those who read the fastest, yet there are many exceptions. An obvious one is the careful, plodding child whose cautious temperament impels him to make quite sure that he understands every point, while at the other extreme is the quick extrovert who finishes first but gains mediocre marks. With older children whose reading rate has slowed down to the point of handicapping them in their studies, then a course to improve speed is warranted. Timed reading of paragraphs, flash card reading of sentences with minimal time for recognition, and exposure of material by means of a simple machine which exposes the material, phrase by phrase, at a set rate may lead to increases in speed of reading. The teacher should, however, link all speed reading with simple questions testing comprehension. We should commence reading practice with selections of two or three hundred words with vocabulary and sentence structure at a level much below that usually read by the group. Two or three check questions should be set on the general meaning of the extract. The difficulty of the extracts should be gradually increased. Some children retard their speed of reading by lip movement and by intermittent breaks in attention. However, the relationship between speed and comprehension is much influenced by the purpose of the reading and by the nature of the material.

Two Approaches

We may make two complementary approaches to training pupils in comprehension, interpretation and study skills.

1. The *first* is through the use of exercises especially designed to emphasise a particular aspect of comprehension.
2. The *second* is to link the vital objective of understanding in reading instruction with activities of a more natural and impelling kind such as those associated with individual interests, projects, visits, lecturettes and so on.

1. *Specific Exercises for Different Aspects of Comprehension*

While the special comprehension exercise has an element of artificiality about it, there is research evidence to show that pupils improve in understanding what they read and in study techniques as a result of practice with such exercises. There is now an adequate supply of well-planned books[1] with extracts and exercises designed to improve comprehension. These range from material for children at the 7+ level up to texts geared to lower secondary classes. The disadvantages of using such texts exclusively with older children is that they may not contribute very much to the child's knowledge. They may produce adverse attitudes towards reading, and they may be so much waste of time with the brighter children who already have an effective technique in silent reading and who are able to take in their stride, and at a much greater speed, all the points so laboriously made in the exercises. In other words silent reading exercises may slow up good readers particularly in the amount they read. Instead of doing comprehension exercises they would be better employed reading and searching for information independently. However, this kind of limitation may be urged against other forms of English teaching in schools.

It is convenient to separate the programmes for the teaching of comprehension to pupils up to say 10+ from that for pupils between 11 and 15/16, although some types of exercises might well apply to both groups.

(a) For Younger Children

With most young children between the ages of 7 and 10 difficulties with sentence structure and limitations in vocabulary might well present obstacles to rapid comprehension, and for this reason the most effective aid to the development of comprehension with pupils of this age range is to increase opportunities for and to improve incentives to reading. We should encourage junior school pupils to read as much as possible by motivating their reading, and by providing them with material that is suited to their reading levels and links with their interests. The slower readers should gain encouragement from being able to see the progress they are making. But for all

---

[1] Variously titled *Reading for Meaning, Reading to Some Purpose, Study Reading*, etc.

young readers, able or slow, a really well ordered class library which the teacher uses as the source of properly planned supplementary reading is a powerful ally in the task of improving powers of understanding what is read.

At the same time a minimum of carefully chosen exercises which whet the appetite and challenge the curiosity of the pupils may be useful. Exercises of the following kinds will add precision and purpose in the achievement of these aims :

(i) We may require pupils to read a paragraph, several paragraphs or even pages to extract the *general meaning of the material* in a clear, concise form. This kind of exercise links closely with much of the pupil's reading, particularly that done in connection with his school work. He is continuously being challenged to assimilate the general ideas conveyed by the writer, and it is sound teaching to require him to show that he can do this by means of carefully framed exercises. Furthermore no one is able to remember all he reads and it is excellent basic training to encourage pupils to select the salient or basic facts in a passage and to be able to reproduce these.

While it is useful to encourage the writing of correct sentences and to aim at producing improvement in each pupil's ability to write varied sentences, yet in comprehension exercises the emphasis should be on brevity of response. We are testing understanding, not literary ability. Therefore we should not require lengthy answers but rather use devices such as underlining appropriate phrases or sentences, selecting the correct answer from a number of answers, giving a one-word answer, or writing short simple sentences in answer to a series of questions.

The following is an example of testing for *general meaning*, the extract having been taken from the *Wide Range Readers*, Blue Book IV, page 97.

The Story of Clocks

Long, long ago the only clock was the sun. People watched it rise above the hill, and knew that morning had come. They looked up when it was right overhead, and knew that the time was midday. They watched it sink lower and lower in the sky, and knew that evening was turning to night.

Shadows helped them too. They noticed that early in the morning, trees and people had long, thin shadows, but later they became short and fat, until at midday there were no shadows at all. In the afternoon the little fat shadows came again, and grew longer and thinner until the sun went down.

Write two short sentences explaining how people told the time before clocks were invented.

(ii) We may, at a later stage with junior school pupils of 9 to 12 years, use exercises which *develop sensitivity to sequence of ideas*—knowledge which will be useful to them in writing a composition or answering questions related to assignments in English, Social Studies, History, Geography, and so on.

This is an example of an exercise framed to test this aspect of comprehension, the extract being from the Great Trek (*Wide Range Reader*, Blue Book VI, page 23).

After the first few days the way was never easy. ' How shall we cross the mountains ? ' asked Piet when he first saw them, rising blue in the distance. The wagons seldom travelled more than eleven miles a day, so it was quite a while before his question was answered. When at last the mountains were reached, the teams of oxen were doubled. Anna Maria, Piet, and their mother sat on a flat stone with other women and children, while the men took the wagons one after another, and helped the oxen to drag them over the huge rocks and up the dry, slippery, stony mountainside, some pulling at the ropes in front, others pushing from the back, panting, heaving, straining with all their might. It was weeks before all the wagons were safely across, and then some of them were damaged or had to have new wheels.

Anna Maria, Piet and Mama followed on foot with the other families, in the scorching sun. Anna Maria grew tired, and stumbled and fell, and cried.

.   .   .   .

When all the families and their wagons and herds were over the mountains and across the empty river bed, Oom Andries called the people together and led them in a service of thanksgiving to God for bringing them in safety thus far. They said prayers and sang hymns, and over the wild South African hills, where before, scarcely a white man had trod, floated the music of brave Dutch voices.

Write six phrases or sentences that tell the order in which things happened to those on the Great Trek as they crossed the mountains, e.g. teams of oxen were doubled.

(iii) We may motivate silent reading by requiring children *to search for information* which is tested by questions or directions that are made known before the material is read. This kind of exercise has value in developing attitudes towards independent study, and in training younger pupils to handle problems which may arise in connection with individual interests.

(iv) As an important form of understanding what is read is continuously revealed in the degree to which an individual can carry out directions correctly, it is advisable to include in any comprehension exercises some measure of *ability to understand directions*. In addition to instructions and directions which may be part of a normal teaching/testing situation, a variety of activities may be linked with such exercises— drawing, making diagrams, crosswords, mapping, writing of simple stories, construction of models, execution of experiments in science and so on, e.g.

Making a Fan (8- to 9-year level) : Take a piece of stiff paper about 12 inches long and 9 inches wide. On each side of the paper paint or draw with coloured pencils a bright picture or pattern. Next fold the paper in half-inch pleats from one end to the other. Then gather the pleats together and fasten them at one end with a paper clip.

Making your own Map (10- to 12-year level): An interesting weekend activity is to make a map of your own neighbourhood or of part of the countryside where you live.

You should take a small notebook and with a friend walk along the streets or roads making a note of the various landmarks you pass. Make a note only of the important features. You would record a church or a school, a railway line or a station, a bridge, a river or a small lake. In the country you might note a large or peculiar tree, a swamp or a wood, a farm or an old hall, a lane or a park.

In order to save space on maps the map-maker uses symbols for many of the features mentioned in the last paragraph. Instead of printing the word CHURCH he would put

                if the church had a tower

                if the church had a spire

                for a bridge under a railway

                for a swamp or a marsh

Before you make your map it might be a good idea to consult an ordnance map, scale 1 inch to 1 mile, to see what kind of symbols and lines a map-maker uses.

(v) We may require *intensive reading* by *demanding the answers to a series of detailed questions*, all of which call for a slow, careful examination of the material.

Example : [1]

Long ago there were no lamps. There were only stars shining in the darkness. There was only the moon to light the way at night.

Then cave men discovered fire, so the first lamp was a burning stick, pulled from the flames and fixed up in a dim cave.

Perhaps one day a spark from the fire fell on to a rock, where fat from a roasted animal had dripped. The burning fat gave a brighter glow than the stick had given. So men made the first oil lamp, by pouring oil into a shell or a hollow stone. Soon they added wicks of grass, which burned more slowly and kept a steadier flame. And when men learned to make pots of clay, they made little bowls for the oil.

For hundreds and hundreds of years lamps were very much like this. People did not worry about making them any better. Day was meant for work, they thought, and night was meant for sleep. So they were quite happy to go to bed at sunset.

But at some time during those years men began to make candles. They dipped a wick of rag or rope into melted fat or bees-wax, and hung it up to cool and harden.

Complete the statements, or answer the questions :

1. The first lamp was a ....

2. An oil lamp was made by ....

3. Wicks were made from ....

4. Pots of clay were made to hold ....

5. For how long were oil lamps the only form of light used ?

6. How did men make candles ?

[1] Taken from *Wide Range Readers*, Green Book VI, page 96

(vi) One form of silent reading which we all use from time to time is *skimming through a passage* to select a point on a particular matter or to verify an idea. This form of reading is of special value when a pupil is searching for information or checking a fact he has recorded. It has, moreover, constant application in the study skills of senior scholars who need to be able to pick out a point from a complex discourse or a detailed description when they are doing assignments or revising for examinations.

(b) For Older Children

In addition to exercises of the kind discussed in the last section for younger children, certain other aspects of comprehension and interpretation assume increased importance for students as the breadth and intensity of their studies increase and as the need for effective study skills becomes more urgent.

Briefly we may list these as:

(i) *Ability to organise information round a topic.*

This skill is of prime importance to the student who must not only

(A) be able to search for and select relevant information from different sources ; but also

(B) be capable of assessing the value of the information, whether it is relevant or not, whether it is of major or minor importance and then of organising it in an effective way.

Hence older students should be able to consult source books and reference books, and here training through a class library is essential. Furthermore they should know how to find their way about a book by using its contents and its index, a point of particular significance in the use of encyclopaedias. It should be the aim of every senior class to possess a set of reference books such as the *Oxford Junior Encyclopaedia* and the *Concise Oxford Dictionary*. We are failing in our job as educators if we do not include such training as this in the objectives of

English teaching for all senior pupils. While the actual use of reference books is dependent on knowledge of how to use them, it is equally dependent on (*a*) their ready availability and (*b*) on school situations and reading methods which prompt and impel young minds to search for information—a point discussed more fully in the next chapter.

(ii) *Ability to read material and then to make a summary of it under headings and sub-headings ;*

Few students know how to organise their reading, so that they will be able not only to understand what they have read but to select the points of prime importance for inclusion in a summary. Too many students think that understanding and making a summary should proceed hand in hand so to speak. They attempt to summarise paragraph by paragraph and in consequence do not obtain a really sound and effective understanding of what they read because a major part of their mental energy is devoted to recording in writing what they are reading. Furthermore, such a practice may lead to lack of balance, conciseness and accuracy in the selection of important points.

First Reading : Students should be advised to *make a first reading* of the material whether it be a paragraph, a page, a section or chapter, without making any notes at all. In this first reading the student should concentrate on understanding the material, making clear in his mind the various relationships between points, deciding on their relative importance for the matter under consideration, and unconsciously recording them in their sequence. All this is a mental process which in the first place should not be hindered or handicapped in any way by writing. Writing, while we are endeavouring to understand what we read, may suggest to the mind that we have recorded the information—unfortunately not in the mind but on paper, with the result that the same initial mental effort is not put forth to understand and assimilate the information. The student will find that this first reading should enable him firstly, to grasp more clearly the author's ideas; secondly, to gain a clearer understanding of the material as a whole, with parts related to the whole ; and thirdly, to become aware of the salient features of the material.

While the student is making this first reading he may wish to underline or put marginal numbers, letters or ' high light ' marks which will help him considerably when he makes his second reading.

Second Reading : In the *second* reading the student should be taught to select the main points using a system of Roman numerals or capital letters for headings, with small figures or lower case letters for sub-headings. The use of explanatory sentences and phrases for expanding the headings and sub-headings should be demonstrated. At times students are inclined to make their summaries too extensive.

Equally important as the selection of main points, is the use of a system of trial recall of the summary. Every student should be advised to test his knowledge of each summary by writing the points or saying them aloud—in this way gaps in the knowledge are revealed.

If the student is uncertain of any phase or part of his summary it is worthwhile making a *third reading* of this section in the book.

(iii) *Ability to read logically ;*

Although skill in this is much dependent on level of intelligence and extent of vocabulary—also highly correlated with intelligence—yet there is evidence that we can bring about worthwhile improvement in the degree to which a student can handle the ideas in printed material so as to arrive at a conclusion. Briefly, we may for convenience of discussion, discern two main forms of logical reading, with certain overlap between the forms.

(*a*) Ability to read material involving a sequence of related steps so that the pupil may arrive at a conclusion.

(*b*) Ability to predict the outcome of events, that is, to make an inference or to solve a problem given certain information.

L

These aspects of reading enter extensively into thinking in problems in mathematics and science, in which the student has to sort out essential from unessential data, understand the relationships between the steps in the data, and perceive the similarity between this and a given rule or law. Undoubtedly some improvement in problem arithmetic can stem from training pupils to tackle problems in a systematic way. They should be taught to read each problem carefully so that they realise what is given and what is required and to determine the relationships between the parts. Too many children proceed in a haphazard fashion in their problem solving.

Likewise in geography or history, where there are cause and effect relationships or time relationships which must be understood to arrive at the right conclusion, training will be of value.

2. *The Activity Approach to Training in Silent Reading*

Without doubt a natural way of training children to understand and interpret what they read is to link the reading with a strong purpose. In most cases purpose is strongest when interest has been aroused and when activity is involved. This is seen when children prepare information preparatory to a school journey or an exhibition, seek help on making a model, or follow up queries which have arisen during a visit to a place of interest in the locality.

The most impelling motivation of silent reading is that associated with the natural and varied interests of the pupils. In these situations pleasure and purpose combine to provide a stimulus which results in concentration, understanding and interpretation at their most effective levels. Edward, age 11, has become intensely interested in cricket, particularly in ways to improve his batting and methods by which he may become a spin bowler. Everything on cricket that appears in the daily paper is read with avidity, while much spare time is devoted to an intensive study of a book on *How to Improve Your Bowling and Batting*, by a former English cricketer. Malcolm, age 10, is just as keen on birds and has built up for himself a small library on birds and bird watching. He can conduct a first-class discussion with adults similarly interested, so revealing the excellence of his understanding of what he reads. Eleanor, his sister, has between the ages of 10 and 14 developed three main interests—dogs, horses and collecting and identifying shells—each receiving varying amounts of attention at different times. Her interest in dogs and horses has resulted in reading books such as : *Black Beauty*, by Anna Sewell (A. & C. Black), *Queenie*, by Harper Cory (University of London Press), *Rover*, by Harper Cory (University of London Press), *The Silver Brumby*, by Elyne Mitchell (Hutchinson), *The Story of Fire-brand*, by J. Selby Lowndes (Collins), *Five Proud Riders*, by Ann Stafford (Puffin Story Book), *Bush Christmas*, by Smart and Borer (Pitman), *Man Shy*, by Frank Dalby Davison (Angus and Robertson).

At the time when these interests were at their peak no student could have applied herself more diligently to her studies than did Eleanor to her self-chosen search for information. Every fact about the horse, its history over the ages, its function in different communities, its anatomy, its care and protection was discovered and assimilated with a quite amazing degree of accuracy and retentivity. The details of all common breeds of dog were similarly well known, and adults in the family circle had to listen to all manner of questions, such as ' Which are the most intelligent breeds of dogs ? Which is the biggest ? Which is the most faithful ? Where do Alsatian dogs come from ? Which dogs are the best tempered ? Which is the best gun dog ? ' Most answers to this increasing spate of questions were supplied by Eleanor herself, whose level of knowledge revealed how effectively she could understand and interpret what she read in her field of interests.

Now the development of reading skill of this kind in children is not a little dependent on the degree of encouragement given to them at home and on the continuity with which suitable books are adroitly placed in their hands. Not all children are so effectively encouraged or fortunately fed at home with reading material linked to their emerging interests, and for this reason the school should be the motivating force and the supplying source in regard to training in individual habits of reading for information.

SCHOOL ACTIVITIES

School methods by which we can arouse interests leading to silent reading of an effective kind should be linked with activities that give scope for individual expression and for group work.

1. The simplest and most effective start that may be made with almost any child, junior or senior, dull or bright, is the compilation of an Interest Book or Travel Book. Children are invited to select a topic about which they would like to gather information and are then encouraged to search for pictures and letterpress related to their topic. Each child uses a fairly large exercise book in which he pastes suitable pictures, the rule being that each picture should be accompanied by at least one written sentence or one paragraph of printed matter. The teacher should assist children in the selection of explanatory material—in so doing he is, of course, motivating and, at the same time, testing the pupil's quality of comprehension. I have seen comparatively dull boys compile most attractive interest books on a very wide variety of topics—Bee Keeping, Fruit Growing, Car Manufacturing, Making Films, Photography, Bicycle Racing, Diving, Aeroplanes, Migratory Birds, Tennis, Cricket, Coal Mining, The Druids, Roman Roads. The resulting amount of reading done was quite extensive and the improvement in silent reading skill quite considerable.

While many pupils add much to their general knowledge by the compilation of an Interest Book or Travel Book, the most important derivatives from such an activity are the attitudes formed towards the search for information and to the necessity to read for meaning.

2. This approach through the Interest Book or Travel Book may later have a useful application in oral reading by inviting boys to read sections of their books to the class. As an outcome of the Interest Books, pupils may be encouraged to prepare a *short lecturette* on a topic, which is discussed with the teacher some weeks before the talk is given. This form of motivated silent reading is effective and popular with the class, if in the preparation of the lecturettes each pupil is aided by the teacher in the provision of sources from which to obtain information and in the selection and sequence of the items to be included in the talk. One class period a week throughout a year devoted to this work, means that there are always ten or twelve pupils who are reading material in preparation for their lecturettes.

The use of reference books and encyclopaedias is a natural outcome of this. But not only does this activity link logically with training the pupils have obtained in the preparation of their Interest and Travel Books, but it provides a situation which helps the blossoming of each pupil's fuller personality, for each is given opportunities to talk to and debate with his peers in a logical, dispassionate way, training of immense significance for after-school life. The gain in understanding and interpreting what is read in preparation for the lecturette is supplemented by the growth of the pupil's confidence to talk to others in a group situation.

3. But perhaps the most significant motivation and training in comprehension in school is connected with *the project, the centre of interest or environmental study*. Here the opportunities for controlled silent reading directed towards particular aspects of the project are considerable. Projects, whether they be related to problems in health or history, geography or general knowledge, science or the fine arts, can lead to better training in understanding, selecting and interpreting what is read. Sometimes this derives from assignments which children have to carry out in small groups, at others it comes from the individual responsibility each pupil has, to prepare

certain material for inclusion in the class venture. But whatever the nature of the project or the extent of it, there is no better way of motivating the search for information, and in consequence the training in obtaining the maximum meaning from the material supplied to the pupils. In the upper classes of the primary school and in secondary or high schools for non-academic pupils, all pupils should at some time derive training in reading for meaning as part of a project.

4. Finally, activities which lead to enhanced appreciation of the meaning of written English are those of dramatic reading and choral speaking. While there are text-books that may appropriately be used for each of these activities, we should also include dramatisation of historical events and civic celebrations.

CHAPTER VIII

TELLING STORIES AND READING BOOKS

THE seeds of an interest in reading may be sown quite early in a child's life. Close contact with children growing up reveals how deeply they may be influenced in their attitude towards books by early story-telling and reading aloud. Not only do these activities create an atmosphere of expectancy and pleasure towards books and reading but such sessions give them information, extend their vocabulary and provide them with a basis for discussion and dramatisation.

Moreover, reading to children creates a vital bond between parent and child, a situation which often evokes pleasure for both reader and listener. For ourselves, some of the richest and most satisfying memories we have of growing up with our children are the evening reading sessions. There was always a source of continuing joy during our reading of such stories as *The Tale of Tom Kitten*, *The Tale of Peter Rabbit*, *The Tale of Samuel Whiskers*, by Beatrix Potter (at 3 years of age) ; of *Winnie the Pooh*, by A. A. Milne, *The Tale of Jemima Puddleduck*, by Beatrix Potter, *The Story of Little Black Sambo*, by Helen Bannerman, *Millions of Cats*, by Wanda Gag, *Johnny Crow's Garden* and *Johnny Crow's Party*, by Leslie Brooke, *When We Were Very Young*, by A. A. Milne (at 4 years of age). The essence of the situation is delightfully expressed by Dorothy White :

> Sharing a story with Carol stirs my memories of both childhood reading and that more recent reading of adult life. Reading to children is not something one does in a vacuum. Children's literature is part of the great whole of literature, and I shall always feel grateful to the

professional training which made me aware of it and left me excited about it—excited in much the same way as those nineteenth century folk-lorists reared on written literature must have been when they discovered a world of poetry and prose in the peasant vernacular. For them ever afterwards, I imagine, the written and the spoken literature would illuminate one another like confronting mirrors.[1]

Reading to young children, with their interpolated questions and spasmodic comments, provides one of the surest ways of knowing the child mind, information which must surely help parents towards greater understanding in bringing up their children. Those who desire an insight into the inner workings of a reading partnership between parent and young child might read Dorothy White's excellent book, *Books Before Five*, in which she describes in diary form the books she and her husband read to their own child, the reactions they evoked and the aspects of emotional and intellectual development with which they became linked.

If we select books carefully—and it is amazing how many books there are for very young children unsuitable both in content and illustrations—we can open up a whole new world for them while at the same time enabling them to play in the old. In the pictures they recognise familiar objects and activities, and enquire about new ones, thus expanding their vocabulary, increasing their ideas, and consolidating the very basis on which later successful reading is established.

As a guide to parents and pre-school teachers who are intimately concerned with the growth and development of young children up to five, I have given below a short list of books which might well form a basis for reading sessions. The source of the list is a record of reading to our own children

[1] *Books Before Five*, by Dorothy White—printed for the New Zealand Council for Educational Research (Whitcombe & Tombs 1954, and Oxford University Press) p. 102

and a few of Dorothy White's selections, together with publishers' suggestions of some recent books. The list is simply a sample to guide parents and teachers in the choice of books for particular ages, but it should be used with caution, for even amongst the very young there is individuality of taste, and what may strongly appeal to one child may be equally vigorously rejected by another. There are many good books for children [1]—this brief list leans towards the inexpensive ones and includes only those published by British publishing houses and hence available in British Commonwealth countries.

Age 2 to 3 Years

This is essentially a picture book stage in which books with large, clear pictures of common objects and activities, with a minimum of background detail, are most suitable. Very young children love to recognise the familiar and are never tired of having recounted to them over and over again a common event, such, for example, as taking baby for a walk, with attention drawn to the things they see. Similarly, a funny incident or a humorous happening such as the dog that dresses up, or the monkey that falls in the whitewash, or the duck that rides in a motor car, are a continuous source of merriment. Children vary greatly in the degree to which they can be interested in books at this age, particularly in the story part of them. For this reason we must not be impatient if they do not wish to listen to stories read from books. In the first half of the third year their interest and capacity for listening is spasmodic and superficial. However, during the latter part of the year greater interest is evinced in the stories that are found in books.

[1] Suggestions for others will be found in *Four to Fourteen*, by Kathleen Lines (Cambridge University Press, 1950), pp. 13-24. All parents and pre-school teachers might well obtain a copy of that excellent catalogue to the School Library Exhibition, National Book League, 1956, from 7 Albemarle St., Piccadilly, London, W. 1. Pp. 5-7 of this useful catalogue contain a list of inexpensive books for very young children.

BOOK LIST
(prices in sterling, 1959)

Age 2 to 3 years

Adams, G. A.—*First Things* (Collins) 6/-. Photographs of
objects which are familiar to young children.

Ainsworth, Ruth—*Charles Stories* (Heinemann) 3/6
More About Charles (Heinemann) 3/6

Binyon, Helen and Margaret—*Polly and Jane* (Oxford) 2/6
Christmas Eve (Oxford) 1/6

Boyce, E. R. (editor)—*Mother Goose* (Macmillan) 4/-

Brooke, Leslie—*The Golden Goose Book* (Warne) 12/6
Ring o' Roses (Warne) 12/6. Book of nursery
rhymes with full page illustrations.

Brunhoff, Jean de—*Story of Babar* (Methuen) 10/6
Babar the King (Methuen). Translated
from the French by Merle Haas. The
pictures appeal in these books; text
can be left till later.
Engines and Trains (Blackie) 4/-

Fletcher, D.; Bakewell, R.; Taylor J.; Ingleby T.—
Before We Read series (Oliver & Boyd):
Ann's Toys—4 titles (pictures with a minimum of text)
Ann's Doll's Pram, *Ann's Doll*, etc.   1/- each
John's Toys—4 titles (pictures with a minimum of text)
John's Steamer, *John's Sand Box*, etc.   1/- each
Animal Books (photographs of animals, with large clear
captions)
At the Zoo, *At the Zoo Again*, *At the Farm*   1/2 each
Interest Books (photographs of children engaged in various
activities, one line of text per page)
What Do You Like? *What are We Doing?* *What are
We Making?*   1/2 each
Red Squirrel Books—6 titles   1/- each
Round and About Books—4 titles   1/3 each
Town Books—4 titles   1/3 each
Helen Books—3 titles   1/5 each

Gabler, Grace—*A Child's Alphabet.* Puffin Picture Book
          (Penguin) 2/6
Hodge, Valerie—*My First Book.* Wonder Colour Book
          (Collins) 4/6
Kersley Holmes, W.—*Zoo Animals ; Pictures and Rhymes for
          Children* (Blackie) 3/6
Lenski, Lois—*Let's Play House* (Oxford) 5/-
Lingstrom, Freda and Maria Bird—
          Andy Pandy the Baby Clown (Faber) 6/6
          Mother Goose, 2 books (Heinemann) 4/6
Petersham, Maud and Miska—
          The Box with Red Wheels (Macmillan, New York[1])
          10/6
          The Circus Baby (Macmillan, New York[1]) 10/6
Potter, Beatrix—*The Tale of Benjamin Bunny* (Warne) 3/6
          The Tale of Peter Rabbit (Warne) 3/6
          The Tale of Tom Kitten (Warne) 3/6
Slobodkin, Louis—*Melvin the Moose Child* (Macmillan, New
          York[1]) 12/6
          The Wide Awake Owl (Macmillan, New
          York[1]) 17/6
Sutcliffe, Jean—*Five ' Listen with Mother ' Tales* (Adprint)
          2/6

Age 3 to 4 years

Berg, Leila—*The Jolly Farm Book* (Collins) 2/6
Bettina—*Angelo and Bosaline* (Collins) 12/6. Attractive
          picture book
          Carmello (Chatto & Windus) 7/6. Attractive
          picture book.
          Cocola (Chatto & Windus) 7/6. Attractive picture
          book.
Binyon, Helen and Margaret—*The Picnic* (Oxford) 1/6
          The Railway Journey (Oxford)
          1/6

---

[1] English edition from 10 South Audley Street, London, W.1

Brunhoff, Jean de—*Babar's Travels* (Methuen) 6/-

> *Babar and His Children* (Methuen)
> Translated from the French by Merle
> Haas.

Burton, Virginia Lee—*Mike Mulligan and His Steam Shovel*
(Faber) 8/6

Farjeon, Eleanor—*Nursery Rhymes of London Town* (Duckworth) 6/

Freeman, Nancy—*The Story of the Little Ant* (Dent)

Gag, Wanda—*Millions of Cats* (Faber) 6/6
> *Snippy and Snappy* (Faber) 7/6
> *First Book of Verse*, (Ginn)

Heath, Irene—*Heard by a Mouse* (Warne)

Lenski, Lois—*Davy's Day* (Oxford) 4/-.

Milne, A. A.—*When We Were Very Young* (Methuen) 8/6

Nicholson, William—*The Pirate Turns* (Faber) 9/6

Oliver, Torfrida—*The Mole and the Mouse* (Warne)

Opie, Iona—*Ditties for the Nursery* (Oxford) 5/-

Potter, Beatrx—*The Tale of the Flopsy Bunnies* (Warne) 3/6
> *The Tale of Mrs Tiggy-winkle* (Warne) 3/6
> *The Tale of Mrs Tittlemouse* (Warne) 3/6
> *The Tale of Squirrel Nutkin* Warne) 3/6

Rey, A. H.—*Raffy and the Nine Monkeys* (Chatto & Windus)

Richards, Dorothy—*A Home for Mrs Fieldmouse* (Faber) 3/6

Ross, Diana—*The Story of the Little Red Engine* (Faber) 10/6.
> There are five other Red Engine stories.

Severn, David—*Wily Fox and the Baby Show* (Lane)

Slobodkin, Louis—*Melvin, the Moose Child* (Macmillan, New
York[1]) 12/6

[1] English edition from 10 South Audley Street, London, W.1

Age 4 to 5 years

Alleyne, Margaret—*The Story of Mr Prettimouse* (Warne) 4/-

Andersen, Hans—*The Snow Queen* (Blackie) 3/-

Ardizzone, Edward—*Little Tim and the Brave Sea Captain* (Oxford) 9/6
> *Tim All Alone* (Oxford) 9/6
> *Tim in Danger* (Oxford) 9/6
> *Tim and Charlotte* (Oxford) 9/6
> *Tim to the Rescue* (Oxford) 9/6

Bannerman, Helen—*The Story of Little Black Sambo* (Chatto & Windus)

Berg, Leila—*Little Pete Stories* (Methuen)

Binyon, Helen and Margaret—*Polly and Jane's Houses* (Oxford) 1/6

Blyton, Enid—*Favourite Book of Fables* (Collins) 2/6

Brooke, Leslie—*Johnny Crow's Party* (Warne)
> *Johnny Crow's Garden* (Warne)
> *Johnny Crow's New Garden* (Warne)

Buck, Pearl—*The Christmas Mouse* (Methuen)

Burton, Virginia Lee—*Choo Choo* (Faber) 8/6
> *Katy and the Big Snow* (Faber) 8/6
> *The Little House* (Faber) 8/6

Chalmers, Audrey—*Hundreds and Hundreds of Pancakes* (Blackwell-Shakespeare Head) 2/-

Chapman, Elizabeth—*Marmaduke and His Friends* (Brockhampton) 6/-

Clarke, Mollie—*Andrew and Sally Series*. 10 books (Wheaton)

Coats, Alice M.—*The Story of Horace* (Faber) 10/6

Colour Photo Books. 12 books (E. J. Arnold) 1/8 each

Craigie, Dorothy—*The Little Train* (Eyre and Spottiswoode)

Derrick, Freda—*The Ark Book* (Blackie)

Drummond, V. H.—*Mrs Easter and the Storks* (Faber). Winner of the Kate Greenaway Medal, 1958.

Edwards, Dorothy—*My Naughty Little Sister* (Methuen)
    More Naughty Little Sister Stories (Methuen)
First Play Books. 12 books (E. J. Arnold)
Flack, Marjorie—*Angus and the Ducks* (Lane)
    Angus and the Cat (Lane) There are several
    other Angus books.
Frank, L.—*That Baby* (Collins). The story of Peter and his
    new brother. This book, illustrated in colour
    photography, is one of those delightfully sound
    and sane books that should be read with children
    in a family expecting a new baby.
Gay Colour Books. 8 books (E. J. Arnold) 2/6 each
Gell, Kathleen—*Nursery Rhymes* (Blackwell) 6/-
Godden, Rumer—*Mouse House* (Macmillan) 10/6
Hale, Kathleen—*Orlando the Marmalade Cat—His Silver Wedding*
    (Country Life)
Heimeran, Ernst—*Paint a Black Horse* (Methuen)
Helps, Racey—*Barnaby and the Scare-Crow* (Collins) 3/6
    The Tail of Hunky Dory (Collins) 4/-
    Two's Company (Collins) 3/6
Jane and Peter Books. 8 books (Chatto & Windus)
Kiddell Monroe, Joan—*In His Little Black Waistcoat to India*
    (Longmans)
    In His Little Black Waistcoat in Tibet
    (Longmans)
Kipps, Clare—*Clarence, the Life of a Sparrow* (Muller) 5/-
Ladybird Books. Various ones, especially *Baby's First Book*,
    Puppies and Kittens, *The Farm*, etc. (Wills and
    Hepworth)
Law, Margaret—*Stories to Tell to the Nursery*, (Oliver & Boyd)
    5/-
Lear, Edward—*Book of Nonsense*, Everyman Edition (Dent). It
    is necessary to select poems suitable for the age.
    Children love the simpler limericks. They also
    like Edward Lear's nursery classics : *The Owl
    and the Pussy Cat, The Duck and the Kangaroo*.

Lenski, Lois—*Papa Small* (Oxford) 5/-
> *Cowboy Small* (Oxford) 5/-
> *The Little Sail Boat* (Oxford) 5/-
> *The Little Aeroplane* (Oxford) 5/-
> *The Little Farm* (Oxford) 5/-

Lida—*Père Castor's Wild Animal Books* (Allen & Unwin) 4/6.
There is a series of these delightful picture-story books translated from the French ; coloured illustrations.

Little Picture Books. 12 books (Warne) 9d each

Macmillan's Colour Pictures. 6 books (Macmillan)

Macmillan's Picture Books. 12 books (Macmillan)

Milne, A. A.—*Now We are Six* (Methuen) 8/6

Picture Book Series. 7 books (E. J. Arnold)

Potter, Beatrix—*The Tale of Jemima Puddleduck* (Warne) 3/6
> *The Tale of Mr Jeremy Fisher* (Warne) 3/6
> *The Tale of Samuel Whiskers* (Warne) 3/6

Reading Through Interest. 12 books (Collins)

Stevenson, Robert Louis—*Child's Garden of Verses*. Poems which appeal at this age are :
> Bed in Summer, Rain, The Land of Counterpane, My Shadow, The Swing, Time to Rise, The Cow, A Good Play.

Tolkien, J. R. R.—*The Hobbit, or There and Back Again* (Allen & Unwin) 12/6

Uttley, Alison—*The Adventures of Sam Pig* (Faber) 10/6.
There are six other Sam Pig Books.
> *The Little Grey Rabbit Books* (Collins) 4/-
> There are now over 20 Little Grey Rabbit Books, one of the latest being *The Little Grey Rabbit's Paint-Box*.

Vanguard Booklets. 8 books (McDougall)

Words in Play Series (Wheaton)

One observation on the above list—I have purposely excluded all stories introducing situations that may frighten children. There is in children's literature today so much of interesting, everyday happenings, so much of the world beautiful, so much of delightful fantasy and repetitive rhythmic story, that there is no need to include stories about wolves and bears, giants and ogres, witches and warlocks, and that collection of frightening events so continuously occurring in Grimm's Fairy Tales.

In reading to our own children we have found—and this is the experience of other parents—that very young children are not able to cope with such strong and unusual imaginative flights. They need time and security to know the real world before coming face to face so starkly with the grossly unreal. Many young children are so disturbed by gruesome events about boys and girls grappling with the wiles and terrors of giants and ogres, of being locked in castle or lost in forests, of being unable to get back to Mummy and Daddy, that their sleep may be disturbed for weeks.

Moreover, there is available to children so much imaginative literature of an acceptable kind.[1] For example, there are : Jean de Brunhoff's classics, the *Babar Books*; *The Useful Dragon of Sam Ling Toy*, written and illustrated by Glen Dines ; *Five Silly Cats*, by Alena Lewitt, illustrated by Lewitt and Huin. There is the delightfully extravagant fantasy *And to think that I saw it on Mulberry Street*, which chronicles a host of magic happenings, representing the embroidery and embellishment by a small boy of some very simple events ; and Edward Ardizonne's series of imaginative adventures, *Tim All Alone* etc., written to satisfy his own children's requests for stories. *The Jungle Book* and *The Just So Stories*, *Peter Pan in Kensington Gardens*, never fail to entrance audiences young and old.

All parents and teachers should be acquainted with the best traditional fairy tales, nursery rhymes and legends, now

[1] *About Books for Children*, by Dorothy White (Oxford, 1949). Read Chapters 3 and 4.

available in excellent editions and often attractively illustrated.[1]
I cannot refrain from mentioning that entrancing book of 800
rhymes and ditties assembled by Iona and Peter Opie in *The
Oxford Nursery Rhyme Book* (Oxford University Press).

In the Infant School

What has been developed within the home during the pre-
school period and supplemented by nursery school or kindergarten should be continued with strength when the child enters
an infant class. It is here that we shall hope to establish for
many children the beginnings of a real love of books, based, of
course, on their own mastery of skill in reading. However,
it is one thing to teach children to read and another to lead
them to read by themselves.

Book Corner

Reading should *not* be associated in the child's mind just
with the school reading books, and for this reason every infant
schoolroom should have its book corner or library shelves.
Here, there should be a collection of well printed, excellently
illustrated books that children are free to handle. They should
be encouraged to come at any time to ponder over the pictures,
and to read just as much as they are able or feel inclined to do.

There should be a plentiful supply of picture books, some
large like the *Wild Animal Books* of Père Castor (Allen &
Unwin), the *Babar Books* (Methuen), Diana Ross's stories of the
Little Red Engine (Faber), Virginia Burton's books such as
Choo Choo, and *The Little House* (Faber), *Crocodile Tears* by
André Francois (Faber), *Millions of Cats* and *Snippy and Snappy*
by Wanda Gag (Faber). Others will be small like the *Before
We Read* books (*Ann's Toys* and *John's Toys* series), *Round and
About Books* and *Town Books*, *Red Squirrel Books* (all published

---

[1] A useful list of eighty titles of books of fairy tales, nursery rhymes and legends
from many lands is given in *One Thousand Books for Boys and Girls*, published by
Dagenham Public Library, Borough of Dagenham, England, 1957. Also in
About Books for Children, by Dorothy White (O.U.P.), see Appendix I, pp. 209-16.
' Myth, Legend and Folk Lore round the World '.

M

by Oliver & Boyd), *Colour Photo Books* (E. J. Arnold), *Colour Picture Books* (Macmillan), *Ladybird Books* (Collins), *Little Picture Books* (Warne), *Beatrix Potter Books* (Warne), books by Lois Lenski, such as *The Little Red Farm, The Little Aeroplane, Papa Small* (Oxford University Press).

The idea of the book corner for young children is to lead them to like books, to feel at home with books, and to derive a sense of satisfaction from books. It is advisable for the teacher to select, or to allow children to select, occasionally from the book corner, books for reading aloud to the class.

Associated with the books which are used during the preparation period of reading, will be books made by the children themselves with the help of the teacher. These might range from individual efforts of a few simple pages of pictures about trains or motor cars, about cats or fish, about the baby at home or the things we see in the street, to co-operative class projects.

Children can be encouraged to collect pictures for the news sheet or for a ' shop ' or ' farm ' book. These are pasted on sheets, bound, and placed in the book corner for all to use. The obvious value of these home-made efforts is to direct children's minds, in a personal and realistic way, to the fact that books are a meaningful part of our everyday life. They deal with people, objects, and activities in the world around us, and if we want to know more about that world, then we can find it in books. The immediate world is our own family, our own friends, our own school and town, with its streets and shops, its traffic and people. The world of other children, other families, other towns, other happenings, forms the content of the story books in the book corner. This relationship the teacher can bring into life by stories read from the books.

In their second year in school, some children will want to read the books or take them home to read. This should be encouraged. The fact that an occasional book is damaged or lost is of minor concern alongside the fact that some children have started on the road towards independent reading. We cannot expect children to know books, to use books, to be friends with books, unless they have the opportunity to handle them frequently. Every class in the infant school should, therefore, have in its library corner a collection of books such as those in the list on pages 178 to 183, with a range in difficulty to cater for pupils of varying reading attainments.

For the youngest pupils of 5+, the main purpose of these books will be to develop favourable attitudes towards books and towards learning to read. For pupils between the ages of 6 and 7+ the library will provide the more able ones with reading material outside the main reading scheme.

Children of, say, 6½ to 7½ who are making slow but steady progress in reading will need some help and guidance in the choice of books from the library corner, otherwise they may be deterred by the number of books which face them. At the same time we should not be too directive in our advice to them. If a child wishes to try to read a book which appeals to him, then provided he has a reasonable chance of succeeding with it, he should be allowed to make the attempt.

Some teachers help children to make their choice by grading the books into groups, placed in particular sections of the shelves or marked with a tag of a particular colour to indicate that they are of ' easy ', ' medium ', or ' advanced ' levels of reading difficulty.

Searching for Information

While these extra books will be mainly for encouraging children to read for the pleasure derived from the stories in them, it is obvious that their value lies beyond that immediate purpose. Through such supplementary reading, children will strengthen concepts, gain new ideas, and above all, will obtain valuable motivation in reading for meaning. Almost every teacher in the infant school now accompanies her teaching of reading from the earliest stages with some practice in comprehension, but for the older and more able children, there is the need to go a step further and give them the opportunity of learning how to gain information from books.

This may sound a little ambitious to some teachers, but the activities of children during their second year in an infant department invariably involve situations in which children ask for additional information on many matters. This is particularly true in connection with their activity work on such topics as boats, trains, houses, aeroplanes, and so on, and it is equally true of their questions relating to natural history—to birds and animals, to insects and fish, to plants and flowers.

I believe that we can canalise some of their questioning into habits of finding out answers for themselves, but this, of course, is dependent on having a supply of books suitable for the purpose

There is little doubt that children who have access to books with a sound, informative content will glean some of the answers to the many questions that come into their minds. Examples of this are given by M. E. Gillett in two recent articles on *Books as Tools* in which a plea is made for more effective training of children in the use of books to ' dig out what they want to know '. Thus ' children in the infant school may be preparing for a play based on a Bible story, and they will want to know many details about the dress and ways of life of the people concerned. They would find it interesting and exciting to read or look at *The Story of David* or *The Story of Joseph* by Maud and Miska Petercham, or *The Story of Joseph and Pharaoh* by Frances Dale, all simply told and charmingly illustrated on almost every page. 7- to 8-year-olds might even browse about in the pages of *Everyday Life in Old Testament Times* by Canon Heaton, or *Everyday Life in New Testament Times* by A. C. Bouquet, both published by Batsford, and illustrated by M. Quennel '.

Writing About Stories

For young children the story read or the story told may provide a powerful stimulus to personal expression. There is extensive evidence to show that infant school pupils between the ages of 6 and 7+ often choose to write about and illustrate stories during their free work periods, that is, where schools are enlightened enough to provide such periods for growth in the creative powers of its pupils. The association of pleasurable activities with the reading of stories is one way of helping to orient children's attitudes towards books

I give on pages 73 and 76 two examples taken from the free workbooks of children who were just 7 years of age.

In spite of the limitations imposed by imperfect spelling and punctuation, the accounts reveal in full the sheer enjoyment and even the gusto associated with reading the stories. The young writers are clamorously keen that we should enjoy the stories with them, and each in his or her own way reveals a buoyancy of narration which is in itself the strongest evidence of the vital link which can be forged between creative writing and reading.

In schools where suitable books are always available and where encouragement and guidance are readily given, children will make their own progress in written English through re-telling the stories they have read or heard and creating stories of their own. Results themselves sufficiently substantiate the value of the free reading and free writing periods at even these early levels of craftsmanship.

CHAPTER IX

PROVIDING FOR PERSONAL NEEDS AND INTERESTS

ALTHOUGH a major aim in teaching reading must be to enable children to master the mechanics of the subject, yet any programme of instruction that does not at some stage arouse in children a desire to read by themselves must be deemed to have failed. While an interest in reading is determined by a variety of factors, some of which are outside the control of the school, yet the school is nevertheless a vital force in arousing and sustaining in its pupils a desire to read. The fact that in some degree the initial growth and the later stability of an interest in reading are both sensitive to influences within the home strongly indicates that home and school should work together where reading is concerned.

In brief, it would seem that the growth of an interest in reading by children is dependent on *five* different factors.

1. Firstly, *home background exerts a powerful influence*, particularly in regard to the formation of early attitudes towards leisure reading, and in feeding adroitly and effectively both transient and permanent reading interests as they emerge during childhood and adolescence.

2. Secondly, the *level of a child's intelligence is closely related* to the development of an interest in reading, but there are many exceptions to this relationship. While it is true that the more intelligent children develop reading interests earlier, broaden them more rapidly and maintain them more permanently than children of low intelligence, yet there are exceptions at both ends of the scale. There are children of limited

intellectual ability who are avid readers, while on the other hand some who are really intelligent are so taken up with activities in the world around that they have neither time nor inclination to 'waste their time' in reading.

3. Naturally a child's *level of reading ability influences*, in the early stages, *his desire to read*—children cannot really read independently or enjoy reading if they have not developed reasonable facility in the skill. For this reason it is vital that instruction in reading should be so planned as to suit the requirements of every child—for some the need for actual instruction in the mechanics of reading may cease by the time they are 7, while for others effective instruction may just be commencing then.

4. The development of an interest in reading is also influenced, in no small measure, by the *kind of activities and other interests which attract children at the primary school stage.* Many boys particularly are often so much taken up with outside activities of a physical or mechanical kind that they rarely settle to reading books. Games of all kinds, minor expeditions and trips of exploration absorb so much time and energy that they seem satisfied during this 'primitive stage' by an intermittent diet of simple comics.

5. An important element in inducing children to start reading for pleasure and to continue with the activity is the *kind of guidance and help they obtain at certain points.* If books, suitable both in level of difficulty and in content, are available at the crucial time, then most children can be started on the road to independent reading. So much depends for so many children on the kinds of books available—here teacher and parent have complementary roles to play.

From 8 *to* 15

From 8 to 15 years—this is the vital period to develop an interest in reading, to satisfy individual tastes and to build the foundations of a love for literature that will persist through a lifetime. It may, with some looseness, be called the ' now or never ' stage in helping children to develop attitudes of reading for leisure and searching for knowledge.

Although strong motivation at later ages will impel adolescents to become students, yet it is extremely difficult, as experience with adolescent youth groups between 15 and 18 shows, to lead them to turn to books for satisfaction during their leisure time, if they have not learnt to read by themselves between 9 and 12.

Naturally, the avidity with which the boy or girl between 9 and 12 or 13 reads, may suffer a temporary decline when the demands of study in the secondary school absorb most free time, but the children who have already developed a love of books in the primary school will always return to reading for refreshment. As one young adolescent of 16, who had just passed through the arid months of preparing for a stiff examination, said to me, ' Now I can do some real reading—there are so many books I want to read in these next two months '.

This junior and early adolescent period is vital in the development of an interest in reading. What should we do about it ? What degree of success is attending our efforts so far ?

What should we do about it ?

Home and school must reinforce each other in this matter. In the home the reading *to* children, characteristic of the earlier period, now becomes, with most boys and girls of 7+ onwards, reading *with* children.

There is still much to be gained in the task of adroitly developing reading tastes in the young by continuing with the evening reading sessions, but these should become a co-operative venture in which youthful listeners take their share of reading aloud with adult storytellers. I well remember this being the case with my own family with such books as the *Epaminondas Stories*, *Heidi* (Johanna Spyri's world famous Swiss story), Carlo Collodi's classic, *Pinocchio* (in a delightfully illustrated Everyman edition), a simple edition of *Robinson Crusoe*, Mortimer Batten's *Stories of the Wild* (McDougall), and *Romances of the Wild* (Blackie), *The Strange Tale of Humpy Horse*, by Rodney Bennett (University of London Press). Later *The Secret Garden*, by Frances Hodgson Burnett, and *Black Beauty*, by Anna Sewell, were treated in this way, afterwards to be re-read entirely on their own.

It is essential that the books selected for this kind of partnership should be suited to the child's reading level in content and in structure. *Wind in the Willows*, for example, while of absorbing interest at 7, has some difficult passages which the adult must paraphrase.

We found that our own children became so absorbed in some books begun in unison during the bedtime story hour, that they read chapters of them between one evening and the next, particularly if other duties meant the absence of parents. Of course, accommodating parents are prepared to be informed of the intervening parts of the story.

Occasionally a child becomes so interested in a book begun with parents that he will request to be allowed to finish it alone. Many books lend themselves to this treatment ; the ones I recall easily were Arthur Ransome's earlier books— *Swallows and Amazons*, *Swallowdale*, and *Peter Duck*. Later Ransome stories such as *Coot Club*, *The Big Six*, *Missee Lee*, and *Picts and Martyrs*, were read independently. Also included in this category were books on natural history, such as the Romany Books—*Out with Romany* etc., by G. Bramwell Evens (University of London Press) ; *Tarka, the Otter*, Henry Williamson (Penguin) ; the Nomad Books—*Over the Hills with Nomad* etc., by Norman Ellison, illustrated by C. F. Tunnicliffe (University of London Press) ; Père Castor's Wild Animal

Books, translated by Rose Fyleman (Allen & Unwin) ; the series by Bernard Rutley, *Kra the Baboon*, etc. (Macmillan) ; and *Bambi, the Story of a Forest Deer*, by Felix Salten (Cape).

Stories with a basis of everyday science, history and mythology are also suitable for reading together. At different times our reading sessions included these: *Bonnie Prince Charlie*, by Henrietta Taylor (Nelson), *Young Fu of the Upper Yangtse*, by Elizabeth Lewis (Harrap), *The Heroes*, by Charles Kingsley (Macmillan), *Fairy Tales*, by Hans Christian Andersen (Dent), *A Book of Fabulous Beasts*, by A. M. Smythe (O.U.P.), *Uncle Remus*, by Joel Chandler Harris (Chatto & Windus), *Nights with Uncle Remus*, by Joel C. Harris (Chatto & Windus), *Stories from the Arabian Nights* (Oxford University Press), *The Heroes of Asgard*, by A. Keary and E. Keary (Macmillan), *King Arthur's Knights*, by Henry Gilbert (Nelson), *Robin Hood* and *Men of the Greenwood*, by Henry Gilbert (Nelson), *The Wonder Book*, by Nathaniel Hawthorne (Dent), *Nonsense Omnibus*, by Edward Lear (Warne), *Just So Stories* and *All the Mowgli Stories*, by Rudyard Kipling (Macmillan), *The Story of Peter Pan in Kensington Gardens*, by J. M. Barrie, *The Cat who Went to Heaven*, by Elizabeth Coatsworth (Dent). (This is a delightful book of a poor Chinese artist and his little cat, Good Fortune.)

The above titles are examples of books suitable also for reading in school to children between the ages of 7 and 10. Teachers will know which are more likely to appeal to 7-year-olds, e.g. *Peter Pan* and *The Cat who Went to Heaven*—and which to pupils of 10 years, for example, *Bonnie Prince Charlie*, and *The Microbe Man*.

' In addition to the experience provided and the pleasure gained by children in home reading sessions, mention might also be made of those progressive children's libraries where special arrangements are made for not only the display of attractive books, but also the telling of stories. This is not a common occurrence in libraries in British Commonwealth countries but it is occasionally seen in children's libraries in continental countries. Thus K. C. Harrison speaking recently on " The World of Books " reports of Swedish libraries :

" Children receive special consideration. Everywhere the children's libraries are gaily decorated, often with striking murals, and nearly every library has a special room for use at story-hour time. At Malmö the children queue up at story-hour time, and there is keen competition to be first in the queue. The first boy or girl has the honour of giving a magic knock and—presto !—a section of the shelving slides back and reveals a hole in the wall. Through this the children pour, and they find themselves in a magical room where stories are told to them by the children's librarian. As the lights are dimmed, special effects show the heavenly constellations in the ceiling." [1]

Personal Possession

A powerful stimulus to developing a love of books in children is to give them the satisfaction of personal ownership. There is nothing like having one's own small bookshelf of favourites, which are always close by, and to which one can turn at any odd time.

Together with the facilities of a really good school class library and an attractive Children's Public Library, the home bookshelf is a major force in attracting children to read for leisure and to search for information.

As well as fiction, the home bookshelf might well contain for pupils of 11 upwards, one set of reference books such as the *Oxford Junior Encyclopaedia*, an excellent source of reference of thirteen volumes, with illustrations and maps—£30 per set (Oxford University Press). However, before embarking on such expense, a parent should assess the child's attitude towards the use of an encyclopaedia by investing in one of the useful, single volume reference books now available for boys and girls, such as *The Children's Illustrated Encyclopaedia of General Knowledge* (Odhams Press, 1956); or Odhams *Encyclopaedia*

[1] Quoted from *The Listener*, 8th October 1959

for Children (Odhams Press, 1956) ; or the *Golden Encyclopaedia*, by Dorothy A. Bennett (Adprint, London)—well illustrated, and suitable for children of 9 and 10.

If books are given as presents for birthdays and Christmas the shelf soon begins to fill. We are now in the era of the well produced paper-back. There was a time when the paper-back was somewhat suspect. Its contents were not what nice people read. Its production was shoddy, with small print, narrow margins, poor paper and limp covers. But that has changed. Many first-class books are now available in paper-back editions and increasing use of laminated covers enhances durability.

Besides the inimitable Penguins, Pelicans and Puffin Story Books, there are Grey Arrow Books (Hutchinson), St Martin's Library (Macmillan), Fontana, Beacon, Four Square Books, Scottie, Pan and Corgi Books. New titles appear at the rate of ninety a month. All realms of fiction and areas of fact are covered.

Many adolescents have built up their own libraries of paper-backs, and owe their reading of Buchan and Bronte, Trollope and Fielding, Hardy, D. H. Lawrence or Aldous Huxley to the once despised paper-back. Surely no ugly chrysalis ever changed to such a beautiful butterfly.

It is an inexpensive item to help children acquire books of their choice from the various paper-back editions now available. Some Puffin Story Books cater for the younger group up to 11. In the Puffin list (all at 2/6 or 3/-) are old favourites such as *Black Beauty*, *Little Women*, *Heidi*, with newer editions such as *The Circus is Coming*, by Noel Streatfeild ; *Cranes Flying South*, by N. Karazin ; *Redcap Runs Away*, a story of 14th century England, by Rhoda Power. There are also titles like Eleanor Doorly's *Insect Man*, the story of Henri Fabre, and the *Radium Woman* (Madame Curie), *Man Shy*, a first class story of a heifer, by Frank Davidson.

Of course, amongst the Penguins (price 2/6 or 3/6) are some books, such as those of John Buchan, which could well find a place on the bookshelf of any boy or girl of 11 to 15.

LIBRARIES IN SCHOOLS

Slowly, very slowly, we are beginning to realise that the school library is not something extra but that it is an essential to modern education. It is as important as a science laboratory or a gymnasium.

We cannot lead children to read books for enjoyment or consult reference books for information unless they have plenty of opportunity to see books, to handle books, to browse through books, and to take away books to read in the quiet of their home. Experience shows that ' the greatest single factor in developing interest in books and the habit of reading is the accessibility of books '.[1] They can do these things if there are libraries.

Gradually the school and class library movement is growing. Special credit is due to the School Library Association and to the National Book League for their part in this improvement. Their lists of well graded books given under subject sections have been a boon to all who seek to interest children in good literature. *School Library Exhibition* (1956), 2/6 ; *School Library Exhibition Catalogue* (1957), 2/6 ; *A Selection of Books for Children Published* 1957-58 (1958), 1/- ; are all obtainable from the National Book League, 7 Albemarle Street, London, W. 1.[2]

The 1956 Catalogue of the National Book League was prepared from a selection of over 16,000 titles submitted from more than 150 publishers—and what an effective guide it has proved. Likewise the Library Association's three lists have been invaluable :

BOOKS FOR YOUNG PEOPLE

Group   I : ' Under Eleven '
New edition, completely revised.
103 pages, 12/-

---

[1] *Administering Library Service in the Elementary School*, by Jewel Gardiner, 2nd ed., 1954, pp. 2-3
[2] See also *The School Librarian and School Library Review*, three times yearly. Annual Subscription 16/-, School Library Association, 29 Gordon Square, London.

Group II : ' Eleven to Thirteen Plus '
3rd edition, revised, 1960.
239 pages, 16/-

Group III : ' Fourteen to Seventeen ', Fiction and Non-Fiction, under subject headings, annotated.
86 pages, 6/-

Kathleen Lines's attractively annotated list, *From Four to Fourteen*[1], has been extremely useful to libraries, teachers and parents. A tribute should also be paid in this respect to *Junior Bookshelf*,[2] published six times a year and dealing with children's books.

School libraries are certainly growing, but there is wide variation in the size, scope and nature of their use within the school. A recent report [3] from 517 schools both primary and secondary, compiled in 1957, showed that 30 out of 32 *grammar schools* have library rooms, 28 have a teacher-librarian, and each library has between 2,000 and 3,000 books.

Out of 63 *secondary modern schools*, 54 have library rooms ; 51 schools have a recognised teacher-librarian. Books are used for reference and home reading in only 43 schools.

While grammar schools have better stocks of books than secondary modern schools, only 10 allow special library periods. In the samples tested, secondary modern schools tend to issue more books per week than do the grammar schools.

Most of the *primary schools* have classroom libraries, but only 17 out of 422 have library rooms. ' The book stock, unsatisfactory on the whole, averages 300 to 400 volumes, although 81 schools have less than 100, and 4 have more than 1,000 ; 148 schools have no books apart from text books '.[3]

Nevertheless, 41 per cent of schools use books for reference

[1] *From Four to Fourteen*, by Kathleen Lines, 2nd ed., Cambridge University Press for the National Book League, 1956
[2] H. J. B. Woodfield, Tower Wood, Windermere, Westmorland, England
[3] Report on schools in Devon and Cornwall by the School Library Association ; summarised in *The Schoolmaster*, 22nd August 1958, p. 308

and home reading, 27 per cent allocate library periods and in 46 per cent of schools, library instruction is given—this constitutes an immense advance compared with conditions ten to fifteen years ago.

Equally startling is the finding that no less than 350 primary schools and 5 grammar schools are unable to purchase any replacements or additions to their library stock.

The Committee compiling the report recommends :

(i) that all schools should have a separate library grant based on the number of pupils ;

(ii) that capital grants should be made to schools whose library stock is insufficient ;

(iii) that teacher-librarians should have at least five periods a week for running the library and giving instruction to pupils about the use of books and libraries ;

(iv) that children should be encouraged to borrow books and read them at home.

Decrease in Comic Sales

Coincident with the increase in the use of and the provision for library facilities in schools, there is evidence of slow but steady decrease since 1953 in the sales of many comics, the exception being the comics Eagle, Girl, Robin and Swift,[1] which have maintained their circulation. In a balanced and interesting analysis of popular comics and of the decline in their sales,[2] one writer comes to this conclusion : ' It is quite certain, however, that children are reading more books than ever before. This is undoubtedly due to the increased reading ability of children in primary schools ; the increased availability of attractive and suitable books in school and municipal libraries, together with the attention paid in schools to recommending

[1] First produced by the Hulton Press after the Second World War
[2] *The Schoolmaster*, 15th November 1957, p. 778

suitable books. More books are being bought too, for the younger children '.[1]

Using a School Library

While I think every school should have a first class central library, I am a firm believer in supplementing it with class libraries, however small and unpretentious they may be. There is just a tendency sometimes for the central school library to be a thing apart, a place where you congregate on Friday afternoons to borrow a book, because you are expected to, or because your pals do so. The class library, even if it consists of only a couple of shelves of books, is a much closer, more intimate thing. It means books, not a place—books that are within easy reach and that can be used, with wise teachers, in between lessons and in library periods, and that can be taken home any afternoon, not just on Fridays.[2]

Only by seeing books, handling books and by reading books, do children become readers of books, and this should surely be one of the main aims of schools. But this aim cannot be realised if the child's school acquaintance with books is almost exclusively in terms of set text books used during class lessons. If we want children to read books and use books intelligently, then we must create situations that will enable them and teach them to do so. ' A good school library grows out of the life and work of the school '.[3]

There are various ways that this can be done, in addition to individual guidance—the use of group work, of projects, of assignment cards, the compilation of interest or topic books and the weekly use of a library hour will all assist, if centered round a class library. I should much prefer teachers to spend money in the first place on class libraries and to show and to

[1] 'Television and the Child' (O.U.P. 1958), reveals that television causes children to read fewer books at first, but later this loss is reduced. Viewing leads dull children to read more books.

[2] ' Head teachers agreed that class libraries are more important than a central collection for children at the primary stage.' From *Reading in the Primary School*, by J. M. Morris, p. 85.

[3] *The Library in the Primary School,* School Library Association, Gordon House, 29 Gordon Square, London, W.C.1, 1958

encourage pupils to use them, than to pander further to the passive pursuits associated with radio, television sets, or projectors. Children will be assailed by the television screen, the cinema screen, the loudspeaker and the radio almost every hour of their out of school lives, but few will be the occasions on which they are introduced to good books.

The class library has the great advantage that it is on hand every hour of the school day—it serves teachers as well as pupils. Teachers can make use of it during lessons by taking books to illustrate particular points during lessons, and can lead children to make use of books for many lessons during the school week. Queries raised and problems posed may be dealt with by teacher and pupil acting together at the exact time the need arises. In addition to its value as a source of information and enjoyment, the class library is certainly the most effective means of training children in the use of books.[1]

It may be urged that cost prevents teachers from establishing class libraries.[2] This is not so. In the first place, class teachers may, with some justification, make a claim for a share of the Education Authority's capitation allowance; in the second, use may be made of County Library loan schemes, where these exist, but perhaps better sources are raising class funds and inviting children to bring books as a condition of membership.

Furthermore, there are today many sources of good books, well printed and attractively illustrated. For younger children there is a fairly constant supply of excellently produced books at prices from 4/- to 6/- each; there are the Puffin Story Books which cost only 2/6 and 3/-. Various classics are available in such series as Collins Classics, for prices from 4/6 to 6/6 (Cloth Editions) and Nelson's School Classics for 7/6, 8/6 and 10/-.

---

[1] As Russell says, 'The companionship of books can permeate much of the day's teaching', *Children Learn to Read*, by D. H. Russell (Ginn) p. 276.

[2] Useful information on establishing a library is to be found in *The School Library*, Educational Pamphlet No. 21, H.M.S.O., 1952; and *The Library in the Primary School*, School Library Assn. See also *School Libraries*, by C. A. Stott, School Library Assn., and *Running a School Library*, by Alexander Neill (Collins).

N

For older children, in addition to the above, there are many suitable titles in paper-backs.

An interesting account of how paper-backs were instrumental in starting many older boys of 13+ upwards in B, C and D streams in a secondary modern school to read for enjoyment is given by Kenneth Methold.[1] The author started a Paper-Back Book Club, the entrance fee to which was one paper-back book in good condition, with a further levy of one paper-back book twice a term. To help with the levy a bookshop was opened, and through this boys were able to cash their 'book coupons', which they obtained after they had accumulated 2/- or 2/6, deposited in small sums with their form master. The idea of the bookshop with its vouchers was mainly to have some control over the type of book brought along to the Book Club. The bookshop is staffed by senior boys and senior girls with the assistance of a teacher. The shop, which carries a stock of almost 200 titles, is now introducing selected volumes from Everyman, Nelson and Collins cheap classics.

The best sellers of the year were *The Dam Busters* (Pan) ; *While the Sun Shines* (a love story written by Laurence Mynell for school girls and extremely well done) ; *The Overloaded Ark*, Gerald Durrell's adventures of animal collecting—(Penguin) ; *Colditz Story* (Pan) ; *Young Nurse Carter, Sue Barton, Student Nurse* (Scottie) ; and *The Battle of the River Plate* (Panther).

The limitations of such a list are apparent—it does not contain any of the usual books that appeal to many 13-year-olds, but it should be borne in mind that this list stemmed from an experiment with a group of secondary modern school boys and girls aged 13+ in B, C and D streams, who showed no interest whatsoever in reading. Their introduction to some contemporary fiction with quick action changed them from a 'no interest in reading' group to pupils who not only began to read for pleasure, but to take active steps to establish their own library.

[1] 'Children and Books', *The Schoolmaster*, 1st August 1958, pp. 206-7

As Methold says, ' if the book club and shop can develop the reading habit in children, they will serve a valuable purpose and do as much, if not more, than I can hope to do in the lessons set aside for reading and talking about books. . . . Supply can create demand. My belief is that if books can become part of a child's environment, both in and out of lessons, then the child will accept them as a normal part of life and not as a subject for enforced study '.[1]

This is sound philosophy which has special significance for our work with the less able 50 per cent of adolescent pupils. It gives, moreover, an appropriate jolt to the traditionalist and purist who would have teachers continue in the old-fashioned way with books that pupils ' must read '—the only result of which is that less able adolescents are turned away and join that all too large band of semi-illiterates who never open a book for leisure or information once they leave school, where books have been so painfully associated with lessons in which they were mediocrities or failures.

It is not a very difficult task to lead adolescent boys from an exclusive diet of war stories and detective yarns, or adolescent girls from love stories made to a particular pattern, to such books as *Prester John, Huntingtower, Thirty-Nine Steps*, by John Buchan, or historical fiction such as D. K. Broster's *Flight of the Heron* and *Gleam in the North*, or G. Trease's *The Hills of Varna*, R. Sutcliffe's *The Eagle of the Ninth* ; or older classics such as *Treasure Island* (Stevenson), *Black Tulip* (Dumas), *King Solomon's Mines* (Rider Haggard) and *Uncle Tom's Cabin* (Stowe).

Evidence from the latest report on standards of reading in English schools shows that an enlightened programme of reading through class libraries and close contact with the public library can do much to counteract the effects of a limited environment, as judged by objective assessments of children's reading ability.[2]

---

[1] 'Children and Books ', *The Schoolmaster*, 1st August 1958, pp. 206-7

[2] *Standards of Reading*, Ministry of Education Pamphlet No. 32, pp. 14-16 and also 36-40 (H.M.S.O., 1957)

Which Books ?

These comments on the reading tastes of less intellectual boys and girls in the third and fourth years of a secondary modern school, bring us face to face with the question, ' What books shall we put in our class and school libraries ? ' The obvious answer to the question is—books they are *able* to read, bearing in mind the wide range of reading skills at all ages, and books they *like* to read, bearing in mind the wide variety of backgrounds and interests of children at all ages. But there are a few other considerations that also enter into an answer to this question.[1]

1. Books we place on the shelves should be attractive, that is, they should be well produced and well illustrated. So often a good book is a combination of good material and good illustrations. There is no need to put up with the second rate in this age of excellent book production.

2. We should not be rigid in our selection. The book lists mentioned previously are an excellent guide, particularly as they have been compiled in many cases by trained children's librarians and represent much of the best in contemporary writing for children, both fiction and non-fiction. Moreover, we must remember that the range in literary tastes between 10 and 14 is immense. Some pupils in this age group will want only simply written, straightforward adventure stories, while my records show that there will be a few who can read and enjoy such books as *The Mayor of Casterbridge* (Hardy), *Tess of the D'Urbervilles* (Hardy), *The Good Companions* (Priestley), *Jane Eyre* (C. Brontë), and *Daughter of Time*, a kind of intellectual detective story with an historical basis, by Josephine Tey.

W. J. Scott's analysis of questionnaires, completed by 3,972 high school boys and girls (ages 13 to 18),

[1] See *The Library in the Primary School* (School Library Association, 1958).

on which were entered 21,507 books relating to their
reading during a sample month, point to the same
' catholicity of the adolescent's taste which can
allow him to enjoy at the same time Scott and
' Sapper ', Dickens and Orczy, Jane Austen and
Ethel M. Dell, *The Champion* and *Girls' Crystal*,
The Saint in New York, *How Green was My Valley*,
Silas Marner, *Macbeth*. Juxtapositions of this sort
occurred in hundreds of questionnaires '.[1]

3. Many children have a strong liking for contemporary
   story tellers. Older pupils will read *Reach for the Sky*
   (Brickhill), *The Wooden Horse* (Williams), *The Ascent
   of Everest* (Hunt), *The Old Man and the Sea* (Heming-
   way), *The Yearling* (Marjorie Rawlings), when they
   will sheer away like unbroken colts from *Rob Roy*,
   Great Expectations, *Last of the Mohicans* and *Tom
   Brown's Schooldays*. We should avoid directing children
   to read what attracted us as children, or what is
   included in a list of children's classics—they will
   come to these all in good time if their literary
   guidance is skilful.

   The able child who reads his full quota of detective
   stories, war yarns, and even comics, is usually the
   one who also reads extensively literature of a higher
   order, while the child for whom these are the sole diet
   is better off reading these than none at all. The
   really important thing is, as Miller says : ' Let
   children discover the pleasure that is to be had from
   books, create the habit of reading and then do all
   you can to refine their tastes.' [2]

4. We should also remember the intense interest of many
   intelligent boys and girls in non-fiction of all sorts.

[1] *Reading, Film and Radio Tastes of High School Boys and Girls*, by W. J. Scott
(Whitcombe & Tombs and Oxford University Press, 1947), p. 25
[2] 'Books in the Primary School V ', 'What is a Good Book ? ', articles by
L. P. F. Miller, in *The Schoolmaster*, 20th September 1957

Interests and Tastes

While it may be regarded as a general broad principle that certain books are suitable and attract children at particular ages, yet we must be acutely aware that reading interests, especially in particular writers or types of books, are created within both home and school. Hence there is the need for skilful, subtle and persistent guidance by parents and teachers in the development of taste. For example, a too early introduction to some authors may turn young readers from their books for ever.

Scott draws attention in his survey to the frequency with which classical novels appeared among the books reported as 'not finished'. He claims that with high school scholars, (13 to 18) there are few failures to finish books by Emily Brontë, Defoe, Hughes, Twain, Marryat and Stevenson, but the numbers rise sharply with Charlotte Brontë, Dickens, Reade, Kingsley, Eliot, Scott and Thackeray. More than one in four do not finish a book by Thackeray, one in five a book by Scott, one in six *The Mill on the Floss*. Among Dickens' novels *Martin Chuzzlewit*, *The Old Curiosity Shop*, *Nicholas Nickelby*, *The Pickwick Papers*, *A Tale of Two Cities*, were not finished by one reader in three, one in four, one in five, and— the last two—one in ten.[1]

On the other hand the young reader needs to be introduced to good books if we are to wean him from a fare of comics and third-rate adventure or detective stories. Here, of course, *reading books with a class* can do much to reveal a writer's craft and at the same time let children see that well written books can be equally as exciting and attractive as poorly written ones. In fact, reading aloud is one of the most effective ways of unlocking doors for many children—it is a craft that should be nurtured, practised, polished, for in this age of button pushing and knob turning, it is steadily being neglected and its very existence imperilled.

[1] *Reading, Film and Radio Tastes of High School Boys and Girls*, by W. J. Scott, pp. 11 and 13

Perhaps one of the important jobs of teacher and parent is to see that reading interests do not become too narrow. There are too many children whose reading consists almost exclusively of a continuing series of books by one particular author, interspersed with some sporadic comic reading. There are some who never get past a succession of William books, Biggles books, or war yarns and detective stories of rather poor quality.

In this I do not include those children who have strong but transient interests in a variety of subjects—they read everything they can obtain in a particular field and then, having satisfied or partially satisfied that interest, pass on to other pastures. I remember these crazes in our own family —every Ransome book was read, one after the other. When an interest in natural history was at its strongest, every BB book, even difficult ones, like *The Fisherman's Bedside Book* and *The Shooting Man's Bedside Book*, were sought and these in turn spread to others like *Half Breed*, the story of ' Grey Owl ' (Peter Davies), *Tarka the Otter* (Williamson), *Bevis, The Story of a Boy* (Richard Jefferies), *The Sun Himself Must Die* and *Adventure Lit Their Star* (Kenneth Allsop).

When bird watching was an intense and absorbing pastime, then books like *The Observer's Book of Birds* (Observer's pocket series—Warne), *Birds of the British Isles and their Eggs* (Warne), *Bird Watcher's Delight* (Country Life), were studied with avidity.

One member of the family became so engrossed in Scottish history that not only did she read books like those of D. K. Broster (*The Flight of the Heron, The Gleam in the North, The Dark Mile, Sir Isumbras at the Ford*), and Maurice Walsh (*The Key Above the Door, While Rivers Run, Blackcock's Feather*) but details of the country—*Scotland's Western Seaboard* (Oliver & Boyd), *Heart of Scotland* (Batsford), *A Short History of Scotland* (Oxford University Press)—were also included.

Parent and teacher are faced in this task of guiding reading tastes and interests with dual objectives. They have ' to take care that reading interests do not become unduly formalised or solidified'; and 'at the same time to make sure that children experience the comfort and relaxation of the familiar in their personal reading'. They have 'to encourage constant progression in taste and in diversity of interests and yet at the same time to be aware of the tendency of the child to get greater enjoyment and relaxation out of what is well within his capacity'.[1]

Sources of Information

There is a need for every library to contain some books of reference, which will be invaluable for the delving that goes on during projects and the writing of Interest Books (see p. 172). It is amazing the number of children who use books of reference in a class library but who will not bother about fiction. Many of them are really keen on 'digging out' information on a wide variety of subjects—music or mammals, canals or cricket, astronomy or animals, ships or space travel.

Use of the reference sections of a library should be encouraged, for in addition to teaching children how to use tables of contents and indexes in these larger books, we should also show them how to skim over the material, without laborious reading, until they find just what they want.

Some teachers encourage reading for information by compiling lists of quiz questions on various topics. Older pupils enter into the answering of these with zest and provided the topics deal with knowledge of value to the child, it is an effective method of motivating the desire to know—the 'what is it', 'how does it work' aspect of adolescent thinking.

'During the short time we have our boys and girls we can do few things more useful than to show them how to use books as tools, as sources of information and as the means of further study. Perhaps if we can teach them how to get fact from print we may be teaching them not to draw opinions from print. The danger of the age is the perpetual vociferation of inflammatory opinion by all sorts of periodicals (and their placards)

[1] 'Reading for Pleasure'—report of lectures by A. M. Kean, *Times Educational Supplement*, 2nd May 1958

at all sorts of prices. If we can make our pupils understand that behind print, even of the largest circulation, there is merely a man of no special importance, we may be doing them and the world a lasting service. We want to create people who can use print, not people who are intimidated by print.' [1]

Teachers of upper primary classes might well use some reading periods for class library sessions. Sometimes pupils may be asked to answer silent reading questions, using sets of previously prepared cards. It is a good plan to buy suitable books for silent reading in sets of six, eight, or ten books, so that children can work in groups.

Books like the Active Readers (Ginn), each of which is a complete story, contain interesting exercises that children are prepared to do because the exercises are ingenious and challenging.

Even where there is a spread of reading ability in an upper junior or lower secondary modern class, we can easily give library work to the better section, while class lessons involving vocabulary and pronunciation are taken with the less advanced pupils.

While some children know what they want to consult in the reference books, and while others just like to browse over them, it is as well to motivate the work by what Griffith calls ' The Little Project ' method—' small groups of children work together upon a subject of their own choice, the result of their work (notes, sketches, plans, etc.) being placed in folders. Alternatively, they may prefer to work on a " Display Sheet " which can be placed upon the library or classroom wall.

' The groups will need guidance, of course ; often their first choice is too vague and unwieldy. Jackson and Walker announced their determination to write about " sport ", but after a conference with the teacher they decided to write an account of " Four Famous Cricketers ". Similarly, four girls

---

[1] From *English for the English*, by George Sampson (Cambridge University Press), pp. 87-8

with an interest in costume produced a folder illustrating the costumes of the flamboyant dressing of the Elizabethan age.

' Small beer ? Perhaps ; but these four girls, in preparing their folder used two encyclopaedias, a school text-book, Iris Brooke's *English Costume in the Age of Elizabeth*, and that charming King Penguin, *Elizabethan Miniatures*. Apart from the fact that at least one aspect of the Elizabethan age took on for these girls an actuality it perhaps could not otherwise have possessed, they were using books intelligently and zestfully. A librarian could scarcely ask for more.' [1]

The important point in buying reference books is to obtain ones suitable for the upper primary or secondary school. Children of 10 onwards are attracted to the *Children's Encyclopaedia* by Arthur Mee (Education Book Co.), while secondary school pupils, 11 or 12 onwards, will learn to use the *Oxford Junior Encyclopaedia* with its thirteen volumes

Vol. 1 Mankind	Vol. 7 Industry and Commerce
Vol. 2 Natural History	Vol. 8 Engineering
Vol. 3 The Universe	Vol. 9 Recreations
Vol. 4 Communications	Vol. 10 Law and Order
Vol. 5 Great Lives	Vol. 11 The Home
Vol. 6 Farming and	Vol. 12 The Arts
Fisheries	Vol. 13 General Index

But these may be too expensive for most class libraries. There are a number of less expensive, excellently produced, one-volume encyclopaedias such as those published by Odhams, Collins, Ward Lock, some of which teachers should endeavour to place in the class library. A selection might be made from these.

ENCYCLOPAEDIAS

Children's Book of Knowledge (Collins) 10/6
Collins' New Age Encyclopaedia (Collins) £1/10/-

[1] 'The Library in the Modern School', by A. Griffith—article in *The Schoolmaster*, 31st January 1958

Everyman's Dictionary of Dates, compiled by C. Arnold Baker and Anthony Dent (Dent) ; reference to important world events

Everyman's Dictionary of Quotations and Proverbs, compiled by D. Browning (Dent)

Golden Encyclopaedia, Bennett (Adprint) 12/6

Hutchinson's Twentieth Century Encyclopaedia (Hutchinson) £1/10/-

Modern Marvels Encyclopaedia (Collins) 12/6

Nelson's Encyclopaedia, H. L. Gee (Nelson) £1/10/-; good articles, illustrated, comprehensive

New Illustrated Encyclopaedia, J. R. Crossland (Collins) 12/6

Odhams Encyclopaedia for Children, editor J. A. Lauwerys (Odhams) £1/17/6 ; illustrated

Pears' Cyclopaedia, annually (Pears) 15/-

Pictorial Treasury of the World and Its Wonders, editor, Carlton Wallace (Evans) 16/-

The Children's Book of Knowledge—Wonders of Man and Nature, editor J. E. Pryde-Hughes (Collins) 10/6

The Children's Illustrated Encyclopaedia of General Knowledge (Odhams) £1/15/- ; illustrated, information on wide variety of topics

The Pictorial Encyclopaedia, W. W. Sampson—£1/12/6 ; many good illustrations on a variety of topics

The Wonder Book Encyclopaedia (Ward Lock) £1/10/-

The Younger Children's Encyclopaedia (Odhams) 15/-

Books of General Knowledge

Some general knowledge books on a variety of topics such as the following, should find a place in the library.

A Child's Book of Ships and Boats, W. M. Hutchinson (Publicity Products) 7/6

Adventure and Discovery for Boys and Girls (Cape) 12/6 each. Excellently written and illustrated ; an annual publication

Adventures in Science, editor B. C. Brookes (Heinemann) 8/6

Adventure of the Sea, James Fisher (Rathbone) 12/6

Adventure of the World, James Fisher (Rathbone) 12/6

An Illustrated History of Science, F. S. Taylor (Heinemann) 15/-

A Pageant of History (Collins) 12/6

A Picture History of Great Discoveries, Hutton Clark (Oxford University Press) 12/6

A Short History of the World, H. G. Wells (Collins Classics) 5/6

Black's Junior Reference Books, school editions (A. & C. Black)—

A History of Houses, R. J. Unstead 8/6

Travel by Road, R. J. Unstead 7/6

The Story of Aircraft, R. J. Hoare 8/-

Buried Treasure, P. Johnstone (Phœnix House) 16/- Archaeological discoveries of recent years

Come Out of Doors, C. D. Dimsdale (Hutchinson) 12/6

Eagle Book of Modern Wonders (Hulton) 10/6

Feast and Famine, Boyd Orr (Rathbone) 17/6

From Magic to Medicine, Ritchie Calder (Allen & Unwin)

Fun With Astronomy, Mae and Ira Freeman (Rathbone) 10/6

Great Moments of Archaeology, L. N. Hume (Phœnix House) 7/6

How and Why It Works (Odhams) 13/6

How Things Developed series (E.S.A.). Volumes on Books, Roads, etc.

Inside the Atom, Marie Neurath (Parrish) 7/6

Instruments of the Orchestra, J. E. Borland (Novello) 5/6

Junior Naturalist (for pupils 9 to 15). Lively articles, illustrated; published bimonthly, 1/3 per copy or 10/- annual subscription. Natural History Museum, Woodend, The Crescent, Scarborough, England

Lands and People Series (A. & C. Black) 7/6 each

Let's Look at the Sky, Marie Neurath (Parrish) 7/6

Life and Food—Science on the March, John Clark and others (Longmans) 3/6

Lively Youngster Series, T. J. S. Rowland (Cassell) 7/6

Lives to Remember (A. & C. Black) 6/6 each. Helen Keller, Isaac Newton, Saint Paul, Dr Barnardo, etc.

Living in Early Times, Marie Neurath and others (Parrish) 3/6

Mankind Against the Killers, J. Hemming (Longmans) 16/-

Man Must Measure, L. Hogben (Rathbone) 16/6

Marvels of Modern Science (Odhams) 10/-

Masters of Medicine, H. Williams (Pan) 2/6. The story of some pioneers

Men, Missiles and Machines, L. Hogben

Modern Transport Series (Blackie) 3/6. Motor cars, aircraft, ships, etc.

Opera Synopses, J. Walker McSpadden (Harrap) 15/6

People's Jobs Series (E.S.A.)

Science Makes Sense, Ritchic Calder (Allen & Unwin) 12/6

Scottish History for Today, I. Gould and J. Thompson (Murray) 7/6

Stories of the Ballet (A. & C. Black) 3/6 each

Thanks to Inventors, A. M. Law (Lutterworth) 12/6

The Changing Shape of Things, P. Redmayne (J. Murray) 10/6

The Children's Book of Achievement—Wonders of Modern Enterprise, editor J. E. Pryde-Hughes (Collins) 10/6

The Golden Book of Astronomy, Rose Wyler and Gerald Ames (Publicity Products). Giant Golden Book Series 15/-

The Outline of Art, edited by Sir William Orpen, revised by Horace Shipp ; new edition and enlarged (Newnes, London)

The Pictorial History Book, R. Haddon and others (Sampson Low) 17/6

The Story Book of Money, H. W. Whanslaw (Wells Gardner) 4/6

The Story of our World, I. O. Evans (Hutchinson) 12/6

The Theatre through the Ages, J. Cleave (Harrap) 15/-

The True Books (Muller). Many titles about space travel, submarines, Everest, Leonardo da Vinci, David Livingstone, stamp collecting, whaling, Helen Keller, films, etc.

The Wonders of Science (Collins) 12/6

They Saw it Happen, 55 B.C. to A.D. 1485, W. O. Hassell ; A.D. 1485 to 1688, W. O. Routh ; 1689 to 1897, T. Charles Edwards and B. Richardson. Eye-witness accounts (Blackwell)

Ward Lock's Wonder Books (Ward Lock) 15/- each. Twenty books illustrated, on various topics—animals, railways, ships, aircraft, nature, science, etc. ; includes volumes entitled ' Do You Know ? ', ' Tell Me, Why ? ' ' How It's Done ', and ' Would You Believe It ? '

Wild Life of Our World—Pageant of Knowledge Series, John L. Crossland and J. M. Parrish (Collins) 12/6

Wild Life Through the Year, Richard Morse (Black) 8/6

Wonder World of Birds, Marie Neurath (Parrish) 7/6. Similar books on plants, seashore, etc.

Catering for Intellectual Interests

The older child's tendency to browse over illustrated non-fiction books and to take them out of the public library ' on spec ' so to speak, is strong evidence of a fundamental desire for facts he wants to know about many things, and, provided a little assistance is forthcoming, he is prepared to do his share in finding the answers to his queries. I have just this week given a pictorial encyclopaedia to my 11-year-old friend, Vicky, whose joy is expressed in his note to me—' I nearly hit the ceiling when Mother brought home the encyclopaedia '.

Allied to this urge to satisfy their curiosity about everyday problems in the world around by consulting books of general knowledge, we note amongst many children of 10 onwards their attraction to books in which facts form the matrix of exciting adventure or attractive story-biography. Nor are backward readers an exception to this. My experience is that many slow-learning boys make their greatest progress when their reading skill reaches a point at which they can manage a simply written book that combines a rattling good yarn with the provision of some information, the understanding of which is aided by plentiful marginal illustrations. I have in mind the pleasure that has attended the use of that excellent series of Active Readers (Ginn).[1] These are stories about Red Indians, cowboys, trappers (White Hawk, La Bonté the Trapper, X-Bar-Y Ranch) exploits under the water (Frogman Diver), the Royal Canadian Mounted Police (Young Mounties), exploits in South Africa (Diamonds in Springbok Valley, Bushveld Adventure). These stories combine action and adventure with information and are written in simple, effective English.

The widespread success of the Wide Range Readers [2] amongst junior school boys and girls has in part a similar basis. Young friends to whom I have given copies invariably tell me

---

[1] *The Active Readers*, 14 titles (Ginn)

[2] The *Wide Range Readers*, Blue Books (6), Green Books (6), by F. J. Schonell and Phyllis Flowerdew (Oliver & Boyd)

how much they enjoy the stories woven round the Great Trek, The Flying Doctor Service in Australia, the Tale the Geese Tell (the old story of the warning of Rome), When Anna Danced (the story of Anna Pavlova), the Boy Who Liked Music (the story of Mozart), The Story of a Road (a short history of the development of roads), The Great Fire of London, The Man with Sixty Thousand Children (the story of Dr Barnardo).

The imaginative embellishment or the dramatic interlude add zest to the account provided it keeps fairly closely to the facts. Personally, I believe that this accuracy of material, even in small points and incidents, is of paramount importance in all material for children, but particularly in the historical novel or the adventure/information story for older boys and girls.

Geoffrey Trease,[1] in discussing the historical novel and the importance of style and accuracy, reminds us that ' George Eliot tore up the first draft of *Romola* because she found so many historical errors in it. . . . Charles Reade spent eighteen months on research for *The Cloister and the Hearth*, the same seriousness applied to the writing of his South Seas novel *Five Ply* '.

Today we have some first-class writers of historical novels for children—writers who take considerable care over historical background and events in the story they are telling. If we add to this factual accuracy, good story telling, acceptable English style and structure, highlighted with good illustrations, then we have the near ideal type of book for voracious readers of 10 to 14 years.

Class and school libraries should satisfy the growing intellectual curiosity of pupils by including in their shelves books with an historical, geographical, or scientific slant. Sometimes this information will be given in story form, such as *He Went with Marco Polo* (Kent), *Blow the Man Down* (Charles Vipont), *The Flight of the Heron* (D. K. Broster), *Cranes Flying South* (Puffin Story Book), *The Hills of Varna* (Geoffrey Trease), *Ben Hur* (Lew Wallace), but older primary school

---

[1] *Tales out of School*, by G. Trease, New Education Book Club

pupils and adolescents are also attracted to good biography, to accounts of exploration—*The Great White South* (Ponting), *With Scott to the Pole*, *Ascent of Everest*—to life and travel in different countries, to general science dealing with inventions, machines, transport.

The type of variety is illustrated by the titles given in Appendix IV, but these again are only samples—much fuller information can be obtained from the book lists referred to on pages 197 to 198. Kathleen Lines's book *Four to Fourteen* (and its recent supplement), and *Books for Young People*, Groups I, II and III (The Library Association), are most helpful because of the annotations under a wide variety of subjects.

COMICS

At this point, a word about comics is relevant. Many periodicals ranging from a short, simple comic strip to a shoddy, garishly illustrated love story are nowadays lumped together under the title of comics. They cater for all ages, from children of 4 or 5 (e.g. Chick's Own, Robin, Jack and Jill), to the adventure-seeking boy or girl of 14. Many comics deal with superman and space stories, detection of crime, science fiction, cowboy and Indian stories, while the better type of comics such as Eagle and Girl, include serialised, pictorial presentations of the classics, together with Bible stories.

According to Pumphrey,[1] the coverage of comics is immense —290 million comics circulate annually in Great Britain and each copy has an average of eight readers. I believe it is correct to say that every boy and almost every girl reads comics at some stage in their childhood—their appeal is powerful, extensive and fairly continuous up to 15 or 16.

The amount of reading of comics and the age to which it is continued are undoubtedly related to the level of education.

---

[1] *Children's Comics*, by George H. Pumphrey (Epworth Press, 1955), p. 24. Pumphrey includes a classification of British comics and other periodicals for children and young people (pp. 29-36) together with comments on the stronger meat of American comics.

O

home background and intelligence of the children. For some, comic reading is discontinued largely by the age of 12 or 13, when reading of books displaces it ; for others, particularly backward boys and girls, it may continue strongly up to 19 or 20 and not be discontinued entirely during their whole lifetime.

I can recall my own period of reading Magnet, Gem and Champion (all of which have now ceased publication)—the next adventure of Sexton Blake and Tinker, and the further exploits of Billy Bunter were things I looked forward to reading each week-end.

Apparently the well illustrated, well produced comic permits of a double reading—first a quick surface reading relying on the pictures and ' gulping down ', so to speak, the main actions and their associated emotional stimulation, and later a more careful reading taking in details of text as well as those of picture.

An analysis of comic reading [1] would suggest that their popularity is due to the following factors :

1. *The ease with which they can be read.* A minimum of text with a maximum of illustration enables even slow and backward children to follow the story. More recently the same idea has been used with some benefit in material for older backward boys (see page 252—Chapter X). The simple strip sequence of pictures with blurbs of conversation, the relative simplicity of vocabulary and sentence structure (or lack of it in the worst type of comics), makes no great tax on either intelligence or reading skill. They are in a sense the counterpart of the loosely written detective story that adults read to while away the time on a train journey—certainly the situations are comparable.

It has been calculated that five of the popular British comics read by 6- and 7-year-olds (Dandy, Beano, Chips,

---

[1] Some comments on the use of comic reading are given in *Studies in Reading*, Vol. I, pp. 173-80. Publication of the Scottish Council for Educational Research XXVI (University of London Press, 1948).

etc.) use 74 per cent of the words found in either the children's own vocabulary or reading experience. This finding is of importance, but relates only to a few comics read by 6- and 7-year-olds, and needs further investigation of comics for older children.

2. *There is a recurring pattern of theme in many comics*—the readers expect and want to read a similar set of events to those in the last issue. Herein lies a real danger. Children may be so conditioned to a particular form of verbal diet that they do not wish to taste other forms. It is, of course, not only the comic that may have this effect ; the same applies to books of some popular writers who churn out much the same type of story year after year—hence the need for guidance, particularly through reading good books *to* children.

3. *The comic does not require any deep thinking.* The emotional reaction engendered by comics of the ordinary type is on the whole shallow and superficial and does not appear to affect children. They read them just as they eat their meals and are satisfied for a short period.

About 98 per cent of children read comics ' between the years of 8 and 14 with the peak at about 11 years. The only difference that intelligence makes is that the more gifted children tend to give them up earlier and the less gifted children tend to give them up later or not at all. Comics are read by those who enjoy literature as well as those who do not or cannot '.[1]

We might therefore conclude that psychologically, the comic stage of reading is for many children normal and perhaps necessary. On the whole, British comics are harmless both in content and in their emotional effect. Although the English may be poor, it is not harmful.

The comics Eagle, Girl, Swift, and Robin, are certainly an advance in production, style, and content, and many children claim that they learn from them.

[1] *British Comics, an Appraisal*, edited by Miss P. M. Pichard

A typical issue of Eagle, a paper that has been called a fusion of the traditional British comic and the traditional British adventure paper, contains Dan Dare, Pilot of the Future ; Cavendish Brown, brilliant surgeon and detective (black and white strip) ; Jack of Lantern, Storm Nelson (black and white strip) ; Riders of the Range (strip form) ; Luck of the Legion ; The V.C. in the Bowler Hat (article) ; Special News for Eagle Readers ; Eagle Sports Page (Choose your Sporting Heroes) ; The Belond A.P. Special (detailed diagram of a well known racing car) ; Big Noise at Northbrook (school story) ; Harris Tweed Extra Special Agent (comic strip); Wonders of Insect Life (details of Emperor Moth, illustrated); Shepherd King, the story of David (illustrated strip. The story of Paul ran for 60 instalments in the Eagle).

A Note on American Comics

Throughout America and British Commonwealth countries there has been strong, and I believe justified reaction against the low level type of American comic, the main themes of which have been crime, murder, violence, horror, and perverted sex. Dr Wertham, Director of the Lafarge Clinic in New York who has studied the effect of comics on children, has produced startling evidence in *The Seduction of the Innocent*. Although attempts were made in the U.S.A. to pass laws, no real change was effected because of the powerful influence of interested parties. In British Commonwealth countries and in France the law has stepped in to protect young minds, and hence such laws as the ' Children's and Young People's (harmful publications) Act of 1955 ', (England).

Conclusion

Whilst comics are read by almost all children, including many intelligent children who read good literature as well, we must not accept this situation in any spirit of complacency. As Scott says, ' An easy toleration of the mass produced " blood " and novel as normal reading for all children, or for all the habitual readers of them, cannot be defended on rational or educational grounds.'[1]

The comic provides for most readers a mild form of excitement, for some a badly needed degree of compensation, for a still smaller group, fantasy or eroticism of a semi-pathological kind. What we have to do is to wean the avid reader of comics away from that fare and to introduce him adroitly to writers who will provide for him similar thrills and adventures, but something extra as well in the form of useful information of an historical or geographical kind, truer and deeper characterisation, incidents that will enable him to bridge the gap to reality more effectively, and emotional reactions that are wholesome, not erotic or spurious.

There is, as I have pointed out earlier, a considerable body of contemporary literature that is no less dramatic or swift in its action than the comic or the ' blood ', but nearer to the world in which these young people live.

Summary

The main aim in the teaching of reading is to enable children to read by themselves, to derive enjoyment and to obtain information. Teachers in the primary school must therefore make use of school and class libraries to achieve these aims.

The growth of an interest in reading and the development of some discrimination in regard to the qualities of books is influenced by five factors—home background, the intelligence of the children, their level of reading ability or skill, the kind of activities and interests that attract them, and the kind of guidance and encouragement they receive in school and home. In the growth of reading interests home and school play complementary roles.

The class library is of paramount importance in attracting children to read books—in fact it can become the most powerful

[1] *Reading, Film and Radio Tastes of High School Boys and Girls*, W. J. Scott, p. 86

influence in leading them to become deeply interested in reading and in forming attitudes of searching for information by themselves. Children will only regard books as their greatest source of satisfaction and knowledge if they can handle books, browse through them, possess their own shelf of favourites and have plenty of opportunities, every day, of taking books from a library easy of access and from a teacher who will guide and encourage them in their reading efforts.

The production of standards and the improvement of reading tastes in boys and girls is a slow and subtle process and is often achieved gradually by carefully considered steps, through class libraries and home book shelves, through teachers with a philosophy and parents with foresight. Methold, as mentioned earlier, began his class Book Club for less able adolescents by giving them a diet of exciting adventure stories —the racy kind of war yarn, detective story and career novel. But this started them reading and was only the first step from which they were led by subtle steps to book fare of greater depth and richer literary qualities. Those of us who have lived and worked with children, and have been intimately concerned with their reading interests, have no doubts of the accuracy of Dorothy White's finding from the records of borrowing of books made over years from her children's library in Dunedin that ' the good finally drive out the bad '.[1]

And in conclusion we should try to see that the attitudes we develop in school carry over into life. Not only should there be a useful class library, in large primary schools, supplemented where necessary by a central school library, but from the age of 9+ or 10+ children should be encouraged to use the public library. Most progressive towns have arranged children's sections within their public libraries, or alternatively a separate Children's Library.

---

[1] *About Books for Children*, Dorothy White, 1949. Published in conjunction with the New Zealand Library Association (Whitcombe & Tombs, and the Oxford University Press)

Far-seeing town Library Committees realise that their juvenile reading members are as important as their adult members and cater for them in an effective and attractive way. This pays excellent dividends, for the well-read child who can use his reading ability to the fullest extent, both for gaining information and for his leisure pursuits, is likely to make an effective adult member of a democratic community.

CHAPTER X

METHODS AND MATERIALS FOR OLDER BACKWARD READERS

I HAVE discussed elsewhere the causes of backwardness in reading and the appropriate remedial measures as they apply to pupils in the primary school [1] and while this information has relevance to the older backward reader, yet there are special aspects of this problem that we should note if we are to be successful in improving the reading attainments of these older children.

Most backward readers at the top of the primary school or in the secondary modern or junior secondary school are boys, whose impoverished verbal levels may be due to a number of interacting conditions.

(*a*) They are often the duller section of their age groups, against whom the dice has been loaded in a number of different ways.

(*b*) They have often had, in their early primary years, repeated absences from school due to illness or migrations or lack of parental interest in their education. Wall, in giving details of a group of soldiers who had poor reading attainments, revealed that curtailment of schooling and irregular attendance were factors in their retardation.[2]

(*c*) They have frequently been handicapped from the earliest stages by a special weakness in those factors, visual or auditory, or both, which underlie reading ability.

[1] *Backwardness in the Basic Subjects*, by F. J. Schonell, 4th ed. (Oliver & Boyd), Chapter X
[2] ' Reading Backwardness among Men in the Army ', by W. D. Wall, *Brit. J. of Educ. Psy.*, *Vol.* XV, Part I, February 1945, p. 36

(*d*) As a result of this particular disability, they have needed specially planned remedial help with additional time devoted to reading instruction, but in point of fact they have often had less than normal time and attention in the junior classes of the primary school.

(*e*) A relatively large proportion of these older children come from homes where social backgrounds do not work to their advantage in school studies. As Spiegler says, ' far more frequently than we imagine, when you " scratch a poor reader ", you discover underneath a history of meagre or impoverished experience where parents are indifferent to reading and where home attitudes are unfavourable to it '.[1]

(*f*) Many have not been strongly motivated in regard to learning to read, and stronger outside interests of a manual, mechanical and athletic kind have acted in opposition to any remedial practice in or out of school hours. Particularly is this so where parents have not taken an active and understanding part in helping to overcome his backwardness.

(*g*) Slowly, as the pupil has proceeded from class to class, his continued backwardness has resulted in a cumulative build up of adverse emotional attitudes. These acquired emotional attitudes arising from continued failure, are often more intense barriers to a pupil's improvement than intrinsic temperamental qualities of an unfavourable kind.[2] Of course, there is always the possibility, as Vernon reveals in her survey of experimental evidence on

[1] Materials for Reading, compiled and edited by Helen M. Robinson, (University of Chicago Press), *Supplementary Educational Monograph*, 1957. Quoted from the section, ' Reading Materials for Retarded Readers ', by Charles C. Spiegler, p. 25.

[2] See *Backwardness in the Basic Subjects*, by F. J. Schonell, 4th ed. (Oliver Boyd), p. 494.

the relation between defects of personality and backwardness in reading, that some backward readers are hampered from the earliest stages in learning to read by defects of personality.[1]

Now all of these causal conditions or accompanying characteristics of the pupil's backwardness in reading must be taken into account if we are to help him effectively. There is no doubt that with some older backward scholars the junior school has made most persistent efforts to teach them to read ; with others their continued failure is in no small measure due to ineffective and insufficient reading instruction of the right kind in junior classes. Both sets of conditions, while making it more difficult to improve the reading achievements of pupils when they are 11 or 12 or 13 years of age, also make it imperative that our methods should succeed this time—in fact, the last time we shall have a chance of redeeming them from a life of illiteracy or semi-illiteracy when they leave school. Teachers of these older backward pupils are thus faced with a difficult psychological/educational problem of which they must understand the elements before they can plan remedial methods and materials.

CHANGE IN PROMOTION POLICIES

The numbers of these retarded readers to be found in upper primary classes and in secondary schools has tended to increase. Change in promotion policies has, in most English-speaking countries, had an effect on the numbers of backward readers now found in the top classes of primary schools or in the lower classes of secondary or high schools. The modern policy is to increase the promotion ratios, so that whereas in the past children who could not read effectively were kept back in classes, they are now promoted with the rest. In England all pupils, irrespective of attainments, go on from primary to secondary school at 11 + ; there are as a result an appreciable

[1] See *Backwardness in Reading*, by M. D. Vernon (Cambridge University Press, 1957), Chapter VI, pp. 132-48.

number of children in the secondary school who still require some help with actual instruction in reading.

In the State school systems of Australia, owing to a marked shift in promotion policies, we now find increased numbers of older, backward children either in top primary classes or in post-primary grades, still needing help with reading. Whereas in the past approximately 30 per cent of children were kept back one year, and 11 per cent two years or more, the inclusive figure has in most States dropped to 10 per cent or less.

In the U.S.A. 'the rate of promotion rose slowly through the years. The situation existing in the seventh grade in 1916 was mainly the cumulative result of an average promotion rate in the elementary schools that had hovered around 88 per cent in the previous years ; each term one out of eight children had been held back ; often the same child was " retarded " more than once. By 1924 the average promotion rate in the first eight grades of the elementary school (junior high school excluded) stood at 90 per cent ; by 1934 it was 95 per cent ; it reached 99 per cent in 1948.

' Meanwhile, more and more children whose reading skills were below average for their age and who had been retained in the lower grades where they were " over-age " were gradually moved upward.' [1]

Older Backward Readers—a Far-reaching and Challenging Problem

This policy of promotion of all children, irrespective of their attainments, so that they work in classes with those who are their peers in chronological age and in outlook as they go through the school, is most universally applied in English-speaking countries. It is, however, by no means common in educational systems. For example, in some Latin American countries the promotion rate, that is, the percentage of the

[1] *The Retarded Reader in the High School*, Board of Education, City of New York: Bureau of Educational Research Publication No. 21, September 1952, p. 8

number of pupils who pass a promotion examination or are otherwise recommended for promotion to a higher grade may be only 60 per cent in Grades I to III, rising to 85 per cent in upper grades. In certain continental countries it is not uncommon for one-third of the pupils in primary schools to fail to gain promotion.[1] However, this policy of such educational systems of ' keeping back ' slow learners is gradually changing.

Naturally, in countries where backward children are sent forward with all others, the range of intellectual levels, reading attainments and experiences found amongst pupils of 12 to 16 in upper primary or lower post-primary grades, is now very much greater than has been the case hitherto. In other words, teachers of these older children, both at the upper primary and the non-academic secondary level must now concern themselves with actual instruction in reading for some children whom they teach. It serves no purpose to maintain that such children should have been taught to read in the lower primary school. While a more scientific approach to backwardness in reading in the junior school will result in fewer children going on to post-primary education still grappling with the mechanics of reading, yet we now have enough research studies to show that there will always be a small group of children who at 11 or 12 years of age are still not able to make use of reading as an almost automatic skill. There will always be a small core of older children who, through a combination of the factors cited above, have not gained sufficient facility in reading to be able to dispense with further instruction in word recognition. There will also be a somewhat larger group, who, while they have achieved satisfactory levels in word recognition, yet require carefully planned lessons in learning how to understand and interpret what they read.

A recent report, based on a survey in which 2,236 pupils aged 11+ (1,106 boys and 1,130 girls) were tested both in word

---

[1] ' See School Failure ', by Fred J. Schonell in *The Slow Learning Child*, Australian Journal on the Education of Backward Children, Vol. 3, No. 2, pp. 66-82.

recognition and comprehension, and in which all backward readers were given a non-verbal test of intelligence, contains this statement. ' A second obvious conclusion to draw is that secondary modern schools must expect a proportion of their entrants each year to be in need of supplementary lessons in both mechanical reading and reading for comprehension, and that many will be reading at a level which is below their innate capacity. The necessary knowledge of appropriate teaching techniques for all stages of reading should therefore be expected of the staff of a secondary modern school as well as of junior schools[1]'.

These older pupils thus constitute a problem of vital and impelling concern, particularly to teachers of courses for non-academic boys and girls. To teach every pupil to read before he leaves school must surely be an objective of over-riding importance for every school. We live in a reading world in which the printed word is of paramount importance, and a scholar who completes his period of formal schooling still unable to read sufficiently well to meet the demands of everyday life, must surely be gravely handicapped—a handicap that may stay with him all his life and may affect not only his vocational choice, but his effectiveness as a citizen and his stability as an individual.

It would seem that once we can bring pupils to a reading age of between 9 and 10 years this degree of achievement is sufficient to enable them to carry on with reading outside school—many newspapers do not require a reading age above 10 years. Pupils with reading ages below that level are in very grave danger of losing what skill they have attained on leaving school.[2]

[1] Report of a Survey of Reading Ability carried out by the Middlesbrough Head Teachers' Association in co-operation with Officers of the Authority, 1953. Obtainable from the Director of Education, Education Offices, Woodlands Road, Middlesbrough, England.

[2] Reading Ability, Pamphlet 18 (Her Majesty's Stationery Office, London, 1950), p. 12

Effects of Illiteracy or Semi-Illiteracy [1]

Case studies of older backward readers in school and of adults, who have experienced the bleakness of a world in which they are denied information through the printed word because of their limited reading skill, almost invariably reveal changes in personality pattern. There is no doubt that ability to read is essential both for the individual and for the race. The various basic or preliminary education courses set up by the British, American, Canadian and Australian Army Authorities to deal with illiterate and semi-illiterate soldiers revealed that such men had limitations both as soldiers and as individuals. They were unable to read a newspaper and hence were denied knowledge of and lacked interest in current events. They were deprived of one of the most effective means of employing their leisure time and of increasing their general knowledge. Moreover as soldiers they were limited in efficiency, because they could not follow printed instructions—in an army camp, let alone in a new town or beyond it, signs, notices and directions meant nothing to them. Printed warnings of danger, printed army regulations, information about health and sanitation, news from their families at home, all had to be transmitted by word of mouth. Such dependence on others and denial of opportunities for gaining information produced in many men marked behaviour reactions. Some became unduly suspicious and unco-operative, others were extremely subservient and inferior and were unable to use their talents effectively ; still others were compensatorily rebellious, defiant and difficult.

[1] Those who wish to acquaint themselves with the wider international issues of illiteracy as they affect children in countries for whom there is an inadequate system of primary education or adults who have been deprived of an opportunity to learn to read and write, should read UNESCO's publications on Fundamental Education. See, for example, *Learn and Live. A way out of ignorance for 1,200,000,000 people* (UNESCO, Paris, 1951). Also *Developments in Fundamental Education for Adults*, by Paul L. Essed, M. B. Lourenco-Filbo, Angelico W. Cass, Review of Educational Research, Vol. XXIII, No. 3, Adult Education, American Educ. Res. Assoc., Washington, 1953. *Progress in Literacy in Various Countries*, UNESCO , Monographs on Fundamental Education, 1953 (UNESCO, Paris).

Interestingly enough, although the six weeks of the special preliminary education courses devoted to improving the reading levels of many of these men were too short for some men, yet quite startling improvements were achieved by others. For the first time some were able to read a letter from their family without help ; they were able to find their way about a town ; they gained what they wanted to know from the daily newspaper and some even read a small book for the first time in their lives. But the major change often came in regard to their attitudes towards printed material, towards other people, towards those in authority, and, most important of all, towards their own abilities. Many became more co-operative, less suspicious, more teachable and generally happier and better adjusted people.

Emotional Changes in Backward Readers in School

Similarly amongst older school children, we find marked emotional changes in older boys and girls who have continuously failed to learn to read. Inability to read, which is made only too apparent not only to peers and teachers but to the world at large, produces in every older pupil a feeling of inadequacy and inferiority. This inability to be like others is often the basis of tension and conflict which issues in behaviour that is not normal. While a few go to the extreme and attempt to compensate in marked anti-social ways, such as delinquency, many develop attitudes towards learning to read which interfere with their efforts to do what, deep down, they wish to achieve—namely, to read. The degree to which there is rationalisation, withdrawal or antagonism, depends of course on the nature of the approach made by the school, and the degree of pressure and censure, or on the other hand, of understanding and encouragement within the home. Almost every backward reader rationalises his inferior position. One older boy said to me : ' My brother can't read much and he's got a good job.' Another, aged 13, said : ' I'm leaving school at the end of the year.' His attitude might well have been

232 THE PSYCHOLOGY AND TEACHING OF READING

expressed as, 'They've tried all this before—for the last eight years I've been submitted to this frustrating and purposeless activity, so you'd better save yourself for someone younger with whom you might achieve success.'

There is clear evidence amongst some boys of 11 to 14, who are very backward in reading, that they have given up hope and have withdrawn from the situation, so that not only are they uninterested and not willing to try but they are, at times, openly antagonistic to further efforts.

Associated with these feelings of inadequacy and inferiority, which are expressed in apathy, rationalisation or defence mechanisms, is the emotional blocking of the pupils' learning powers. They are unable to use during their remedial instruction such intellectual power and qualities of concentration and persistence as they possess.[1] The more the pupil tries, the more does he become, as a result of his feelings of inadequacy, tense and uncertain of himself, and the more is he thus prevented from learning, while he is in a state of emotional turmoil. Time and again those who have participated in remedial work with older backward pupils know that the greatest measure of success comes when tension has been dispersed, when the pupils feel they are making progress, when there is clear evidence that they are ' not duds ' and that they will succeed this time. As I shall show in the next section, the therapeutic aspects of remedial reading with older pupils are all-important.

It should be remembered that the backward reader's disability is advertised hourly in almost every situation in which he finds himself. Ability to read enters into every aspect of his school work, and he is constantly being paraded as a failure, constantly being denied information in fields in which he could display his powers if only he knew what to do. He cannot understand his arithmetic problems, although he can calculate

---

[1] For useful supplementary information see *Clinical Studies in Reading*, I, Supplementary Educational Monographs No. 68, June 1949 (University of Chicago Press), particularly pp. 114-52.

quite well, he cannot read the instructions in general science although he is interested in the experiments, while in even simple assignments in geography or history, the way is blocked to him. It is little wonder that disability in reading creates a sense of frustration and inferiority unparalleled by any other insufficiency or shortcoming in the individual's life. It is for this reason that we must put in first place and keep in first place, the objective of seeing that no pupil leaves school unable to read.

Six Fundamentals

There are six fundamental points which should be carefully considered when planning the reading lessons for these backward readers.

(1) Most of these pupils of 11 to 14, although backward in school work, have the outlook and interests of the average boy of 11 to 14. They do the same things, play the same games and are interested in the same topics. Although their reading age may be only 7 or 8 years, yet they differ very much in their understanding, speech and interests from the 7- or 8-year-old boy. *This means that somehow we must use reading material, sufficiently simplified, suited to the interests, activities and conversation of average 11- to 14-year-old boys and girls.*

The most vital aim of the teachers of these older backward readers is to break through the verbal isolation in which they live. They must seek to get them to read something whatever it is. Many of them have never read a book of any sort of their own volition. Therefore each boy should be treated individually in regard to his reading requirements. By personal appeal, in which a challenge is issued by the teacher, supported later by guidance and encouragement from him, every backward boy is led to select a very simple book, suited to his reading level, and whenever possible, connected in some way with a topic or event in which he is interested.

As one American writer has observed, ' it's not so much a matter of Johnny doesn't read because he can't, as Johnny

P

can't read because he doesn't '. This observation is of special significance for our remedial approach. Somehow, ' get them reading something ' should be our slogan—comics or books, it doesn't matter in the first instance.

There is now an increasing variety of suitable books on all kinds of subjects for older backward readers. The teacher responsible for the reading instruction of this group of children should be familiar with these books—he should know the reading age levels of each book, which books are best suited to the very dull senior pupils, as compared with those that attract the more intelligent retarded reader, and which are best suited to girls and which to boys.

(2) These pupils represent a residue of really difficult cases of reading disability, where specific mental handicaps, sometimes accentuated by general intellectual weakness, have rendered progress by ordinary methods of reading instruction almost impossible. It is therefore necessary to make a specialised scientific approach to their difficulties, and *to use modern diagnostic measures to find out the causes for their continued failure.*

(3) Nearly all older backward readers have failed for six or seven years with the usual methods of teaching reading as generally used in infant and junior school classes. It is therefore useless to continue with the same kind of instruction now that these pupils have entered a new department or have come under the care of a different teacher. *We must devise a new approach which will, at least in the initial stages, have novelty and ensure immediate success.*

(4) Because these pupils have failed for so long, and because the consequences of their failure have been so apparent to them and to others, they have lost confidence in themselves and failed to maintain normal self-esteem. Differently with different children this has resulted in apathy or boredom, and a longing to be free of the whole atmosphere of school and scholastic failure. With others it has resulted in fierce antagonism towards a system which so condemns and perpetuates their disability—there are things they *can* do, but so seldom

are they given a chance to show this. Others of these handicapped children have sought compensatory satisfaction in anti-social behaviour and even in delinquency. Therefore the reading programme for backward readers must be intimately linked with a reorientation of their whole school programme. They must be provided with plenty of opportunity for expressing themselves and thus regaining their lost self-esteem and diminished self-confidence. *That is, not only their reading lessons but the whole of their school work must be planned along therapeutic lines.* The reading must be woven skilfully into other activities, and these must be activities which they like, and which they can do. Doing and learning must be not. merely a catch phrase but a dominant characteristic of their curriculum.

(5) For the adequate treatment of older boys and girls who are still grossly handicapped by very low levels of reading attainment there is the *need for special organisation within the school to meet their special needs.*

For the more intelligent backward ones, I believe that a *coaching or adjustment group,* which meets every day, or where necessary twice a day, for special assistance from a teacher well versed in the principles of remedial reading is the best way of dealing with the problem. The members of this coaching group will be drawn from different classes and naturally will have to miss certain other lessons. The important point is that they should not be absent from expressional activities like craftwork, woodwork, domestic science, art, music, which they can enjoy and at which many of them will get satisfying success of a compensatory kind. Nor should they miss lessons in mathematics, absence from which will produce its own backwardness. They will probably lose least by absence from history or geography or social studies, inasmuch as they will not be able to make use of the textbooks in these subjects and furthermore, when they are able to read they can catch up with the sections or chapters missed.

For the really dull children requiring a modified syllabus,

instruction is best given through a *small* special class, where special methods with plenty of sympathetic consideration can be given to each individual. Such special classes, whether they be at the top of the primary school or in the secondary modern or junior secondary school, provide an ideal way of enabling such children to regain lost confidence and to develop levels of literacy before they leave school at 15 or 16. A wisely administered syllabus, with a strong bias toward practical work which may be the medium through which such children learn to apply their reading skill in a meaningful way, can have invaluable, far-reaching effects on the rehabilitation of the personalities of young adolescents who have hitherto regarded themselves as failures. But the success of such special classes depends greatly upon the teachers responsible for the bulk of the instruction. They must have not only special technical knowledge to grapple with such problems as these older backward children present, but they must be able to make rapport and develop deep and satisfying relationships with each and every one of their ugly ducklings—no mean task, but one well worth while and immensely satisfying when the metamorphosis to swan-like qualities begins to appear.

(6) Because of the requirements listed not only in the last section, but also in sections 1 to 4, *teachers who undertake work with adjustment groups or special classes should have had opportunities of attending special in-service training courses.* Such courses should include not only training in diagnostic testing and remedial teaching, but in the equally important part of their work, namely the therapeutic approach to the retardation of the older backward pupil. They should know how to devise new approaches to reading to dispel the effects of failure, how to involve the dull boy in activities in which his success will spill over to his efforts in reading and spelling, in short how to use modern methods of the project and activity kind to rehabilitate children whose learning powers are being inhibited by the effects of continued failure and frustration. They should be acutely aware of the effect of creative and expressional work

on the personalities of backward children, and of the vital need of successful accomplishment in areas other than those of a verbal kind.

PLANNING THE METHOD

In planning the method there are again six important aspects of the problem which should be covered.

(1) *Accurate Assessment*

Teachers should *accurately determine each pupil's reading age, both for word recognition and for comprehension.*

(a) Word recognition level, which is the basis of reading ability, may be obtained by giving the Graded Word Reading Test as set out on pages 256 and 257. A qualitative record of errors should be made as well as a quantitative estimate of reading age, which in itself will immediately give the teacher a fairly accurate idea of the amount of reading backwardness present, and of the vocabulary level of material that the pupil can be expected to attempt.

(b) But in addition to assessing word recognition, the teacher will need to know how well the pupil can read continuous prose and the extent to which he understands what he reads. This can be judged from his results in

Test R2—The Simple Prose Reading Test [1]
or Test R3—Silent Reading Test A [1]
or Test R4—Silent Reading Test B [1].

The results of these tests will also help the teacher to decide whether meagreness of vocabulary is an element in his poor reading attainments.

(2) *Careful Diagnosis*

This step should be followed by an application of a number of diagnostic reading tests. The teacher can obtain help here from Chapter VIII, *Backwardness in the Basic Subjects*, in which details are given of a simple diagnostic testing programme. In

---

[1] These are given in *Diagnostic and Attainment Testing*, by F. J. & F. E. Schonell (Oliver & Boyd), 4th ed. pp. 43-63. They are also available separately.

particular the teacher should note the kinds of perceptual errors made by the pupil (as evidenced by Tests R5 and R6) seeking to obtain answers to the questions, ' Does he systematically look at words or transpose letters ? ' ' Has he adequate knowledge of common phonic families ? ' ' Is he familiar with common consonantal and vowel digraphs ? '

Diagnosis must be continuous and the teacher should seek to unravel the nature of the pupil's poor reading :

(*a*) Does it lie in an inability to distinguish likenesses and differences between words ?

(*b*) Does he require systematic training in recognising common phonic families and their longer derivatives ?

　　e.g. *now*, down, drowned
　　　　long, along
　　　　an, tan, hand, stand

(*c*) Does he require help in breaking up longer words ? (Scrutinise his result in the last thirty words of Test R5.) Some pupils profit considerably from a systematic course in syllabising words linked with word building based on common phonic families, e.g. be-ginn-ing, cov-er-ed, win-ter-ing. Varied word building and making small words into larger ones and vice versa, have a place for these children.

(*d*) Is his ability to develop adequate perceptual habits, such as a careful and persistent scrutinising of words from left to right, and an ability to remember differences in visual patterns of words, due to counteracting emotional attitudes ? (See Chapter II.)

(*e*) Is his weakness in word recognition accentuated by his impoverished language background ?

It will be realised that diagnosis must be continuous and comprehensive ; in fact, we can really only diagnose the nature and cause of a pupil's reading disability when we have studied him closely in all kinds of situations over a number of weeks. Tests are only a part of the diagnostic programme. We shall be adding to our diagnostic information as the result of each day's remedial teaching, and in fact modifications in remedial methods and material will be made as we unravel the various forces at work in the pupil's disability. For some there will be the need for strong and continuing doses of therapy, for others success in reading will be the main thera-peutic element in the boy's progress. But there will always be a few for whom insecurity, tension and conflict must be dissi-pated by other means before any progress at all can be made with reading. Here work with the hands, painting and handi-craft may prove invaluable. Others appear to be ready to go forward with the job of learning to read through a therapeutic approach of a verbal kind such as is provided by puppetry and drama.

Then again, the home situation of some boys is such that there is the need for parental guidance and re-education in respect of the backward boy. That is why in the diagnosis it is vital to talk to the child's parents. Much can be gained from such interviews. For many of the older pupils who have attended our Remedial Education Centres, diagnosis of their disability has suggested a remedial approach along three major lines—through remedial teaching of a scholastic kind, through therapy of a directive or non-directive kind and through parental re-education.

(3) *Home Coaching*

For older pupils who have failed continuously in the verbal field it is useful if *the school can enlist the aid of someone outside the school to supplement and consolidate what is being done inside the school.* But for the older pupil it is important that any such person who helps with home coaching should be fully sympa-thetic with the backward reader. He or she should be on extremely good terms with the pupil, and the work should be undertaken in a spirit of friendship, encouragement and mutual satisfaction. For this reason it is necessary for the teacher to have a talk with whoever agrees to undertake the coaching, and to outline the principles that should guide such coaching. Sometimes a parent or an older brother or sister or an older friend will help, but in no circumstances should the coaching be done unless the pupil agrees and unless it will be carried out in the right spirit.

The main points in such coaching are :

(*a*) Each pupil should be given a suitable book which he takes home for reading practice ; the aim is to help children to learn to read, not to keep books clean in a school cupboard. Buy extra books from school funds if parents are not able to provide them. Books should be of equivalent difficulty or slightly easier than the one being read by the pupil at the time.

(*b*) Teachers should set a daily ration of reading from the book—two to six pages per day according to the boy's ability— for a week. This will obviate the backward pupil's being asked to do too much.

(*c*) Helpers should be given precise instructions not to criticise children, but to praise and encourage them.

(*d*) Each week the teacher should check progress and set new assignments. Occasionally short, written exercises might well be included in the work.

(4) *New Method*

The next step is to *introduce the boys to a method which will be different* from the type of reading lesson they have usually had, and which will therefore not suffer from the negative effects of past reading failure. Here again I have outlined elsewhere in some detail what I have found to be a useful approach (*Backwardness in the Basic Subjects*, pages 216 to 220 and pages 244 to 247).

It is essential with backward readers to give, where possible, two short lessons per day. The gain in reading attainment, the consequent improvement in other school work and, above all, the consequent improvement in personality adjustment and development make this fully worth while.

(5) *Comprehensive Approach*

There is the need to introduce into remedial teaching for older children who have failed continuously a comprehensive teaching approach that involves using as many interrelated forms of learning as possible. For this reason while we use reading material that has been carefully compiled in terms of vocabulary load and repetition of new words, yet we must also give the boy a chance to strengthen his word recognition by word drills and workbook exercises. The workbook which has plenty of exercises in discrimination and consolidation of word power is useful. The teacher will be aided in this by reference to Happy Venture Workbooks Three and Four (Oliver & Boyd), by those accompanying the First and Second Story Books (Nelson), and by the exercises in The Pathfinder Books (Oliver & Boyd), Introductory A, B and C, Books One, Two and Three.

But perhaps the most useful correlation of approaches derives from a blending of reading, writing and spelling, particularly by introducing writing and tracing as an aid to reading. Where a pupil finds it difficult to remember a word, encourage him to trace it, say it and write it. Much will be gained by his writing difficult sentences or paragraphs. When vocabulary controlled reading books are used containing word lists of new words as they appear in the book, the teacher should require pupils to write the new words before and after each page is read.

An effective supplement to remedial reading is obtained by a systematic study of word families. This may be done by using Groups One and Two in the *Essential Spelling List.*[1] Group One, for ages 7 to 8, contains 396 common words and Group Two, for ages 8 to 9, contains 456. These words are continuously occurring in the pupil's reading and written

[1] *Essential Spelling List,* 3,200 everyday words carefully selected and graded into six lists suitable for children of ages 7 to 12, by F. J. Schonell (Macmillan). See also *Essentials in Teaching and Testing Spelling.* This contains graded dictations on the spelling lists.

material. As they are arranged in short sets of similar structure, the pupil is also receiving basic phonic training.

Thus set 23 from Group One is as follows :

pipe	feed	now
wipe	need	cow
ripe	sheep	how
were	paper	down

All these words appear repeatedly in the simple material many pupils deal with in their reading books. Hence systematic study of them, writing them and doing exercises on them, considerably improves powers of word recognition, in addition to reviewing and consolidating common words.

For this purpose the *Essential Read-Spell Books*,[1] each one of which is geared to a group of words in the *Essential Spelling List*, provide useful remedial material for backward readers and spellers.

The principle on which the books are based is illustrated by the following examples from Book I and Book II of the *Essential Read-Spell Books*. The first example embodies Set 23, Group One, of the *Essential Spelling List* and is suitable for a reading/spelling age of 7 to 8 years.

pipe	feed	now
wipe	need	cow
ripe	sheep	how
were	paper	down

On the Farm

I live on a farm. We have some cows
and sheep and pigs.
I have a cow of my own.
Now I know how to feed her
and what she needs to make her
give a lot of milk.
Her name is Snowdrop.

[1] *Essential Read-Spell Books*, by F. J. & F. E. Schonell (Macmillan)

She is as white as paper.
I wipe her coat to make it shine.
One day when all the cows
were in the yard,
I found Snowdrop lying down.
She was ill from eating ripe berries.
' Oh, Father, Snowdrop is ill,' I cried.
Father poured some oil down a pipe
into her mouth.
She was better in a few days.

A. Write these sentences, filling in the gaps.
   These words will help you : paper, cow, were.
   1. I have a . . . of my own.
   2. She is as white as . . . . .
   3. All the cows . . . . in the yard.

B. Here are two lists of words. Each of the words in the
   first line rhymes with a word in the second line, like
   this : ripe-wipe. See if you can pair the others.
   1. ripe, feed, town, now, keep
   2. need, down, how, wipe, sheep

C. Write down three animals they have on the farm.

The second example is taken from Book II, *Essential
Read-Spell Books* and embodies the words in Set 7, Group 2
of the *Essential Spelling List*. It is suitable for a reading/spelling
age of 8 to 9.

meet	rake	list
street	wake	lift
sheet	awake	mist

week   three   named

UP EARLY

Last week Tom and his three brothers
had to rake the garden for Mother.
They said that they
would wake up very early to do it.

Tom was awake first, so he called the others.
' Come on, you chaps,' he shouted.
It was so early that the mist hung
like a white sheet over the pond
at the bottom of the street.
It did not lift until nine o'clock.
There were lots of birds singing in the trees.
Ned tried to make a list of them
but did not know some of their names.
He named ten birds.
While they worked the birds sang,
and the sun came up to meet the soft white mist.
Soon Mother called them to breakfast.

A. 1. What did the boys have to do for Mother ?
    2. Who was awake first ?
    3. What did Ned try to do ?

B. Put a box round the little word in the big word :

meet	sheet	list	mist
named	lift	they	them

C. Write the names of three birds you know.

D. Put these words in four lists of

   5 letters   6 letters   7 letters   8 letters
   brothers, mother, others, awake, first,
   bottom, singing, worked, street, called,
   garden, named, shell, sheet, birds, spoon.

(6) *Selection of Material*

But perhaps the most important part of the remedial reading programme lies in the selection of material for the backward reader. In this aspect of our work we have been helped considerably in recent years by the production of books specially suited to older children with low reading attainments. These books deal with topics of interest to pupils of 11 to 15 years, but with reading ages of only 7 to 10. There is also a limited amount of material with a very light vocabulary, geared at the 6 to 7 reading age level, which is suitable for extremely retarded older boys and girls. While in the main it is advisable to use this special material, yet at the same time teachers in special classes and reading centres have taught many hundreds of backward boys of 11 and 12 to read by use of the *Happy Venture Reading Scheme*. While this is eminently suited to backward readers up to 10+, its use with poor readers above this age must depend very largely on the pupil's reaction to such books. In most cases they will react better to the schemes specially prepared for older boys or girls.

I would therefore suggest that, bearing in mind the points enumerated above, our procedure might be characterised by four stages. Stage C (reading from the *Wide Range Readers*) might be commenced before Stage B is completed.

Stage A. Pupils build a simple book related to their own interests.[1] The objective of this is to create a favourable attitude towards reading instruction and at the same time to lay the foundations of more effective word recognition.

Stage B. Once the pupil has acquired a sight vocabulary of forty or fifty words, connected with his Interest Book, we may then proceed to the second stage, namely the use of one of the vocabulary controlled basic reading series given on pages 246 to 249. We must use, for these backward pupils, a reading scheme in which vocabulary and sentence structure are controlled and graded. Most of these books are accompanied by some workbook exercises involving written work.

Stage C. To stimulate interest we move on to *Wide Range Readers* (see page 250). These graded reading books may be introduced as soon as the pupil has a reading age of 7. Their great value lies in the quality of the stories which have an appeal to all children, young or old, backward or advanced. Through them the child is inspired to read more ; through

[1] See *Backwardness in the Basic Subjects*, 4th ed, pp. 245-6.

them he begins to feel the joy of reading and to be attracted by the information the printed word can provide.

Stage D. When Stage B has concluded and Stage C is proceeding satisfactorily, we may introduce some of the books described on pages 251 to 254. My own choice has been to introduce children with reading ages of 8½ onwards to those excellently written and produced books, *The Active Readers* (page 254). There is no doubt that White Hawk, X-Bar-Y Ranch, Frogman Diver, La Bonté the Trapper appeal to the boy who is just climbing up the reading ladder.

Finally, throughout the entire period of instruction it is essential, as I have indicated earlier, to help children with the reading and spelling of that matrix of common, simple, everyday words that form about three-quarters of all reading matter. For this reason an extremely effective aid is provided by allowing pupils each day to do some work from *Essential Read-Spell Books* (see pages 242 to 244), commencing with Book I. I suggest that all children with reading ages below 9 do both Books I and II of the *Essential Read-Spell* series.

A selected list of suitable books for Stages B, C and D are given on the following pages.

STAGE B MATERIAL

The Escalator Reading Scheme, by W. U. Dalby and P. M. Bland (Oliver & Boyd). An excellent series to commence remedial reading with older boys or girls whose reading vocabulary is very limited.

Controlled vocabulary and sentence structure ; based on family life and everyday incidents of six boys and six girls ; plenty of action ; 30 stories, presented as 15 separate booklets, graded in difficulty into 3 series of 10 stories.

	Reading Age	Number of pages
' C ' Series		
5 Booklets . .	6+ . .	12
1 set Reading Cards		

	Reading Age	Number of pages
'B' Series		
5 Booklets	7+	16
1 set Reading Cards		
'A' Series		
5 Booklets	8+	32
1 set Reading Cards		
Teachers' Manual.		

The Griffin Readers, by S. K. McCullagh (Arnold). Vocabulary carefully controlled ; interesting subject matter ; well illustrated ; equally suitable for boys and girls.

	Reading Age	Number of new words
Book 1	5 - 6	46
2	5 - 6	56
3	5 - 6	
Books 4, 5, 6	6 - 7	
Books 7, 8	7 - 7½	
Books 9, 10	7½ - 8	
Books 11, 12	8 - 8½	

The Pathfinder Books, by J. and P. Bradley (Oliver & Boyd). Graded books, with vocabulary control ; based on interests of the 10 to 15 years age group ; *particularly suited to older backward boys*.

	Reading Age	Number of new words
Introductory Book A	7	42
Introductory Book B	7	64
Introductory Book C	7	80
Book 1	8+	445
Book 2	9+	537
Book 3	10+	
Book 4	10+	
Book 5	10+	

Each chapter is followed by word lists, comprehensive exercises, revision, and puzzles.

Adventures in Reading and Writing, by G. Keir (Oxford University Press). Vocabulary controlled in early books ; short books of 16 or 32 pages ; variety of interesting topics.

	Reading Age	Number of pages
First Series :		
6 Adventures in Reading .	6 - 7 .	. 16
5 Supplementary Adventures in Reading		
6 Adventures in Writing .		
3 Crossword Puzzle Books .		
Second Series :		
6 More Adventures in Reading	7 - 8 .	16
5 Supplementary Adventures in Reading . .		
6 More Adventures in Writing		
3 Crossword Puzzle Books .		
Third Series :		
6 New Adventures in Reading	8 - 9 .	. 32
6 New Adventures in Writing		
3 Crossword Puzzle Books .		

Adventures in Writing are workbooks which accompany Adventures in Reading. The Crossword Puzzle Books are useful for vocabulary consolidation.

Family Affairs, by P. and J. Bradley (Oliver & Boyd). This series has been designed specially for backward senior girls aged 11 + to 14 +. Carefully graded ; vocabulary controlled ; word lists at end of each book. Each book contains word building and comprehension exercises.

The Teacher's Book contains introductory stories for reading to the girls before they start on Book I.

	Reading Age	Number of new words
Book 1	6+ - 7+ .	. 142
Book 2	6+ - 7+ .	. 91

	Reading Age
Book 3	7+ - 9
Book 4	7+ - 9
Picture Book . . .	
Teacher's Book . .	

Active Reading Scheme, by J. E. Miles (Ginn). Very useful for older backward boys ; carefully graded ; useful workbooks.

	Reading Age	Number of pages
Part I		
Reading Book—Bonfire Night	7 - 8 .	. 50
Reading Game — Pieces of Eight		
Workbook — Getting Ready for Bonfire Night	. .	. 64
Part II		
Reading Book — London Express	8 - 9 .	. 64
Reading Game—Cardsharp .		
Workbook — Getting Ready for London Express	. .	. 64
Part III		
Reading Book — Derwent Adventure	8 - 9 .	. 112
Reading Game — Take a Chance		
Workbook—Getting Ready for Derwent Adventure		

Teacher's notes accompany each part.

Highfield Series, by D. Highfield (Nelson).

	Reading Age	Interest Age	Number of pages
First English Workbook (Picture Section)	7 - 8	10 - 13	16
First English Workbook .	.	.	. 63
First School Story Book .	.	.	. 87

Q

This is an excellent series for older backward pupils. Attractively printed and illustrated with controlled vocabulary and adequate repetition. Approximate vocabulary in the three books 300 words.

STAGE C MATERIAL

Wide Range Readers, by F. J. Schonell and P. Flowerdew (Oliver & Boyd). Parallel with, or on completion of, reading from one of the above series, pupils might well be introduced to the Wide Range Readers which never fail to satisfy reading tastes of children from 7 to 15.

The Wide Range Readers consist of two parallel series, each of six books—the Blue Books and the Green Books. The books, which commence with a reading age of 7 to $7\frac{1}{2}$, are graded by a control of vocabulary and sentence structure according to reading age.

The scheme is as follows :

	Blue Books *Reading Age*	*Green Books* *Reading Age*
Book I	$7 - 7\frac{1}{2}$	$7 - 7\frac{1}{2}$
Book II	$7\frac{1}{2} - 8$	$7\frac{1}{2} - 8$
Book III	$8 - 8\frac{1}{2}$	$8 - 8\frac{1}{2}$
Book IV	$8\frac{1}{2} - 9$	$8\frac{1}{2} - 9$
Book V	$9 - 10+$	$9 - 10+$
Book VI	$10+ - 11+$	$10+ - 11+$

The amount and nature of the material together with its grading and construction provide continuous reading practice for pupils of all reading levels. The fact that in each book, vocabulary, sentence structure, and idiom have been carefully considered at each reading age level, makes them entirely satisfactory for older backward readers with *reading ages* between $7\frac{1}{2}$ and 11 years.

But it is in the nature of the material, almost all of it original matter specially written for the series, that its appeal and value lie. In addition to stories well told, the aim has also been to give pupils accurate information in story form. There are stories of the Wright Brothers, of Robert Louis Stevenson's childhood, of how the first boat was made, of writing, of clocks, of ships and of houses, of Magnus Barefoot and Leonardo da Vinci, of Tycho Brahe, of Anna Pavlova, Jenny Lind and Helen Keller, of the Great Trek, and the Run for Oklahoma, the Flying Doctor Service of Australia, and stories of fish and insects, birds and beasts in many lands, and innumerable other tales that tap the interests of history, geography, travel, famous men and women, natural history, science, music and art. All of these and many other topics are treated with a realism and an accuracy of fact interwoven in stories of real literary value and strong human interest.

STAGE D MATERIAL
Supplementary Readers

No. 5 Charles Street, by J. Butler and B. Whatley (Wheaton).

		Reading Age	Interest Age	Number of pages
Book I	At Home	8+	10 - 15	32
Book II	Going Out	8+	10 - 15	32
Book III	Start of Work	9+	10 - 15	32

This is a very useful series for older *girls*, and deals with activities within the home, in everyday life and at work. Simply written and illustrated. Vocabulary appropriate.

The Peter Brown Stories, by T. N. Pinder and E. O. Hann (University of London Press).

	Reading Age	Interest Age	Number of pages
Books 1-4	7 - 9	9 - 12	32

Suitable for *boys and girls*. Carefully graded vocabulary. Stories about the adventures of Peter and Molly.

The Ready Readers, by J. Hemming (Longmans).

	Reading Age	Interest Age	Number of pages
Series A (12 titles) . .	7 - 8	8 - 12	16
Series B (8 titles) . .	7½ - 8½	9 - 12	16
Series C (8 titles) . .	8 - 9	9 - 14	48
Series D (8 titles) . .	8½ - 9½	10 - 14	64

Series A and B, in black and white comic strip style, appeal to older backward pupils. Vocabulary and sentence structure simple. Series C provides interesting, longer stories, simply written. Series D deals with various leisure pursuits and social services, illustrated by photographs.

Far and Near Readers, by various authors (Chambers).

	Reading Age	Interest Age	Number of pages
Red Series, Books 1-4 .	7 - 9	9 - 12	24
Blue Series, Books 1-5 .	9 - 10	9 - 14	32
Green Series, Books 1-4 .	10+	10 - 14	32 - 52
Teacher's Book . .			52

Well printed, adequate illustrations in black and white, graded vocabulary and simple sentence structure. Very attractive to older backward *boys and girls*. Stories have a suitable range of topics, while the Green Series contain simple versions of classics.

The Story Path to Reading, by L. F. Hobley and P. H. Leyden (Blackie).

	Reading Age	Interest Age	Number of pages
Books 1-3 . . .	7 - 8	9 - 14	42 - 56
Textbook for Books 1-3			110
Books 4-6 . . .	8 - 9	9 - 15	58 - 64
Books 7-12 . . .	9 - 10	9 - 15	66 - 138
Textbook for Books 4-12			88

Well printed, well illustrated. Controlled graded vocabulary. Book 1 uses just over 200 different words, Books 2 and 3 use approximately 250 words. Subsequent books in the series use an increasingly large number of words up to 650 in Book 12. These are excellent books of well written adventure stories which appeal strongly to *boys*. Sample titles are Rob, Joe and the Smugglers, Burwood Tyler Flies to U.S.A., The Hope Diamond, The Secret of the Island. The textbooks provide an adequate supply of exercises and games to help boys consolidate their learning of the vocabulary of the books.

The Challenge Books, by A. E. Smith (McDougall).

	Reading Age	Interest Age	Number of pages
Nine titles . . .	7 - 8	9 - 15	32

The easy vocabulary of these books of adventure stories makes them very useful supplementary readers. Sample titles are The Garage Gang, The Night Mail.

The Burgess Books, by C. V. Burgess (University of London Press).

	Reading Age	Interest Age	Number of pages
Four titles . . .	$7\frac{1}{2}$ - $8\frac{1}{2}$	9 - 14	32
Workbook for each title			
Teacher's Book . .			

These are short stories written in a bright, vigorous manner. Older backward boys enjoy them because of their humour and adventure. Sentence structure simple, vocabulary easy.

The Discovery Readers, by J. Anderson (Harrap).

	Reading Age	Interest Age	Number of pages
Eleven titles . . .	7 - 8	8 - 12	32

Well illustrated, adequate repetition of vocabulary. Stories are much enjoyed by very backward readers of 11 and 12.

Onward Readers, by G. R. Crosher (Cassell).

	Reading Age	Interest Age	Number of pages
Twelve titles . . .	$7\frac{1}{2}$ - $8\frac{1}{2}$	10 - 15	52 - 62

Fairly easy vocabulary. Simple sentence structure. Vigorous, interesting adventure stories which appeal strongly to older backward children of both sexes.

Forward Books, by G. R. Crosher (Methuen).

	Reading Age	Interest Age	Number of pages
Eight titles . . .	8 - 9	10 - 14	44

These short books provide useful supplementary reading matter for senior boys and girls who are just beginning to read by themselves.

Adventures of Bill and Betty, by E. Owen (Oxford University Press).

	Reading Age	Interest Age	Number of pages
Six titles . . .	8 - $8\frac{1}{2}$	10 - 14	32

Clear, well-printed and usefully illustrated. Lively style appeals to older children.

Active Readers, by various authors (Ginn).

	Reading Age	Interest Age	Number of pages
Twenty-three titles .	$8\frac{1}{2}$ - $9\frac{1}{2}$	9 - 16	160+

These are excellently produced; vigorous interesting stories based on factual material. Liberal illustrations assist the reader. Strong appeal to both boys and girls.

GRADED WORD READING TEST

tree	little	milk	egg	book
school	sit	frog	playing	bun
flower	road	clock	train	light
picture	think	summer	people	something
dream	downstairs	biscuit	shepherd	thirsty
crowd	sandwich	beginning	postage	island
saucer	angel	ceiling	appeared	gnome
canary	attractive	imagine	nephew	gradually
smoulder	applaud	disposal	nourished	diseased
university	orchestra	knowledge	audience	situated

physics	campaign	choir	intercede	fascinate
forfeit	siege	recent	plausible	prophecy
colonel	soloist	systematic	slovenly	classification
genuine	institution	pivot	conscience	heroic
pneumonia	preliminary	antique	susceptible	enigma
oblivion	scintillate	satirical	sabre	beguile
terrestrial	belligerent	adamant	sepulchre	statistics
miscellaneous	procrastinate	tyrannical	evangelical	grotesque
ineradicable	judicature	preferential	homonym	fictitious
rescind	metamorphosis	somnambulist	bibliography	idiosyncrasy

INSTRUCTIONS FOR GIVING, SCORING AND INTERPRETING THE GRADED WORD READING TEST

PRECAUTIONS

THE test should be given to one testee at a time and the testing should take place in an atmosphere of quiet and calm. Distraction prevents the testee from concentrating upon the material and it may prevent the tester from hearing accurately the pupil's pronunciation of the more difficult words. Only the printed form of the test, as given on the preceding pages should be used, as in this form care has been taken to select a size of print appropriate to progressive reading levels.

PRELIMINARY ATTITUDE

The most important point to observe in giving the test is that an atmosphere of friendliness and co-operation should prevail between tester and testee. This, in most cases, is easily and quickly achieved by a smile, a few friendly words, a greeting, a jest—any such suitable attitude to reassure the child that this is a joint affair between you and him, that it is in no way a vital examination, and that you will be pleased if he will just try to read as many words as he can. I always call the pupil by his Christian name—it is more personal and is one way of establishing rapport.

After taking the child's name and age, frame an introduction on these lines : ' Well, Jim, I've a lot of words here and I want to see how many you can read. The first words are fairly easy and then they get a little harder. Now, let me see how many you can read, please. Read across the page.' (Quickly run your finger from word to word across the *first* five words with which the testee is to commence.)

Obviously there must be some minor modification of the initial approaches to suit individual cases. If one can see (or has had previous knowledge) that the testee is nervous and apprehensive, it is usually advisable to talk to the pupil for a little while, asking her a few questions about herself. ' Do you live far from the school, Bessie ? ' ' Have you got any brothers and sisters ? ' ' You're lucky having two brothers, I've only got one,' (or some such remark appropriate to the case). Obviously, too, with backward readers or with very dull children, one would omit the opening remarks about the first words being easy. It is also necessary with such pupils to praise liberally. ' Good, that's right, now try the next line.' A halting reader, who is apprehensive of his own achievements or of what you are thinking, may also need additional sympathetic encouragement.

The examiner must use his knowledge of child psychology to detect quite early the child's attitude towards him and the test, and to mould his opening statements in accordance with the demands of the situation.

RECORDING

Young testees up to the age of 9 should start the test from the beginning—the printed form should be squarely placed in front of the child—and the examiner should record the responses on a separate sheet. The recording should not be made too obvious ; it should not be so apparent that it might distract the pupil. At the same time the recording should be carefully and systematically done for each pupil. *Do not try to count orally the number of words correctly (or incorrectly) read by the testee, and do not try to score on odd bits of paper.* The record should be so made that the calculation of the number of words correctly read, and hence of the reading age, may be done at some convenient break or pause after the conclusion of the testing. The most convenient way of recording is to make a dot for each word correctly read and a cross for each word wrongly read. The marks should be made in rows of five following the pattern of the test—a small space left after each ten words will later facilitate finding the total words correctly read.

e.g.   Peter S., $8\frac{5}{12}$

```
 .     .     .     .     .

 .     .     .     .     .


 .     .     .     .     .

 .     .     .     .


 .     .     .     x     x


 .     x     x     x     x

 x     x     x     x     x
```

Total score : 29 words

GIVING THE TEST

If the pupil reads too fast for the purpose of recording, he may be asked to read more slowly, or to re-read a line some words of which the examiner was not sure about. There should not be any prompting of the pupil during his reading of the words. Allow the pupil adequate time if he wishes to analyse and recombine the words. Some pupils are very slow readers, but show a fairly well-developed power of word analysis and synthesis if given sufficient time—this is one of the things revealed by the test. The pupil should not be hurried and self-corrections should be counted as correct. *At the same time any attempt at coaching or teaching a testee should be studiously avoided.* Thus a slow pupil reading the word *shepherd* may say *she* (as in she) *p-her-d*, then half say to himself *she(e)pherd*, finally giving the correct form *shepherd* ; this is counted as correct.

On the other hand a pupil reading the word *postage* may say *post* (as in box) *age* instead of *post* (as in low) *age*, and the examiner, not quite sure of the testee's pronunciation, may ask him to say it again. If the pupil repeats the first-named form the word is counted as wrong. Asking for a repetition of the word should be used only when the examiner is not sure of what the pupil has said. If the word is clearly said wrongly, as *can'ary* instead of *ca'nary*, then there is no need to ask for a repetition. Asking the pupil to re-read the word or words should not be used to indicate ' You had better look at it again, there is something wrong with it '. The only cases in which one would allow this is when an obviously bright pupil or good reader makes a slip in an earlier word. For example, a bright 10-year-old pupil reading quickly may leave the *s* off *downstairs*, but on being asked again to read the word will usually give it correctly.

Words should not be pronounced for pupils even when they stumble over them except on the rare occasion in the early stages of testing with a hesitant pupil who is apprehensive and lacking in confidence. One may then pronounce a word with the object of encouraging him to move on to other words with which he may be able to register a success, and thus give him confidence to try further words. Usually, however, the injunction, ' We will leave that one and try this word ', is sufficient.

The usual pronunciation of words (e.g. see the *Oxford Dictionary*) is accepted. Guessing should *not* be discouraged ; in fact, intelligent guessing is one means by which pupils make progress in reading. Pupils above the age of 9 years may be allowed to commence the test at the third, fourth or fifth group of ten words (according to age), i.e. a 10-year-old may commence at *dream*, a 13-year-old may commence at *physics*. The point at which the testee should commence is left to the discretion of the examiner,[1] but the first word of the group at which older or brighter pupils commence should be recorded to enable the examiner to calculate the score correctly.

[1] One technique with older pupils is for them to read down the left-hand column, then to commence at what seems to be the appropriate ten words.

Should a testee fail with any word of a group of ten words, when he has started at a point beyond the initial group of ten, then he should be taken back to read the preceding group of ten words.

e.g. A testee commencing at *smoulder* and failing on any word within this group should go back and read the group commencing *saucer*. Care should be taken that all backward readers and dull pupils commence the test from the beginning.

All testees should continue with the test until they fail *in ten successive words*. This margin of failure is sufficient with most pupils, but with older and brighter testees of 10+ onwards it is sometimes advisable, even after this limit of failure has been reached, to let them skim over the successive groups of words to see if there are any further words they recognise.

CALCULATING READING AGE

The reading age is calculated from the total number of words correct. For example, here is the record sheet of Robina C., $9\frac{4}{12}$:

```
tree    .      .      .      .
        .      .      .      .      .
        .      .      .      .      .
        .      .      .      x      .
        .      x      x      .      x
        .      .      x      x      x
        x      x      x      x      x
        x      x      x      x      x
```

Score : 23 words correct

$$\text{Reading age} = \frac{\text{number of words correctly read}}{10} + 5 \text{ years}$$

$$= \frac{23}{10} + 5 = 7\cdot3 \text{ years}$$

Record sheet of John B., $10\frac{4}{12}$:

dream		.		.		.		.
.		.		.		.		.
.		.		.		.		x
.		x		x		.		x
.		x		x		x		.
x		.		x		.		x
.		x		x		x		x
x		x		x		x		x

Score $= 41$ ($21 + 20$ words in 2 groups prior to *dream*)

$$\text{Reading age} = \frac{41}{10} + 5 = 9 \cdot 1 \text{ years}$$

(Remember that the reading ages are found in years and *tenths* of a year.)

SUGGESTIONS FOR COMPILING EXERCISES AND WORKCARDS OR WORKBOOKS

THE exercises suggested below should be regarded simply as a supplementary means of assisting pupils in word discrimination and in phrase and sentence recognition. As I have indicated in foregoing chapters, specific word or phrase drill is no substitute for actual experience with meaningful reading material. The child learns to read most effectively if given full preparatory reading experiences, followed by frequent practice and adequate help with simple material. There is an immense gap between the exercise type of reading matter and the content of up-to-date reading books.

On the other hand there are many children in the initial stages of reading instruction, and later, a smaller group of less able pupils, who profit considerably by a little additional help with special aspects of learning to read. Exercises can be devised to assist their somewhat uncertain power of discriminating similar word patterns, e.g. of discriminating *stop* from *shop*. The development of rapid phrase recognition and later, of phonic analysis, can also be aided. This help is most efficacious if the exercises are linked with such useful activities as drawing and colouring, and if they are so framed as to contain some of the elements of the game or the puzzle.

Reading exercises may be used as preparation or as revision for reading selected pages of a book, but they should never be allowed to replace the creative appeal of a centre of interest or the pleasure of dramatisation. Moreover, we should always remember that our final objective is to give the child sufficient facility in the technique of reading to enable him quickly to understand what he is reading. Hence the best kind of exercise is that which directs or tests powers of comprehension. Here we should be ready, with our most forward group of readers, to give them opportunity for silent reading, motivated or checked by questions or activities.

The exercises reproduced in the following pages are merely samples of given types. There is no limit to the examples an enthusiastic and ingenious teacher can construct on these lines. Obviously the number and kind of such exercises should be suited to the reading level of the pupils and to the progress they are making. Some children do not need to do such exercises, but nevertheless they enjoy the fun of doing them quickly, especially those questions of a game or puzzle kind.

How to Use the Exercises

In the early stages of reading, the instructions for doing the exercises should be read orally with the pupils. In fact some of the exercises can be taken orally from the blackboard ; the teacher will readily recognise these and will construct similar ones for the requirements of particular groups of pupils. In the main, however, the exercises are intended to be a means of linking up reading with drawing and writing. For this purpose the class teacher can trace off the line drawings given in the book and can then reproduce copies of the drawings and the exercise by means of some form of duplicating machine. It is as well to remember when doing this to run off extra sheets for another year's pupils. Additional exercises can be constructed and prepared by the teacher, as the single line drawings required do not demand a very high level of artistic ability. The exercises can be used a single sheet at a time, or can be made into a small booklet.[1]

Introductory Book (Matching Cards)

A useful device in these early stages of reading for the slower and less able children is to provide them with dictionary or

[1] There is no need for this additional preparation for those using the *Happy Venture Reading Scheme*. Teachers can now procure the Happy Venture Card Material (Oliver and Boyd) which consists of sets of graded exercises to aid word recognition and comprehension—one set for each of the five Readers. There are also the Happy Venture Workbooks, publication of which will begin in 1960.

R

matching cards. These simply consist of small manilla cards, about the size of a playing card, on which is a picture of a character, object or activity which appears in their reading books. Under each picture is the correct word or phrase. The teacher may also prepare slips of thin cardboard on which appear the names (words or phrases) only. The pupils may use (*a*) the cards with names on as dictionary cards, (*b*) the cards and the slips for matching one with the other.

SPECIMEN EXERCISES

THE EXERCISES ARE GRADED TO FIT IN WITH THE APPROXIMATE ORDER OF PROGRESS IN READING ABILITY

MATCHING CARDS

Dick

Fluff

Dick

Fluff

a big ball

Dora runs.

a big ball

Dora runs.

DRAW A PICTURE OF NIP PLAYING WITH DICK

COLOUR THE PICTURES

This is Dora.   Here is Nip.

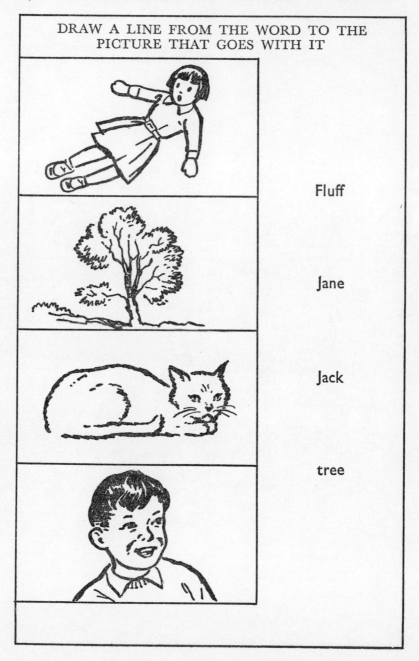

DRAW A LINE FROM THE WORD TO THE
PICTURE THAT GOES WITH IT

Fluff

Jane

Jack

tree

PUT A RING ROUND THE SENTENCE THAT
IS THE SAME AS THAT IN THE PICTURE

Mother has the ball.

Mother plays with Dick.

Mother has the ball.

Dora plays with Jane.

Dora has a doll.

Dora plays with Jane.

FIND THE LINE IN YOUR BOOK THAT SAYS:

> Jane is in the mud.
>
> Fluff is in the tree.
>
> Dora fell with the cat.

PUT A LINE IN GREEN CHALK UNDER 'BRING THE BALL'. PUT A LINE IN RED CHALK UNDER 'BY A TREE'.

> Fluff is in the tree.
>
> The cat sits by a tree.
>
> Nip sits by a ball.
>
> Bring the ball.
>
> The ball is in a tree.
>
> Jack will bring the ball.
>
> The ball is by a tree.

DRAW A LINE UNDER THE WORDS IN THE SENTENCE
THAT LOOK JUST LIKE THE WORDS ON THE RIGHT

Jack is in the tree.	the tree
Dora will bring Jane.	bring Jane
Nip sits with the ball.	Nip sits
Nip will play with Dick.	will play

DRAW A PICTURE TO TELL US ABOUT THESE

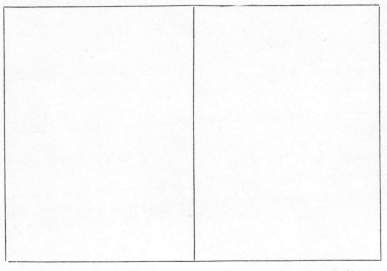

| The ball stopped in the tree. | Nip brings the ball in his mouth. |

DRAW A LINE FROM THE PICTURE TO THE
SENTENCE THAT TELLS ABOUT IT

Dick has
the ball.

Fluff is
in the tree.

Mother is
on the seat.

DRAW A LINE UNDER THE WORD THAT TELLS ABOUT THE PICTURE

	ball basket dog
	basket little kitten
	sit Nip bit
	mud tree shoe

DRAW A LINE UNDER THE WORD THAT IS LIKE
THE WORD IN THE BOX

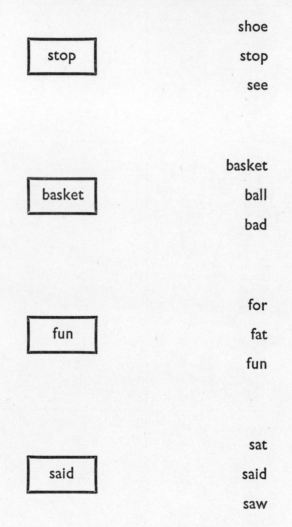

shoe

stop

see

basket

ball

bad

for

fat

fun

sat

said

saw

Draw these :   a little kitten

a green basket

a big shoe

a rag doll

WHO SAID ?

DRAW A LINE TO THE ONE WHO SAID THESE :

' You cannot sit in the mud.'   Fluff
                                       Mother

' I am wet with mud.'   Fluff
                                       Dick
                                       The kitten

' I can hop on a line.'   Nip
                                       Dick

' Bow-wow, bow-wow.'   Jack
                                       Jane
                                       Nip

' My knee is cut.'   Dick
                                       Dora

BLACKBOARD GAME

PUT A RING ROUND THE RIGHT ANSWER

Dick is a boy.   (Yes) or No

Jack is a girl.   Yes or No

Dora sleeps in a basket.   Yes or No

The kitten is little.   Yes or No

Nip sleeps in a shoe.   Yes or No

Dick throws his bat at the ball.   Yes or No

Jack can hit the ball with his bat. Yes or No

Dora skips well.   Yes or No

You can wash a cat.   Yes or No

You can wash a dog.   Yes or No

A jumping jack is a toy.   Yes or No

Mother tied up Jack's knee with
    rag.   Yes or No

PHONIC PRACTICE
PUT A RING ROUND THE WORD THAT TELLS ABOUT THE PICTURE

cat

hat

rat

fog

dog

log

sun

gun

run

hop

mop

top

big

dig

pig

hill

mill

pill

bed

led

red

sick

stick

Dick

DRAW A RING ROUND EACH WORD THAT ENDS OR
BEGINS LIKE THAT PART OF THE WORD WITH
A LINE UNDER IT IN THE BOX

ba<u>ll</u>	t<u>op</u>	<u>sh</u>op
small	shop	shoe
nest	cut	bring
wall	skip	ship
sing	stop	stick

ri<u>ng</u>	w<u>ell</u>	take
throw	tell	cake
bring	little	knee
line	fell	jump
jumping	small	make

QUESTIONS TO TEST COMPREHENSION

(Pages 30, 31, Book One, HAPPY VENTURE READERS)

Who went to the shop ?

What can you see in the toy shop ?

Draw some of the toys you can see in the toy shop.

Draw the toy Dick got.

What can a jumping jack do ?

Draw Dora's toy.

Who wanted a small ball ?

(Pages 18 to 23, Book Two, HAPPY VENTURE READERS)

PUT IN THE WORDS LEFT OUT

Mother Hen has —— —— chicks.

Little ———— Chick ran away.

'No, no, no,' said Pig,
    'I must get my ————.'

White Horse said :
    'I must go —— —— ——.'

The Mother Hen found White Chick
—— —— ——.

s

COMPREHENSION EXERCISE

DO YOU KNOW?

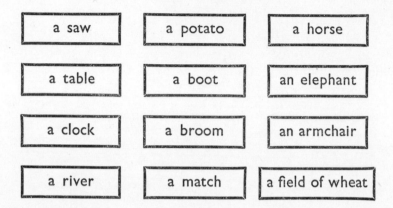

a saw	a potato	a horse
a table	a boot	an elephant
a clock	a broom	an armchair
a river	a match	a field of wheat

1. What has arms but cannot move them ?

2. Which has teeth but cannot chew ?

3. Which has a face but does not wash it ?

4. What has a mouth but cannot drink ?

5. What has a head but cannot turn it ?

6. What has hair but does not comb it ?

7. Which has legs but cannot walk ?

8. Which has eyes but cannot see ?

9. What has a tongue but does not speak ?

10. What has shoes but does not take them off ?

11. What has ears but does not hear ?

12. What has a trunk but does not pack his clothes in it ?

COMPREHENSION EXERCISE
PUZZLES

I have four legs.
I have a back.
I cannot walk.
People use me at table.
   What am I ?

I have wings.
I give light.
I come out at night.
I am very small.
   What am I ?

Sometimes I am small.
Sometimes I am tall.
I am not there at all if
   there is no sun.
   What am I ?

I like apples.
I like eggs.
I have brown eyes.
I have golden hair.
I am called Mar . . . . .
   Who am I ?

I have a head.
I have a foot.
I am not alive.
People use me at night.
   What am I ?

I can fly very fast.
I am pretty.
I can carry messages.
I sometimes save life.
   What am I ?

I shine brightly.
I guide men on their travels.
I cannot be seen when there
   is a lot of cloud.
   What am I ?

I can be used for cooking.
I come through pipes.
I am made from coal.
I give light.
   What am I ?

PUZZLES (Continued)

I have a handle.

I am made of iron.

I have a claw.

I make a noise when I work.

I am used by a carpenter.

What am I ?

I am made of glass.

I have a neck.

I hold all kinds of liquids.

I am closed by a stopper
or a cork.

What am I ?

I am light.

I grow on a tree.

I float on water.

I am brown in colour.

What am I ?

I come from Africa.

I grow on trees.

I am gathered and sent to
be crushed.

I am put in tins.

I am used to make some-
thing to drink.

What am I ?

I am made from soda and fat.

I smell nice.

I dissolve in water.

I am used to make things
clean.

What am I ?

SAMPLE LISTS OF BOOKS OF A HISTORICAL, NATURAL HISTORY, GEOGRAPHICAL AND BIOGRAPHICAL NATURE

HISTORICAL

1. ANCIENT TIMES (up to 1066)

Fidler, Kathleen : *The White Cockade Passes*

Lutterworth Press

Mitchison, Naomi : *The Conquered*   Cape
(the story of the Roman conquest of Gaul)

Mitchison, Naomi : *The Land the Ravens Found*   Collins

Severn, Dorothy : *Kerin the Watcher*   Dent
(about tribes, Druids, etc. 250 B.C.)

Sutcliffe, Rosemary : *The Eagles of the North*   O.U.P.

Sutcliffe, Rosemary : *Outcast*   O.U.P.

Trease, Geoffrey : *Word to Cæsar*   O.U.P.

2. MIDDLE AGES (1066-1485)

Doyle, Arthur Conan : *White Company*   Murray

Doyle, Arthur Conan : *Sir Nigel*   Murray

Hodges, W. C. : *Columbus Sails*   Puffin

Kent, L. A. : *He Went With Marco Polo*   Harrap

Kent, L. A. : *He Went With Christopher Columbus*   Harrap

Lewis, Hilda : *The Gentle Falcon*   O.U.P.
(the story of Isabella, Richard II's wife, 1377)

Power, Rhoda : *We Were There*   Allen & Unwin
(eleven stories set mainly in the Middle Ages)

Reason, Joyce : *The Secret Fortress*   Dent
(Cumberland in early Norman times)

Rush, Philip : *Queen's Treason*   Collins
(England, 1324)

Seaby, A. W. : *Alfred's Jewel*　　　　　　Harrap
Seaby, A. W. : *The Ninth Legion*　　　　　Harrap
Stevenson, R. L. : *The Black Arrow*　　　　Nelson
Trease, Geoffrey : *The Hills of Varna*　　Macmillan
　　(the story of Erasmus)
Trease, Geoffrey : *The Secret Fiord*　　Scottie Books
　　(England and Norway under the Hanseatic League,
　　1400)

3. 16TH CENTURY ONWARDS

Blackmore, R. D. : *Lorna Doone*　　　　　Harrap
Broster, D. K. : *The Yellow Poppy*　　　Duckworth
　　(France, early 19th century)
Broster, D. K. : *The Flight of the Heron*　Heinemann
　　(1745 Jacobite Rebellion)
Broster, D. K. : *The Gleam in the North*　Heinemann
　　(Scottish Jacobites after Culloden)
Buchan, John : *John Burnet of Barns*　　　Nelson
　　(Covenanters)
Cooper, J. Fenimore : *The Deerslayer*　Everyman's Library
Dumas, A. : *The Three Musketeers*　　　　　Dent
Dumas, A. : *The Black Tulip*　　　Nelson's Classics
　　(Holland in the 17th century)
Forester, C. S. : *Hornblower Goes to Sea*　Michael Joseph
　　(British Navy early 19th century)
Henty, G. A. : *With Wolfe in Canada*　　　Blackie
Henty, G. A. : *With Clive in India*　　　Foulsham
King-Hall, Magdalen : *Sturdy Rogue*　　　Nelson
　　(Elizabethan England)
Kingsley, Charles : *Westward Ho !*　Everyman's Library
Lewis, C. Day : *Nick Willoughby*　　　Blackwell
　　(Elizabethan England)
Macfarlane, Kenneth : *The Young Jacobites*　Cape
Needham, Violet : *The Boy in Red*　　　　Collins
Niven, John : *Gypsy in Scarlet*　　　　　Faber
　　(Crimean War)

Oman, Carola : *Baltic Spy*   Pitman
   (Europe, 1808)
Orczy, Baroness : *I Will Repay*
   (French Revolution)
Orczy, Baroness : *The Scarlet Pimpernel*
Ross, Sutherland : *Three Steps to Tyburn*   Hodder
   (London, 1724)
Seth-Smith, E. K. : *When Shakespeare Lived in Southwark*
   (a story for children of London in Tudor times)
                                            Harrap
Stevenson, Robert Louis : *Kidnapped*   Puffin
Sutcliffe, Rosemary : *The Queen Elizabeth Story* O.U.P.
Sutcliffe, Rosemary : *Brother Dusty-Feet*   O.U.P.
   (Elizabethan England)
Trease, Geoffrey : *Cue for Treason*   Blackwell
   (Tudor England : intrigue and the stage)
Trease, Geoffrey : *In the Land of the Mogul*   Blackwell
   (a story of the East India Company's first venture in
    India)
Vipont, Charles : *Blow the Man Down*   O.U.P.
   (life on the sea during the Commonwealth period)
Vipont, Charles : *The Heir of Craigs*   O.U.P.
   (Jacobite England and America, late 17th century)

NATURAL HISTORY

Batten, H. Mortimer : *Tales of Wild Bird Life*   Blackie
Batten, H. Mortimer : *Romances of the Wild*   Blackie
Batten, H. Mortimer : *Red Ruff*   Puffin
Batten, H. Mortimer : *Starlight*   Puffin
Bianchi, Vitaly : *Mourzouk*   Puffin
Bronson, Wilfred S. : *Children of the Sea*   Museum Press
Chipperfield, Joseph : *Gruka, Eagle of the Hebrides*
                                     Hutchinson
Cory, Harper : *Rover, A Collie Coyote*   U.L.P.
Ellison, Norman : *Over the Hills with Nomad*   U.L.P.

Evens, G. Bramwell : *Out with Romany*　　　　U.L.P.
Grey Owl : *The Adventures of Sajo and Her Beaver People*

　　　　　　　　　　　　　　　　　　　　　　　　Davies
Haig-Brown, R. L. : *Panther*　　　　　　　　　Cape
James, Will : *Smoky*　　　　　　　　　　　　　Puffin
Knight, Eric : *Lassie Come Home*　　　　　　　Cassell
Lippincott, Joseph W. : *Wilderness Champion*　Hutchinson
Lockley, R. M. : *The Way to an Island*　　　　　Dent
Martin, Dorothy : *Munya the Lion*　　　　　　O.U.P.
Rawlings, Marjorie K. : *The Yearling*　Four Square Book
Richmond, Kenneth : *Twelve Deeds of Greywing*

　　　　　　　　　　　　　Routledge & Kegan Paul
Rutley, C. Bernard : *Lotti the Wolf*　　　　　Macmillan
　　(series of 12 Wild Life story readers)
Salten, Felix : *Bambi, The Story of a Forest Deer*　　Cape
Seton, Ernest Thompson : *The Best of Ernest Thompson Seton*
　　　　　　　　　　　　　　　Hodder & Stoughton
Sewell, Anna : *Black Beauty*　　　　　　　　　Puffin
Verrill, A. Hyatt : *Strange Birds and their Stories*　Harrap
　　(for older boys and girls ; about unusual birds all over
　　the world)
Watkins-Pitchford, D. J. : *Wild Lone : The Story of a
　　Pytchley Fox*　　　　　　　Eyre & Spottiswoode
Williamson, Henry : *Tarka the Otter*　　　　　Putnam
Williamson, Henry : *Salar the Salmon*　　　　　Faber

GEOGRAPHICAL

Borer, M. Cathcart : *Kilango*　　　　　　　　Pitman
Buckley, Peter : *Cesare of Italy : Luis of Spain*
　　(Around the World To-day books)

　　　　　　　　　　　　　　　　Chatto & Windus
Busoni, Rafaello : *Somi Builds a Church*　　　Muller
Churchward, Robert : *Explorer Lost !*　　　　Nelson
　　(the story of Colonel Fawcett)

Columbus, C. : *The Log of Christopher Columbus's First Voyage to America in the Year* 1492

Davis, Norman : *Picken's Great Adventure*   O.U.P.

Davison, F. D. : *Man Shy : A Story of Men and Cattle*

Puffin

Dawlish, Peter : *He Went With Drake*   Harrap

Dobie, J. Frank : *On the Open Range*   Pitman

Elips, Julius : *Tents in the Wilderness*   Harrap

Fitzpatrick, Percy : *Jock of the Bushveld*   Longmans

Forbes-Watson, R. : *Shifta*   O.U.P.

Gatti, Attilio : *Saranga the Pygmy*   Hodder & Stoughton

Harrop, Hilda M. : *The Young Traveller in New Zealand* (this is one of a traveller series of books by various authors for readers of 12-15 years)

Phœnix House

Haslund, Henning : *Tents in Mongolia*

Routledge & Kegan Paul

Lenski, Lois : *Blue Ridge Billy*   O.U.P.

Lewis, Elizabeth F. : *Ho-Ming, A Girl of New China* Harrap

Lewis, Elizabeth F. : *Young Fu of the Upper Yangtze* Harrap

Lindbergh, A. M. : *North of the Orient*   Chatto & Windus

Moon, Grace : *Daughter of Thunder*   Blackwell

Morice, Stella : *The Book of Wiremu*   O.U.P.

Morrow, Honore : *The Splendid Journey*   Hutchinson

Patterson, J. H. : *The Man Eaters of Tsavo*   Macmillan

Peach, L. du Garde : *The Story of Captain Cook*

Wills & Hepworth

Seredy, Kate : *The Good Master*   Harrap

BIOGRAPHICAL

Burnett, Constance B. : *The Shoemaker's Son*   Harrap

Curie, Eve : *Madame Curie*   Heinemann

Doorly, Eleanor : *The Insect Man*   Puffin

Doorly, Eleanor : *Ragamuffin King : Henry IV of France Called the Great*   Cape

Ford, Donald : *Dr Barnardo*   A. & C. Black
    (Lives to Remember series)
Graham, Eleanor : *Story of Charles Dickens*   Methuen
Gray, Elizabeth Janet : *Young Walter Scott*   Puffin
Grey Owl : *Pilgrims of the Wild*   Davies
Larsen, Egon : *Men Who Fought for Freedom*

        Phœnix House
Lewis, Lorna : *Nansen the Adventurer*   Heinemann
Manton, Jo : *Elizabeth Garrett Anderson*   A. & C. Black
    (Lives to Remember series)
Mason, Cora : *Socrates, The Man Who Dared to Ask*   Bell
Meynell, Esther : *The Story of Hans Andersen*   Methuen
Mountevans, Admiral Lord : *Man of the White South :*
    The Story of Captain Scott   Nelson
Noel-Baker, Francis : *Fridtjof Nansen*   A. & C. Black
    (Lives to Remember)
Scott, J. M. : *Hudson of Hudson's Bay*   Methuen
Scott, J. M. : *Captain Smith and Pocahontas*   Methuen
    (other titles in the Story Biography series)
Southey, Robert : *The Life of Nelson*   A. & C. Black
Taylor, Boswell : *Joseph Priestley*   Macmillan
Taylor, Boswell : *Edward Jenner*   Macmillan
    (other titles in They Served Mankind series)
Trease, Geoffrey : *Fortune, My Foe : The Story of Sir Walter*
    Raleigh   Methuen
Wheeler, Opal and Deucher, Sybil : *Mozart : The*
    Wonder Boy   Faber & Faber
Wheeler, Opal and Deucher, Sybil : *Franz Schubert and His*
    Merry Friends   Faber & Faber
Wheeler, Opal : *Ludwig Beethoven and the Chiming Tower*
    Bells   Faber & Faber
Wymer, Norman : *Great Inventors*   Blackie

INDEX

Reading, lip movement in, 160
    material, 15, 19, 21, 30, 32, 33, 34,
        41, 92, 95, 98, 100, 116, 133-8,
        143, 176-85, 245-54
    methods, 15, 19, 41, 45, 82-112,
        132-8, 148, 237-44
    oral, 138, 146-50
    preparation for, 21, 25, 29, 30, 45,
        47-81, 113, 185
    progress in, 151, 161, 187
    radio, 38, 156
    reactions, early, 11, 12, 40
    readiness, 25, 45, 48, 49, 52-62, 71,
        95, 115
    readiness books, 59, 71, 108
    readiness tests, 60-2
    revision of, 100, 103, 105, 108, 117
    sheets, 67, 77, 79, 116
    silent, 130, 137, 141, 148, 153
    speed of, 159-60
    tests, 55, 130, 133-6, 143, 151-3, 237,
        255-63
    understanding directions, 164-5
    units, 17, 33, 88
Recognition of phrases, 34
Relationships, 26, 27, 28, 35, 40, 43
Reliability ratio, 25
Remedial—Centre, 41, 46, 138, 239
    work, 31, 44, 121, 133, 139, 225, 226,
        232, 235-6, 239, 244
Research, 17, 29, 30, 35, 36, 39, 47, 56,
        91, 93, 140
    Scottish Council for, in Education,
        21, 36, 37, 99, 218
Rhymes, 19, 39, 51, 65, 70, 128, 185
Richardson, J. A., 38, 39, 42, 43
Robinson, H. M., 225
Rorschach, H., 18
Rudisil, M., 107
Russell, D. H., 81, 201

Sampson, G., 209
Schonell, F. E., 130, 139, 237, 242
Schonell, F. J., 17, 23, 31, 34, 58, 66,
    92, 104, 137, 138, 215, 224, 228, 242
School Library Association, 197
Schools, home and, 45
    primary, 18, 48, 50, 131-54, 190, 209,
        226, 228
    promotion, 226-7
    secondary, 132, 168, 174, 202, 204,
        209, 229

Scott, C. A., 201
Scott, W. J., 204, 206, 221
Security, 27, 36, 39, 40, 44, 59
Sensory powers, 30, 53, 57
Sentence—method, 82, 89-91, 93, 94,
        98, 100, 118, 145
    structure, 31, 48, 59, 67, 90, 116
Serjeant, F. I., 31, 63, 68
Sex differences, 27
Sheldon, W. D., 37
Simpson, D., 56
Social—conditions, 36, 38, 53, 54, 56,
        63
    development, 29, 35
Solomon, A. H., 18
Sounds, blending of, 34, 125
    consonants, 84, 125
    letters, 84, 94, 112
    vowels, 84, 111, 127
Spache, G., 46
Span of recognition, 13, 33, 147
Speech, 18, 19, 36, 55, 57, 63, 98
    defect, 57
Spelling, 44, 87, 131, 138, 139, 241-2
Spiegler, C., 225
Stories, 39, 40, 49, 55, 78, 96
    telling, 175-83
Study skills, 158, 160, 168
Summaries, 168-9
Supplementary reading books, 104-6,
        118, 129, 141
Syllabic method, 83
Syllables, 13

Tachistoscope, 71, 108, 123, 159
Taylor, J., 20
Television, 156
Terman Merrill Intelligence Test, 18,
        42
Tests (see Reading tests)
    projection, 42
Therapy, 239
Timetables, 66
Tracing, 12, 22, 23, 51, 241
Training Colleges, 50
Transfer of knowledge, 140
Type, size of, 31-3

Understanding, reading (see Reading—
    comprehension)
Unesco, 230
Units, reading (see Reading—units)

PRINTED IN GREAT BRITAIN BY
OLIVER AND BOYD LTD.,
EDINBURGH